Literate Systems

and

Individual Lives

SUNY Series, Literacy, Culture, and Learning:
Theory and Practice
Alan C. Purves, Editor

Literate Systems and Individual Lives

Perspectives on Literacy and Schooling

Edited by
Edward M. Jennings
and
Alan C. Purves

State University of New York Press

Published by
State University of New York Press, Albany

© 1991 State University of New York

For information, address the State University of New York Press,
State University Plaza, Albany, NY 12246

Production by Christine M. Lynch
Marketing by Fran Keneston

Library of Congress Cataloging-in-Publication Data

Literate systems and individual lives : perspectives on literacy and
    schooling / edited by Edward M. Jennings and Alan C. Purves.
        p.   cm. — (SUNY series, literacy, culture, and learning)
    Includes bibliographical references.
    ISBN 0-7914-0513-3 (alk. paper). — ISBN 0-7914-0514-1 (pbk. :
    alk. paper)
    1. Literacy—United States. 2. Literacy—Social aspects—United
States. I. Jennings, Edward M., 1936-   . II. Purves, Alan C.,
1931-   . III. Series.
LC151.L53   1991
302.2'244—dc20   90-33715
                                                                 CIP

10 9 8 7 6 5 4 3 2 1

CONTENTS

I

SETTING THE STAGE

1

Introduction

EDWARD M. JENNINGS
AND
ALAN C. PURVES

The essays in this volume, besides being contributions to different, on-going discussions, come together to help place "literacy"—the state of being comfortable inside a sign-sharing community—within a broad context of perennial puzzles.

Not too many years ago a cartoon strip summarized a large chunk of the rationale for promoting literacy. Mr. Grimmis, an elementary school principal, is telling some obstreperous kindergarteners why they have to stay in school: "The law requires you to go to school, because we cannot have a generation of illiterates running the country in a few years. You MUST stay!" We are familiar with his argument; he speaks for the American Education Establishment. But the paradoxes and questions surrounding "the literacy issue" belie the simplicity of Mr. Grimmis's self-satisfaction.

"Literacy" has become an increasingly important topic of discussion around the world. The year 1990 was declared International Literacy Year by UNESCO, which estimates that by 2000 the total number of illiterates in the world will surpass one billion, or about one-third of the adult world population, and that four out of ten children in the developing countries will not complete primary education. In the two most populous countries, India and China, the illiteracy rates are nearly 57 percent and 31 percent respectively. In addition, the illiteracy rate for females in the Third World outstrips that for men by over 20 percent.

Within the United States and other industrialized societies the number of absolute illiterates—those who cannot read or write in any language—is relatively low: less than 5 percent of the population. At the same time the literacy demands for most jobs exceed the level of education of a large proportion of the young adults. Less than a generation ago many entry-level positions called for a reading level of about sixth grade. In many industrial plants that are retooling, job entry requirements are jumping to a level higher than the twelfth grade. The American educational system is failing a significant portion of the population

who seem unable to read or do mathematics above a simple and superficial level. They can read the want ads but not the editorials in the daily
papers. The gap most affects minority groups and immigrants or "guest
workers." These people can get employment, but it is not steady and the
wage is often substandard. The migrant group places demands on our
social and educational institutions, demands which in some cases had
not been encountered before, or anticipated.

This context of pressing global and national need makes the promotion of literacy look like a matter of highest priority. Such urgency, as
perceived by development-devoted governments of the Northern
Hemisphere, may occlude some of the paradoxes and potential errors
that lie in wait to trip up smug evangelists.

Mr. Grimmis was lecturing to schoolchildren. For those mature,
adult parents who pay his salary, his "insider" position is attractive.
Knowledge is power, and inferiority accompanies ignorance. But, over
at the other end of the cartoon strip, we onlookers are asked to reconsider the relationships between teacher and pupil, parent and child,
member and aspirant: One of the precocious kindergarteners asks a co-
conspirator at the back of the room, "NOW do you know what they
mean by 'political prisoners'?"

As the fortunate possessors of the ability to read and write, our duty
to those less fortunate looks transparently clear: help "the illiterate"
learn to do what we can do. We think our life is better than theirs, and
we want to share the specific ability that we take to be the cause of that
betterness. When Mr. Grimmis's altruistic giving takes on a resemblance
to Torquemada's earnestness, however, when the offer of assistance becomes the insistent war cry, "It's for your own good," when liberation is
also obliteration, that transparent simplicity clouds over very fast.

Does the gain compensate for the loss? What motivates the givers?
Are there unintended consequences? Are we, the literate, actually in the
grips of an addiction and desperately trying to force others to join us? Is
literacy an "absolute" concept, determinable once and for all, "where is
and as is," or is it a slippery notion, varying in different locales and different circumstances? If it is not measurable on a universal scale, who is
entitled to talk about "literacy" outside of its immediate context? Is the
"literacy problem" actually a fraud being perpetrated by educationist
xenophiles?

The phenomenon of irreversibility surrounds these complexities.
Once one has learned to read and write, one cannot willfully erase the
competence. Once we have learned to read we cannot "unlearn," and
we "know" that knowing how is better than being ignorant. Having acquired the credentials, furthermore, we patronize the unfortunate who

have not qualified for membership. It is only natural that we should seek to share our good fortune. Yet it is these assumptions that deserve some consideration before we turn them into action. It is possible to allege that literacy is more curse than cure.

The monotype of such one-way journeys is The Fall, the drama of original sin played against the backdrop of Creation. Once innocence is lost, there's no getting it back. You can't go home again. Ludwig von Bertalanffy once hypothesized a specific connection between language use and the psychology of the fall. In his speculation, oral communication "beyond the grunt," so to speak, sparked the original sin. He wondered if Genesis dramatized the first opportunity say one thing while thinking another. Using language to lie, that is, is the essence of original sin, at least as crucial as disobedience or pride. It was after the fall that wise people made sure there was a third person in the room when an oral agreement was reached.

We can speculate, by stretching the analogy further, that the next stumble occurred when it became easy for a patent-medicine pitchman to *think* in terms of greed, *speak* to his audience in terms of cure, and provide exculpatory conditions only in the fine *print* on the label. Writing added a layer of complexity to the opportunities that voice had given us for role-playing. The "blind carbon," the copy sent "secretly" to a third party, became an instrument of conspiracy. Literacy compounded the corruptions of orality. This innocence-experience model is essentially one of instant corruption, of a fall away from gracious simplicity into (some would say) Western, capitalist, modernist materialism.

There is another model of irreversible change, a progressive version that emphasizes upward mobility and positive development. This cultural-evolution model generally associates "language" with memory, history, and culture—and aligns writing with science, credit, and constitutional governance. It connects written records with consistent measurement and calculation, with fractional-reserve banking, and with reverence for government by document. This thoroughly secular model, in which natural chaos and divine design are gradually nudged aside by calculations of likelihood and by long-range planning, leads to a set of assumptions about prediction and property and progress that look remarkably like materialistic, modern, Western capitalism.

In either model, the ability to record and use records—to write and to read—is implicated in the generation of significant change, whether gradual or sudden, whether for "the culture" as a demographic whole or for individuals one at a time. What is more, the transition cannot help but look oppressive and exploitative. In Jack Goody's words (out of a legal, marriage-registration context): "The written law is thus highly partial in every sense of the word, favouring the literate few at the expense of the illiterate many" (158). Less obvious but even more important, the illiterate are absolutely prevented from knowing the consequences of literacy before they "give it a try"; "choice" is meaningless because experimenting with one alternative—writing and reading—makes the other alternative—illiteracy—impossible. There have been circumstances, to be sure, where a few elite have wanted to restrict the privilege of literacy for the same reason that a few others want to promote it—because it will lead to revolution. But neither the pushers nor the proscribers have pretended that the literate can choose to return to blissful ignorance any more than theologians can argue that the burden of making choices can be refused. From this point of view, it looks as if the literate Mr. Grimmises have all the power, and are either tempting or forcing those without it to leave their innocence behind.

But this interpretation is misleading. It perverts the inevitable gap between knowledge and ignorance by portraying the older and more experienced dwellers on the "later" side of the gap as somehow conspiratorial, as selfish indoctrinators taking advantage of the less fortunate. The bridge across that gap runs in one direction: Those who "know more" cannot choose to erase what they have learned, and those who "know less," having become suspicious about the motives of their "superiors," will remain antagonistic until they too have gained the experience that takes them across the one-way bridge.

Neither being aware of the gap and the bridge, nor recognizing the theological fall and the secular transformation of culture, nor even being wistful about having left Eden, makes the preservation of apparent innocence a sensible goal, even for the most romantic idealists. Even if later is not better, if knowing more is not definitively superior, there is indeed no going back. The move to help others acquire abilities we possess is a sincere attempt to give power away, not a selfish attempt to indoctrinate and control the uncorrupted. The extension of Western standards of living and planning and controlling may not be entirely altruistic on the part of every participant, but at this point change is not a matter of choice: the globe is hurtling down a one-way street, and bringing ourselves together to learn to steer seems more sensible than trying to stop and find reverse gear.

All of this is little more than a backdrop for arguing that we who can read this volume have a responsibility to realize that we are all in Mr. Grimmis's position. We have been released from the relative "innocence" of oral acculturation through an initiation rite of schooling into a patronizing and mutually congratulatory oligarchy of literacy. We, of the Northern Hemisphere and Western civilization, ought to be conscious of what we think we are doing as we offer to share our power with—or impose our values on—those we perceive as less fortunate. The essays in this volume all help us stand back from unexamined immersion in the crusade, help us recognize the maelstrom of complexity lurking just behind pious policies.

There are those, for instance, who say there is a crisis in literacy and basic education. The problem and its potential solutions raise questions of language and cultural policy, economic planning, political and social mobilization, and materials production, not to mention issues of pedagogy, teacher training, and assessment. At the same time these various figures and programs make the issue of literacy seem a large and impersonal phenomenon. Yet again, we know that learning to read and write, or failing to be able to read and write in a literate society, are personal and human concerns. Literacy is not simply a statistic; it impinges upon and shapes the lives of individuals. Literacy programs see people in terms of groups and numbers and classes. For the person, however, it may be a matter of dealing with the local market or settling one's spiritual affairs.

Educational systems have long recognized but they have not reconciled this tension between the group and the individual. The goals of education as propounded in the Faure Report of UNESCO, *Learning to Be* (1972), suggest that developing the broader social polity through schools must be prior to and then be fitted with the development of individual potential. In regard to literacy, however, writers tend to look at the phenomenon from a broad demographic view—what is called the etic view—and not from the view that situates the individual within a particular social and cultural system—what is called the emic view. The same may be said to be true of educational systems that are primarily the instruments of the state or organized religion, and only secondarily comprised of individuals who seek to foster the growth of other individuals. Yet literacy for each person is—or may be—quite different from literacy for groups and subgroups. Literacy is situated in the present; it is not an abstraction.

Another way of viewing the dilemma is from a sociocultural perspective. Providing basic education for all may undermine the existing cultures of the society and move the society willy-nilly into a standardized society. In a recent article in *The Courier*, Federico Mayor wrote, "... culture should be regarded as a direct source of inspiration for development, and in return, development should assign to culture a central role as a social regulator. This imperative applies not only to developing countries, where economic extraversion and cultural alienation have clearly and sometimes dramatically widened the gap between the creative and productive processes. It is also increasingly vital for indus-trialized countries, where the headlong race for growth in material wealth is detrimental to the spiritual, ethical and aesthetic aspects of life, and creates much disharmony between man and the natural environ-ment" (1988, p. 5). The implication of such a statement for literacy edu-cation is that while it may be important to see education internationally as a race that will lead to monoculturalism and economic gain, such a single-minded approach may cause great harm. Education leads people away from their past and their family; it is the main cause of alienation as well as the main cause of acculturation. One set of questions some of the essays in this volume raise may help to determine which educa-tional programs serve best to educate people for development without destroying their cultural heritage and cultural pride.

Education must meet the needs of society by fostering the broadest range of social communication, and education must be used for individ-ual development and to foster freedom from the dominance of systems. In reading and literature education, these polar goals lead some educa-tors to assert that there is a common, consensual, or correct meaning to a text that is to be learned, and lead others to claim that the critical re-sponse of the individual reader is to be fostered and to be seen as hav-ing ascendancy in educational life. In writing education, the goals are often represented by the slogans "product" and "process," with the for-mer suggesting a conformity to certain text models and the latter imply-ing the development of individual freedom in composition. Often the adherents of one or the other of the goals have couched the debate in political terms, as can be seen in the writings of Allan Bloom and *The Closing of the American Mind* on the one hand and Paolo Freire and *The Pedagogy of the Oppressed* on the other.

This volume seeks to address this and other tensions and paradoxes by bringing together a group of distinguished authors who view liter-acy and schooling from the perspective of the individual or that of the social system, but who are acutely aware that their view is only a part of the whole. We hope that by bringing these views into juxtaposition we can help the reader recognize some of the complexities that envelop the multitude around the world who seek to promote literacy among its populace.

The tension is particularly apparent in schools. They are for the most part institutions of the state or of a religious group, yet their teach-ers must deal with individual children, not abstractions of public policy. The authors deal here with literacy in both industrialized and develop-ing nations, for they see the differences between the two as differences less in kind than in degree.

Taken together, the essays in this volume answer almost as many questions as they ask. Yes, literacy is a complicated, paradoxical concept. Yes, it is self-righteous to utter the syllables "the illiterate." Yes, what goes on in Africa is pertinent to John Teacher and Jane Pupil in rural America and urban Paris. And yes, policy and reform and inertia in Norman Rockwell villages are good illustrations of global dilemmas.

The University at Albany

2

Literacy as Culture: Emic and Etic Perspectives

DANIEL A. WAGNER

A Moroccan Vignette: Oum Fatima and Print

Oum Fatima has labored virtually everyday of her fifty-five or so years of age, and with a chronically ill husband unable to help financially, she could only hope to do housecleaning in the wealthier homes of the labyrinthian *medina* (old city) of Marrakech.

Beyond regular washer-woman duties, it was normal for Oum Fatima to handle a gamut of contacts between the "outside world" and the home and children for which she worked so hard. Such activities varied enormously. On some days, the mailman would arrive with letters; Oum Fatima would deliver each to the addressee, knowing simply by the type of handwriting or script used—Arabic or French—who should receive which letter. Once a month, the "electric man" would arrive to collect money for the month's charges; Oum Fatima handled this affair with just a question or two, drawing from a earthenware jar stashed with odd coins and bills which she always maintained in anticipation of his visits. At the *souk* (market), Oum Fatima's prowess with money was legendary. Not only could she switch effortlessly in mental calculations between the several parallel money systems in use—dirhams, francs, and rials (with a base-five system)—but her frugality and ability to negotiate the lowest possible price made her a well-known figure in the *derb* (quarter). To those of her social class, as well as to those "higher up," Oum Fatima was a woman worthy of great respect.

Never having gone to school, Oum Fatima could neither read nor write in any language, nor do simple arithmetic on paper.

While both local educators and international policy makers would label Oum Fatima as "illiterate," most people in her *derb* know her as a shrewd bargainer, astute with money, and among the most competent individuals they know. The use and misuse of the label of literacy (or illiteracy) is one principal focus of this volume. How one interprets Oum Fatima's ability and behavior in this one, relatively narrow, segment of

11

her life has become one of the key social issues of our time.

"Literacy" is a remarkable term. While seeming to refer to simple individual possession of the complementary mental technologies of reading and writing, literacy is not only difficult to define in individuals and delimit within societies, but it is also charged with emotional and political meaning. It was not long ago that newspapers and scholars referred to whole societies as "illiterate and uncivilized" as a single referent, and "illiterate" is still a term which carries a negative connotation, as it might still to many contemporary observers of Oum Fatima.

Defining literacy as an individual cognitive phenomenon was once thought to be simple: it simply entailed testing for reading and writing skills. This could involve, as in relatively recent American voting laws, the ability to sign one's name. Or, as is generally done by international and national organizations for statistical and methodological expediency, literacy may be simply inferred from school attendance: those with four (or eight or twelve) years of formal public schooling are assumed to be literate. We now know that such approaches to presumed literacy may be misleading, if not often incorrect. When considered as a cultural—as contrasted to a cognitive—phenomenon, literacy is even less well defined, since its functions, meanings, and methods of transmission may vary greatly from one cultural group to the next.

As social scientists seek to compare and contrast cultural differences in cognition, language, and literacy, an important conceptual distinction must be addressed. First introduced by Pike (1966), and then elaborated by Berry and Dasen (1974), the distinction between "emic" and "etic" concepts is crucial to the present discussion. Emic concepts are those that can be understood only within a single cultural system or society, and can be measured only according to criteria relevant to and understood within that single system. Etic concepts are those which are deduced or derived from a position outside of any particular system, and have as a primary goal the analysis of more than a single society—in sum, cross-societal or cross-cultural comparisons.

In the context of the present discussion, an etic perspective on literacy assumes that skills such as decoding, word-picture-matching, and reading a medicine bottle's instructions ought to have substantially the same meaning to different individuals and across different cultural groups. An emic perspective on literacy would encompass other types of meanings and skills associated with literacy within cultural groups. In the Moroccan vignette, an emic definition of literacy would incorporate Oum Fatima's "script recognition" skills, as well as knowledge about the uses of print by the Moroccan government, and even oral recitation of the Quran. That these practices are thought of—by actors and local observers alike—as constituting "literate behavior" in Morocco demonstrates the importance of an emic definition of literacy. In the context of the present discussion, then, emic literacy skills would be those which have not only not been "imported" from some other source (such as keyboarding skills in Morocco), but also are embedded in the social life of individuals. What is particularly crucial in the emic-etic distinction is that the emic skills be those which can only be adequately understood within a given cultural framework, and were not created for historical convenience by those who desire a common or universal system of measurement.

Does an interest in emic skills and behaviors necessarily call into question the utility of etic measures? Not really. Etic measures are also important in understanding how people acquire literacy, and how educators and policymakers view literacy; furthermore, the etic perspective has played a critical role in the vast majority of literacy studies in contemporary educational research. Since the measurement of literacy has, over the last century, been associated with school achievement, it was to be expected that quantifiable tools would be developed to compare etic-based norms for the comparison of individuals and groups. But the convenience of such psychometric measurement of literacy need not and should not be the only way we view the acquisition of literacy. Indeed, the psychometric tradition of measurement purposefully ignores most of the process and context features of literacy which affect its acquisition and use.

BECOMING LITERATE

While a review of the origins and history of literacy is well beyond the scope of this paper, it is useful to highlight some areas which are relevant to the present discussion. Turning points in the production of literate materials—from the Dead Sea Scrolls to the Gutenberg Bible to the word processor—have served as markers of social and cultural change. Conversely, historical changes in society have played major roles in the popular use of literate materials, as evidenced, for example, by the need of thirteenth-century British landlords to control the intergenerational transfer of property through legal documents, and the rise of mass public education in nineteenth-century France. These and other historical perspectives on literacy are described in recent volumes by Graff (1981), Eisenstein (1979), and Clanchy (1979). What is most impressive in historical accounts of literacy is the importance that reading and writing—often as separate activities—have been given over the centuries. That clergymen of many of the world's great religions were also the possessors of one or both of these skills signifies not only the sometimes "restricted" (Goody and Watt, 1968) nature of literacy, but its social and moral power as well.

On the one hand, the history of literacy parallels and has been implicated in several of the greatest changes in social history, such as religion, public schooling, and even the establishment of democracy. On the other hand, such an over-the-shoulder look at history tends to obfuscate the presence of many traditional forms and emic dimensions of literacy in contemporary societies of both the developing and industrialized worlds. Morocco, as we shall see, provides an interesting case in point, as it contains dimensions of literacy which reflect its stance partway between each of these worlds, and between emic and etic conceptions of literacy as well.

Setting aside for a moment the aforementioned definitional issues, it has generally been taken for granted that literacy was and still is a major factor in the economic development of nations, whether industrialized or Third World. This assertion derives from three rather different presuppositions. First, there are those who believe that literacy is an active and important component in the process of social development, and is linked in a causal way to economic growth. In this context, literacy is perceived as being able to change attitudes and bring new information to people previously deprived of sources of information beyond their village limits. Second, it is commonly believed that the tasks of economic productivity are themselves directly dependent on the ability of individuals to utilize the tools of literacy. Recent reviews of this issue by various social scientists (Chall, 1987; Miller, 1988) make it abundantly clear that the average expected standard of skills for workers is far higher now than only a few decades ago.

Third, and with respect to Third World countries in particular, it has been frequently claimed that "minimum functional literacy skills"—as evidenced by four to six years of primary schooling—are required among the citizenry in order to attain sustained economic growth. The argument is that a "threshold" number of years of education is required for more or less *permanent* literacy to be acquired by the individual (Fagerlind and Saha, 1983). Interestingly, little in the way of empirical research has been done to support such claims of literacy retention, which are, nonetheless, crucial to the argument that formal schooling is the route to social and economic development. Such societal-level claims are based primarily on cross-national comparisons of presumed literacy rates with economic growth (usually gross national product), using national census data.

Until recently, most specialists typically thought of literacy as a phenomenon that was perhaps the most central consequence of formal schooling. After all, the curricula of schooling the world over have the teaching of reading and writing as a major pedagogical goal. It comes as no surprise, then, that the vast preponderance of research on reading and writing involves how the individual learns these skills, and what pedagogies are optimal for teaching them.

Historical and anthropological work now shows, however, that literacy was and is often transmitted outside of the normal channels of schooling. For example, as early as the sixteenth century, reading was said to be widespread in Sweden as a function of family efforts to read the Bible at home (Graff, 1981). In contemporary Liberia, the Vai people still teach each other the indigenous Vai script, completely beyond the confines of any schooling experience (Scribner and Cole, 1981), while the Native American Cree of Northern Canada maintain the use of their syllabic script as a source of cultural identity (Bennett and Berry, 1987). Naturally, before the rise of mass public education in the nineteenth and twentieth centuries, literacy was provided by other channels, most notably that of the religious school, a topic to which we shall return later on.

An important locus of out-of-school learning is the home. Where literacy exists in the household, among parents and/or older siblings, the child has an opportunity to learn a great deal about the functions and uses of print—and how to employ them—well before setting foot in school. In the United States, there has been a dramatic increase in research on the nature and influence of home learning of reading and writing skills. It has been found that families in which parents read storybooks to their children (Teale and Sulzby, 1987) and provide helpful learning environments (Snow, et al, 1991; Heath, 1983; Wagner and Spratt, 1988) tend to produce children who learn to read well in school. Conversely, in homes where such supports are lacking, children are far less likely to become proficient readers in school.

TRADITIONAL WAYS OF BECOMING LITERATE

As mentioned earlier, religious schools—Jewish, Christian, Islamic, and Buddhist—have been among the major providers of literacy over the past two millennia. From the great Islamic universities of Spain and North Africa to the Buddhist monasteries of Thailand and Sri Lanka, scholars and their students gathered to share the wisdom of the ages through the reading and interpretation of ancient texts and exegeses (Eickelman, 1978; Tambiah, 1968). These schools shared a number of common characteristics, such as the presence of a "master" and his "apprentices," often with children, adolescents, and adults clustered together in the same class. Teachers were almost always male, and had considerable power over their charges, as well as in the community at large.

While most of the traditional masters were expert in the reading and writing of religious texts, what is less well known is that below this elite was an ever-widening pyramid of students and a religious public who were much less able to utilize "full" literacy skills. Some, for example, could engage in religious recitations that required decoding but little comprehension, while others might use writing skills acquired in religious school for use in personal letters or business transactions. Such religious literacy is still maintained in diverse geographical areas of the Islamic world, where a traditional pedagogy continues to be used in Quranic schools. In spite of a lack of transferable "etic" literacy skills, many Quranic school teachers are considered to be "literate" by the community, since they have the accoutrements of literacy (such as owning books, presiding over books, and recitation ability), and because they are simply the *most* literate individuals in their town. Further research on Quranic schooling and religious literacy in Morocco has been described elsewhere (Wagner, 1986; Wagner and Lotfi, 1980, 1983; Wagner, Messick, and Spratt, 1986).

As in many Third World settings, adult women in Morocco are, on the average, considerably less schooled and less literate than Moroccan men—women average about one year of schooling versus four for men. Yet, most Moroccan women in our study had considerable knowledge of the functions and uses of literacy in Morocco, and how to "get" literacy if and when it was needed. The examples cited by illiterate Moroccan women were quite varied: ranging from how to interpret modern medical instructions (by asking a literate eldest son) to finding the appropriate traditional doctor who could write the needed amulet for protection from evil spirits (Wagner, Messick, and Spratt, 1986). Perhaps most interesting was the women's expressed need for having *access* to literate persons who could accomplish literacy acts when required. Thus, it is *not* the case that most Moroccan women felt the need to be literate themselves, nor that they felt that each of their children needs to be literate, but rather that the family must have available at least someone who can deal with such matters as decoding and/or encoding print. The implications for this type of finding are serious, especially when considering the oft-accepted notions of "universal" literacy adopted by numerous international organizations and individual countries.

The findings from our Moroccan research suggest that one can be considered to be "literate" without a full mastery of etic literacy skills in any language; conversely, one may be considered to be "illiterate" (*maqariash* or "nonlearned" in Moroccan Arabic) if not in possession of the *right kind* of emic literacy skills (such as the ability to recite by heart certain passages of the Quran, or knowledge of traditional medicine). From an emic Moroccan perspective, individuals are often classified as "literate" or "illiterate," but these culturally based categories may differ dramatically from those used in industrialized societies.

POLICY IMPLICATIONS OF EMIC DIMENSIONS OF LITERACY

Vignette: At the Gas Station

It is a bright sunny April day as Si Mohamed drives the office car into the brand new Afriquia gas station in Berrechid, Morocco. When Allal, the gas station attendant, has filled the gas tank, Si Mohamed asks for a *facture* (receipt) for reimbursement. Allal rummages briefly through his leather money bag and carefully extracts a pad of blank *factures* and a blackened rubber stamp with the station's name and address. With a deep breath he exhales on the rubber stamp, moistening it slightly, and then presses it with deliberation into the *facture* paper. This small rubber stamp, like tens of thousands all over Morocco, serves as the guarantor of official literacy in Morocco. Allal, who cannot read or write, then hands the stamped paper to Si Mohamed, who fills in the date, amount of gas, and the price.

This joint literacy act of Allal and Si Mohamed provides another exemplar of the notion of an emic or culturally derived definition of literacy. There is a tendency among specialists to treat literacy as something to be understood as affected *by* various cultural factors. Here it is suggested that literacy may be thought of as being as much a *part* of culture as is, say, language—and just as difficult to disembed and isolate as an independent factor or element.

The implications of such a proposition are, I think, rather serious. If literacy is culture, then interventions in or "tampering" with literacy—i.e., through campaigns of any kind, and even schooling—is to change, sometimes forcibly, the way people live. Because policymakers and educators have often treated literacy as essentially separate from culture (what Street, 1987, refers to as an "autonomous" model of literacy), relatively little attention has been paid to the *negative* consequences (not to mention the actual financial costs) of becoming literate. The very idea of negative effects may seem antithetical to many, and yet there is ample evidence that the failure of many, if not most, literacy campaigns, derives heavily from *resistance* to outsiders' intrusion into the lives of people who have coped with little or no literacy over long periods of time (Wagner, 1990); this same type of resistance has been proposed by Giroux (1983) and Gilmore (1986) as being partly responsible for the failure of minority children to learn in American classrooms.

Taking this argument one step further, policymakers may need to pause and reconsider the high priority given to the achievement of *universal* or *minimum basic* literacy among adults in low-literate societies or in low-literate "pockets" of industrialized societies (sometimes referred to as the Fourth World). An alternative policy would suggest that resources be invested in a more constrained fashion, directing more funds to pre- and primary schools, or to specific groups of adults. In this way, some individuals—those less resistant to and more motivated for change—would have access to resources for becoming literate or more literate. Indeed, recent evidence on volunteer literacy effort in the United States suggests that the least literate portion of the population is remarkably resistant to literacy training, often exhibiting much higher rates of program attrition and skill loss after one or two months of program completion (Mickulecky, 1986).

Yet, how do we come to grips with the common sense notion that literacy *ought* to be provided to all, in the same way that governments try to provide health services? If the present analysis has some validity, mass literacy programs that are broadly and etically conceived are not only likely to have minimal success, but are also likely to be least successful among those people who are most illiterate and furthest from the mainstream dominant culture. Such large-scale programs may be counterproductive in the long term simply because they pose a challenge to the cultural lives of the people "targeted" for participation. By contrast, literacy programs which have been adapted through meaningful understanding of *local* contexts and *specific* needs—essentially an emic framework—seem more likely to succeed in the long run.

CONCLUSIONS

In the popular media and in academic circles it is not uncommon to hear that the low level, or lack, of literacy is among the chief problems facing contemporary America, and indeed the rest of the world. There are numerous arguments that would support concern for such a point of view, ranging from the economic pressure on the American workplace to the advent of robotics, to increased farmer productivity in developing countries, and the major problems endemic in today's urban secondary schools in the United States. Literacy is part of policy discussions in all of these areas, and yet it has remained unclear as to whether simply more literacy would help to alleviate the perceived problems. I have tried to suggest that both industrialized and developing nations have a common literacy "problem." That is, literacy—when seen in emic terms—is an inherent part of the cultural fabric by which peoples everywhere live their lives. A very small percentage of twentieth-century adults can still be labeled as "naive illiterates"—those with absolutely no knowledge of the existence and use of written language. The literacy problem is not a matter of illiteracy in extreme forms, but rather a matter of varying degrees and types of literacy skills, behaviors, and beliefs.

Any attempt to intervene in order to change an individual's literacy status means change not only in a set of etic skills (as measured by most tests and taught in most schools), but also in the emic, socially constructed and mediated behaviors and beliefs that define each individual, the rest of his or her community, and, ultimately, the communities and societies themselves. Resistance to individual and cultural change is not a new topic in social science, and yet it has remained relatively unexplored in current conversations about literacy. We may ask ourselves whether the very high dropout rate from American adult literacy programs is related to such a cultural discrepancy between recipients and providers, or whether the limited successes of Third World literacy campaigns may be a function of resistance to national (often revolutionary) authority. As various policy options toward trying to improve literacy are considered, the issue of its cultural roles and emic dimensions needs to be better understood. Literacy as a cultural entity is already a part of virtually all of today's societies, whether industrialized or developing. To change it is to change the individual and ourselves.

The University of Pennsylvania

II

LITERACY FROM
SOCIETY'S PERSPECTIVE

3

Literacy, Economic Structures, and Individual and Public Policy Incentives

DOUGLAS M. WINDHAM

INTRODUCTION

This paper reviews the assertions commonly made for literacy in justifying it as an activity worthy of promotion and social support. The discussion leads to an analysis of how the interactive relationship between literacy and economic structures presents configurations of incentives (negative and positive) that vary among individuals and within and among nations. These incentives, in both monetary and nonmonetary forms, ultimately determine both the societal and individual justification for support of and participation in literacy programs.

The reciprocal relationship between literacy and economic structures is stressed in the discussion of how literacy can encourage or discourage certain forms of technological innovation, and how innovation itself changes the rewards for literacy acquisition and use. Within this context of reciprocity, a variety of political and administrative challenges faced by literacy programs is reviewed.

THE JUSTIFICATION FOR A LITERACY EMPHASIS IN PUBLIC POLICY

The following assertions commonly are made concerning literacy: (1) literacy is a basic human right; (2) literacy promotes an improved quality of life; (3) literacy is a basis for enhanced lifelong opportunities for education and personal development; (4) literacy reduces social and economic disparities; (5) literacy promotes national health, nutrition, and population goals; (6) literacy promotes political and economic freedom; and (7) literacy encourages national economic development and adaptation to technological change. However, the validity and relevance of each of these assertions is context-specific. Any effective policy approach to literacy has "to be tailored to the particular . . . conditions existing in each country. It will only work where this is done" (Lind and Johnston, 1986).

In this essay, the "particular conditions" imposed by economic structures on the promotion of literacy and how these interact either to encourage or to constrain the wider access to literacy skills will be discussed. Both the status of literacy attainment and the nature and development of economic structures within a given country will determine if any of the aforementioned seven assertions concerning literacy are deemed to have either political or economic merit.

The assertion of literacy as a basic human right has general political acceptance in most societies; however, as with all such assertions of "rights," it is meaningful only to the extent that a society has the ability and the willingness to make the right a reality. As indicated in Table 3.1, almost 890 million illiterate adults are estimated worldwide and nine countries have more than ten million citizens without literacy skills (ranging from India with 264 million and China with 229 million to Iran

TABLE 3.1
The Incidence of Illiteracy

Country	Illiteracy Rate (1985)	No. of Illiterates	Proportion of World Total	
	(%)	(millions)	(%)	(cum. %)
India	56.5	264	29.7	29.7
China	30.7	229	25.8	55.5
Pakistan	70.4	39	4.4	59.9
Bangladesh	66.9	37	4.2	64.1
Nigeria	57.6	27	3.0	67.1
Indonesia	25.9	26	2.9	70.0
Brazil	22.3	19	2.1	72.1
Egypt	55.5	16	1.8	73.9
Iran	49.2	12	1.3	75.2
Subtotal (9 countries)		699	75.2	
Other Countries		220	24.8	
World Total		889	100.0	

Source: UNESCO, Office of Statistics, 1988.

with just over 12 million). While the percentage of adults who are illiterate has declined in the last twenty years, there is no assurance this decline can be maintained, because developing nations face increased future population growth in the over-fifteen-year age cohort and reductions in basic educational opportunities and/or effectiveness. For example, the UNESCO estimates of primary education gross enrollment ratios (the number enrolled as a proportion of the "official" age group for primary education) indicate that eighteen of forty-three sub-Saharan countries (with comparable data) reported a *decline* in enrollment ratios between 1980 and 1986. More generally, literacy has the potential of becoming more of a privilege than a right in many countries by the beginning of the next century, when UNESCO predicts the number of illiterates will exceed one billion worldwide.

To gain support to offset these trends and to mobilize new support for literacy activities, public policy attention is being directed to the effects of literacy. The ability of literacy to promote an improved quality of life for the individual and to serve as a basis for enhanced lifetime opportunities is a conditional ability at best in many countries. The achievement of literacy is a necessary but far from sufficient premise for these asserted effects. The nature of educational access and effectiveness, and the ability of the economy to absorb literate and post-literate labor and of the political structure to adapt to the empowerment of the individuals, will be the ultimate determinants of whether literacy can achieve these benefits for the individuals and their societies.

Even more problematic are the assertions concerning the effect of greater literacy on social and economic disparities, on national health, nutrition, and population goals, and on the encouragement of aggregate economic development and adaptation to technological change. Again, the attainment of greater literacy among a population is only a partial determinant of these desired outcomes.

Reducing social or economic disparities assumes a relative demand for literacy skills that is sufficient to result in higher real incomes for previously disadvantaged populations. However, if the supply of new literates exceeds the demand, then the social and economic benefits to new literates may be delayed or even denied altogether. This can occur even in a competitive labor market; if, as is often the case in less developed regions or nations, there is significant labor market oligopsony (a restriction on labor hiring by collusion among or limitation in the number of employers), the benefits of literacy may go predominantly to the employers rather than to the newly literate workers. Finally, if racial, ethnic, or some other form of market discrimination is effective at segmenting the labor market, the newly literate entrants may find themselves receiving wages significantly less than those available to equivalent members of the present labor force.

This pessimistic situation is not inevitable but is more than just possible: without proper political and legal infrastructure for the economy, exploitive practices toward this new segment of the labor force are quite probable. Thus, even if literacy can be accepted to have the productivity-enhancing effects many are prepared to assign to it (Lockheed, Jamison, and Lau, 1980), a question remains about the extent to which the benefits of this additional productivity will accrue to the worker, the employer, or to the nation.

The gains anticipated in health, nutrition, and population are dependent upon the extent to which literacy increases are concomitant with increased availability of information, technology, and resources. In each of the three areas of health, nutrition, and population, literacy skills among adults can greatly advance dissemination and use of relevant knowledge. But this knowledge will not be effectively used unless the "tools" for implementation are provided. It simply is not adequate to teach people the need for vaccinations or for boiled water, the types of food that are nutritious, and how to avoid unwanted pregnancy. These programs must be judged by changes in behavior, not simply changes in understanding, and the latter is not sufficient to cause the former.

Literacy programs in this context must not be designed as if literacy is other than a mediating goal; the final goals are larger, more complex, and require a wider range of resources (and delivery agents) than that of literacy. The larger goals can be obtained without literacy, but the existing body of research indicates that literacy training is the most cost-effective means of promoting a synergistic program wherein the larger goals of health, nutrition, and population programs can be achieved concurrently with the other benefits that literacy can promote.

In recent years, increased attention has been directed to the benefits of greater political and economic freedom. At the end of a decade that has seen a significant increase in democratic political structures, and in market rather than bureaucratically controlled economies, the importance of literacy is underlined. For individuals and subgroups within a polity to be able to exercise their influence, they must be able to comprehend their own self-interests and then get around administrative barriers to the exercise of their political rights.

Similarly, as more reliance is placed on market forces, there is a danger that predatory practices by employers and sellers will take the place of the ineffectiveness and corruption of planned economies. In fact, given the continued role of government in the new "mixed economies" of Eastern Europe and Asia, the opportunity for merging the worst—rather than the best—of both systems is a real hazard. A major check against this is a population of voters, workers, and consumers who, being literate, can understand their political and market options and will exercise them in a manner that promotes their own enlightened self-interest.

The "consumer sovereignty" that characterizes a market economy can only be beneficial if the consumers have a basic understanding of their options and of the implications of each choice. Literacy is, once again, the most cost-effective means of promoting this ability. Obviously, just as political democracies are subject to demagoguery, so market economies are subject to producing tawdry products and unfair employment practices. The ability of a more literate population to help assure an equitable environment for both political and economic freedom is one of the strongest arguments that can be made for literacy. As we enter the 1990s, that argument has greater merit than ever before.

THE RECIPROCITY OF LITERACY AND ECONOMIC STRUCTURES

The complexity of the relationship between the level of literacy in a society and the society's economic structures is especially complex because each adapts to changes in the other. Obviously, the labor market for workers will adapt to changes in the supply of literate workers. This is perhaps the most direct relationship and the easiest to understand. If, for a given period of time, the increase in the supply of such workers exceeds the increase in demand for them, then this condition will have a negative effect on workers' wages. If the change in demand for such workers exceeds the change in supply, then wages will face an upward pressure. As noted earlier, however, even these relationships can be complicated where oligopsony or other anticompetitive market forces exist.

Less well understood is the ability of the economic structures to adjust over time and how the incentives to acquire and maintain literacy are altered as the economic structures evolve. It is this recurrent reciprocity between the two that is the most significant characteristic in the study of literacy as a cause and as a result of economic change.

The least adequately discussed of the earlier assertions concerning literacy has been the way it can encourage national economic development and adaptation to technological change. Increased literacy can, in concert with appropriate production technologies and resources, increase a worker's productivity (Jamison and Lau, 1982; Jamison and Moock, 1984; Cotlear, 1986). If the value of this increased productivity exceeds the cost of literacy training, then this justification alone is sufficient to rationalize the investment in the literacy program for that individual. However, there is no natural congruence between the justification for the nation investing in literacy training and for the individual investing in it. The ultimate rationale must depend upon the relationship of benefits to costs (in both monetary and nonmonetary forms).

It has already been noted that the benefits of literacy programs do not accrue solely to the individual: other workers may benefit (from the greater productivity of their peers), employers may benefit (from a greater increase in worker productivity than in worker costs), and the nation may benefit (from enhanced tax income, human resource availability, political participation, cultural involvement, and international trade advantages). In addition to these overtly "economic" benefits, we also must consider the benefits of individual self-esteem and dignity and the effect of a literate citizenry on national goals of political or economic liberty.

This calculation of the benefits and costs of literacy must consider four aspects: (1) the amount of benefits and costs; (2) the incidence of benefits and costs; (3) the form of benefits and costs; and (4) the certainty of benefits and costs. To compare the amount of benefits and costs without consideration of the other three aspects of the benefit/cost relationship can lead to policy anomalies of the type that often burden literacy programs: e.g., why potential clients do not join or persist in programs or why political will for illiteracy eradication often is lacking even when the economic capacity is more than sufficient.

The incidence of benefits and costs relates to the question of who receives the benefits and who pays the cost. In any program, the incidence of costs will vary among the individual, the employer, and the nation (usually represented by the central government); from program to program (and even more so from nation to nation), the pattern of incidence will vary among these three parties. For example, a "free" program may have no money cost for participants (who still may have to sacrifice productive and/or leisure time), but must impose costs on private agencies or the government (which may or may not finance these costs through taxes that affect employers, workers, or consumers).

It is quite easy to envision a program which one or two of the three parties would support but another would not. A reason for nonparticipation or non-continuance could be that participants feel they bear too much of the costs and receive too small a share of the benefits from enhanced literacy. Similarly, if the government feels that literacy benefits accrue primarily to individuals and not to the government (or to specific parties, politicians, or political alliances) then the government may not support the further extension of literacy even when it can afford to do so. The true measure of a nation's commitment to literacy is indicated by the level and effectiveness of its expenditures, not by its rhetorical zeal for literacy as a "basic human right."

Related to the issue of the incidence of benefits and costs is the form that benefits and costs take. If the benefits are primarily nonfinancial and collective, and the costs are financial and individual, then the participants are unlikely to be able to justify joining the training program even if the program is rational in terms of the collective benefits and costs. Psychological benefits to individuals from literacy training are very real and legitimate considerations—it is not, however, realistic or legitimate to expect economically disadvantaged individuals readily to sacrifice scarce monetary resources to finance the acquisition of non-monetary psychological benefits. The reason literacy programs require subsidization (and they often are undersubsidized in this context) is that the form and the incidence of benefits are not such that literacy programs can be sustained in a participant-financed system, especially when the desired participants are from economically disadvantaged populations.

Another aspect of incidence is the issue of when the benefits or costs will occur. It is an almost universal characteristic of education and training programs that they involve investments in the short term in exchange for benefits received over the long term (it is this relationship which has led to the economic methodologies of the "human capital" approach to education and training). Given the time-preference of individuals, politicians, and even governments, an equal nominal value of immediate costs and future benefits will not be judged as equal by the recipient. Thus, the future value of benefits must exceed the current value of costs sufficiently to encourage an investment to be made in literacy.

The third consideration, along with benefits and costs, is the issue of the certainty of the benefits or costs. The provider of a literacy program might have a high expectation of the value of the benefits because of greater experience with the outcome of such training and a greater understanding of the nature of labor market supply and demand. The participant, on the other hand, might value the benefits too low, or even too high, depending on their personal experiences. Given that many adult illiterates may have had negative experiences with formal schooling, these potential clients (or parents of potential clients) may undervalue the benefits to be received from an opportunity to engage in training in literacy skills.

Similarly, different individuals may assign different values to the probable costs of the training. Individuals will differ in their opportunity costs and in their ability to finance these costs. A more consistent pattern will exist, however, in the certainty of costs relative to benefits. This again is related to time preference in that, because costs are immediate, they are more certain and because benefits are delayed, they are less certain. In any case, the combination of time preference and the relative certainty of costs versus benefits creates a negative bias by participants toward the literacy program. This bias may not be sufficient to prevent participation, but its presence may necessitate additional subsidization of the program or an energetic demand-mobilization effort as part of the marketing of participation opportunities.

A special case of the benefit-cost consideration exists for parents who must decide whether to have their children participate in basic schooling through the literacy achievement level (Bequele and Boyden, 1988). Even in those countries where the physical capacity of schools and effective government enforcement of compulsory attendance make universal primary education a reality, a lack of parental support for schooling activities can hinder literacy attainment. A more serious situation exists in those countries that lack adequate spaces in schools for the full primary school age cohort, that fail to have or enforce compulsory education laws, and where regulations governing child labor are either inadequate in extent or ineffective in application. Child labor prohibition and the enforcement of compulsory school attendance laws have the effect of reducing the relative cost to the family of having their child in school.

In reality, these laws and regulations are often difficult to enforce, especially in the more rural areas and in the poorest sections of urban areas (for example, see Myers, 1988). Too often, family survival depends on the availability of child labor; even parents supportive of education often have to remove their children from school during planting and harvesting seasons.

In developed nations the greatest problem area is among the urban poor and migrant agricultural workers. Like the rural and urban poor populations of developing nations, these individuals suffer from what is best described as a "convergence of disadvantage." These families face a variety of economic and cultural disadvantages, including: a lack of positive prior experience with education and training; inadequate information and inability to use it effectively; discrimination as a result of being an ethnic or racial minority; instructional resources (teachers, facilities, and materials); a lack of supportive literacy resources such as libraries or museums; less-educated peers, siblings, parents, and other adult role models; and a lower probability of being able to capture the economic benefits of literacy even if literacy is attained. Given this convergence of disadvantage, it is hardly surprising that many of the urban, poor students often are only physically present in schools, rather than being actively engaged in learning, and that absenteeism and truancy are epidemic within schools serving both the urban and rural poor. The special disadvantage to migrant workers of not having a fixed residence further lessens the probability of their children benefiting from basic literacy training within traditional primary schools.

This discussion of the benefits and costs of literacy training is the framework within which the reciprocal nature of literacy and economic structures can best be understood. Changes in economic structures can alter either or both the benefits and the costs of literacy acquisition. The alteration may occur in the amount of benefits, their incidence, their form, or their probability. Similarly, this will lead to a change in the possession of literacy by the population, and this can further change the future costs and benefits of literacy acquisition for new populations. It is an iterative, reciprocal relationship that can be understood only in terms of a dynamic interaction which does not lead directly to an inherently stable equilibrium result.

An example of this can be seen in the case of the introduction of a new technology into the production process. The issue will be whether the new technology enhances or reduces the demand for literate workers (Levin and Rumberger, 1986). Traditionally, it was common to assume this was a unidimensional relationship—that new technology always increased the demand for (and value of) literacy. However, advances of the last two decades in computers and robotics have shown an almost bipolar phenomenon in terms of skill demand. While the creation of such technological changes increases the demand for high levels of postliteracy skills (engineering, electronics, advanced mathematics), the implementation of these technologies in the production process may reduce dramatically the skill demands of certain entry-level production workers. As workers find less demand, and therefore fewer rewards, for literacy skills, new workers will have a reduced incentive to acquire the skills. Then, if literacy becomes a less common entry-level skill, it will become easier for companies to justify new technologies that further reduce the requirement for literacy—and the cycle continues.

It is impossible to forecast the future direction of these effects with any level of acceptable certainty, but one must recognize that there no longer can be an assumption that the labor market demand for literacy skills continually will be increasing. Existing market-based incentives for the already disadvantaged segments of the population may not be sufficient in the future to encourage them to acquire literacy. Collectively, it may become politically more difficult for a nation to justify the financing necessary for universal literacy (however "universal" and "literacy" are defined) when the labor market demand for literacy does not provide appropriate rewards in the form of either higher wages, productivity, or even a greater employment probability.

Given the reciprocity of the relationship between literacy and economic structures, we must expand our views beyond the financial effects of wages and employment to the other structural effects of political participation, the promotion of enlightened consumer sovereignty, and the implications of literacy for other social programs such as health, nutrition, and population to create the incentives for greater literacy demand by individuals and the justification for wider social support. As literacy levels increase, the technology of our societies will adjust to make use of the newly available human resources. While no certainty of employment will exist, the probability of self-sufficiency is increased for individuals and families and the efficacy of transfer and other assistance programs will be reinforced if clients are literate. The wage and employment effects of literacy programs can be reinforced if they are instituted simultaneously with programs that provide incentives for employers to use labor-intensive alternatives in production. Another complementary program that has been shown to be effective combines literacy provision with access to venture capital funds, so that small-level entrepreneurial enterprises can be established or expanded. One means of obviating employer exploitation of the newly literate worker is through greater opportunities for self-employment.

GENDER AND COMMUNITY: SPECIAL LITERACY ISSUES

Within the economic structures and the literacy incentives that exist for individual and public policy support, special issues exist in regard to gender and community. In terms of gender, it is critical to recognize the special role of literacy as it affects the social and economic productivity of women. It is important to stress that although a substantial increase in the educational attainment of the female population has been made in developing countries, a significant proportion of this population still is without adequate schooling (see Table 3.2). Within the low-income countries of Africa and South Asia, nearly four out of five women over the age of twenty-five years have had no schooling. Females are less likely to enter school and, except in certain parts of the Caribbean and the more prosperous areas of Latin America, they are less likely to complete primary education successfully.

Obviously, like all equity issues in education, the access, retention, and achievement problems for women vary by country and within each country. However, I would assert that the issue of female equity deserves priority over other forms of inequity because of the centrality of the women's role in the transmission of the immediate and intergenerational benefits of economic and social reform to the family and community. Examples of this are the following areas where the women's role often is critical:

— health practices
— nutritional patterns

— utilization of contraceptive alternatives
— agricultural initiatives
— small-scale entrepreneurial activities
— home management
— attitudes toward education and career choices of children.

TABLE 3.2
Illiteracy Rates in the World and Major Regions by Gender
1985

| Region | Illiteracy Rates Age 15+ | | | |
	Total	Males	Females	Female Rate Minus Male Rate
WORLD	27.7%	20.5%	34.9%	14.4
Developed countries	2.1	1.7	2.6	0.9
Developing countries	38.2	27.9	48.9	21.0
Africa	54.0	43.3	64.5	21.2
Asia	36.3	25.6	47.4	21.8
Latin America and the Caribbean	17.3	15.3	19.2	3.9
Least-Developed Countries	67.6	56.9	78.4	21.5

Source: UNESCO, Office of Statistics, 1988.

In many of these activities the women may work in concert with their families or larger social groups (including but not restricted to women's organizations). In others, women have their major effect through the cumulative impact of their individual decisions and behaviors. In both cases, the effect of altering the immediate learning opportunities for women is to change (and, in fact, to improve) the long-term opportunities for all.

If one accepts the idea of gender equity as a priority issue, what constraints do we face in attempting to facilitate increased female achievement in basic learning activities? The discrimination against women that exists in the education and training system may best be viewed as a residual form of the larger biases extant in the community and labor market environments. While no generic condition exists to fit all national contexts, there is a pattern of cultural bias within which girls and women are treated as the marginal participants in education and training activities. They often are the last to benefit when programs are initiated and the first to lose when programs are reduced. Obligations of family service, differential expectations for their success, and gender-identified social roles all act against community support for female education when rationing of opportunities occurs.

Within the labor market few formal barriers or constraints on women are required because the informal ones have been so effective at limiting their opportunities. Even in developed nations, the biological link to pregnancy and the cultural link to child-care responsibilities have promoted an aversion by the labor market to equitable participation of women. Maternity and child-care benefits are a solution in some environments, but in others they raise the specter of higher costs that the reluctant employer can use as an additional excuse to avoid employing women or paying them equitably. In developing nations, the first generations of successful women have often been drawn disproportionately from the social elite, substituting one form of inequity for another.

The education and training system exists between these cultural and labor market sources of disadvantage. Unfortunately, rather than serving as the force for greater equity that many assert it should be, the system often maintains or even compounds the inequities of the external environment. Through inadequate remediation, a paucity of female role models, inappropriate materials and facilities, a biased curriculum, and gender-linked programs of study, the formal education and training system exacerbates the inequities promoted by the home and community and facilitates the biases of the labor market. Also, nonformal literacy and skill programs sometimes appear to equate relevance with a justification to restrain access to nontraditional roles for women. In both general literacy and specific income-generation programs, the nonformal activities often implicitly endorse traditional male conceptions of the female's role and substitute a local and immediate definition of relevance for the more general and long-term one that guides many programs for males.

While this convergence of discriminatory practices is discouraging in the extreme, the linkage of the sources of bias can, in fact, offer encouragement for reform. The powerful intergenerational effects of education can mean that the present generation of educated women will have a disproportionate effect on the attitudes of future generations. What remains obvious is that the role of women as facilitators of social and economic assistance programs will remain an important consideration for development strategies for the foreseeable future.

Paralleling this gender issue is the issue of community rather than individual levels of literacy. The economic and social effects of literacy attainment by an individual are reinforced and expanded by the attainment of literacy by other community members. Hunter (1989) has asserted that "community literacy" is a more appropriate concept to guide literacy work than is individual literacy attainment.

The community dimension recognizes that all groups require literate individuals to allow them to interact with the larger society. It also explicitly recognizes the ability of literate members of a community to complement (and sometimes even substitute for) formal literacy training opportunities. Finally, a literate community will evolve wherein literacy materials are more common and stronger incentives exist to acquire and use literacy skills. Group acquisition of literacy is a cumulative and self-reinforcing process; a community basis for literacy programs offers much long-term encouragement to counter the short-term frustrations often encountered in the early stages of literacy training for individuals.

SUMMARY

The level and distribution of literacy will determine the viability of the existing economic structures in a society; the nature of economic structures will determine the motivation of individuals to acquire and use literacy skills. Economic structures can adapt to any level of literacy, but with dramatically different implications for the quality of life for individuals and society. To assume that greater literacy will, by itself, promote aggregate economic development involves a fallacy of composition (what works for an individual worker does not necessarily apply if all citizens obtain literacy skills) and a fallacy of causality (other concomitant changes are required to make the new literacy skills effective economic tools). However, the policy analysis of literacy must look beyond the easily quantified labor market benefits to the political and economic externalities and to the longer term personal and aggregate developmental effects for which literacy is a prerequisite.

One learns only by experience. Literacy is the most cost-effective means of acquiring the experience of others and adapting it to one's own life needs. Even though the current society provides the greatest quantity of nonliteracy-based information ever available, the premium on literacy skills has increased both as a goal in itself and as a facilitator for further skill and knowledge acquisition. The current stress in society on "computer literacy," "economic literacy," or "artistic literacy" suggests that new forms of social and economic stratification are evolving that will place greater emphasis on literacy's facilitating role. This is an especially important consideration in understanding that literacy acquisition is the first step in attacking the convergence of disadvantages faced by society's poorest members. All other forms of "literacy" are dependent upon the prior possession of the ability to read and to write.

Without this foundation, personal improvement cannot be expected to occur and aggregate national development will be constrained.

Both developed and developing countries face challenges to their ability to organize and finance such literacy programs, but the major barrier to reform will be the question of society's willingness to pay. Many developing countries are becoming poorer and are financially constrained by existing levels of debt; almost all nations suffer from an increased skepticism about the ability of social programs to achieve their goals. Only when citizens and leaders are convinced that the cost of ignorance is greater to society than the cost of literacy programs will true reform occur. And because so many of the short-term costs of ignorance are borne by the politically inactive or ineffective segments of the population, there currently exists an inadequate political motivation in many nations to support wider access to literacy programs. This will change only as part of a more general transformation of society's economic structures; while the nature of change is uncertain, the fact of change is immutable.

Our responsibility is to work to bring the political and economic and the individual and collective incentives into congruency. Only then will the growth of literacy change our other social programs from transfer activities designed to promote survival to human investment programs designed to assure success.

The University at Albany

4

Literacy and the Politics of Language

PHILIP FOSTER

INTRODUCTION

In considering the issue of "literacy in whose language?" or more precisely the problem of national language policies in multilingual states, we should first note that what appears to be a simple distinction between multilingual and monolingual polities is rather more fuzzy than we often suppose. Even in ostensibly monolingual nations, dialectal variation based on ethnic, regional, or social class provenance may be substantial enough to raise serious issues concerning the "standard" spoken and written forms of the national language. In the United States, for example, we should not forget the use of "Black English," nor the growing influence of West Indian dialectical forms in the United Kingdom. Indeed, the movie fans among us will have already noted that in both countries what passes for standard spoken or written English has been substantially modified over the last fifty years to include new vocabulary, idiom, or syntax originating from ethnic, regional, or class minorities.

Thus the tension between the so-called standard language and local dialectical variants can raise legitimate and important policy issues even in ostensibly monolingual states. However, in this essay I shall confine my discussion to those nations where fragmentation is related to differences significant enough to be regarded as "language" rather than "dialectically" based. Thus, cockney may be a dialect rich in vocabulary or idiom that may render it incomprehensible to other English speakers, but a dialect it remains. Welsh, by contrast, as a distinct language with its own rich spoken and literary heritage, raises far more profound questions for the policymaker and the schools of the United Kingdom.

First we must acknowledge that purely monolingual polities are a good deal thinner on the ground than we suppose. The notion of the "nation-state" usually conjures forth the image of an aggregation unified not only by common political institutions but through possession of a shared culture and history and above all through a common spoken or written language. Thus a leading candidate in terms of this definition might be Japan, but in fact there are very few other nations that would qualify. Even in those countries of Western Europe which are usually regarded as being linguistically and culturally homogeneous, shared political institutions mask a variable degree of cultural and linguistic diversity. In Belgium the century-old confrontation between Fleming and Walloon over national language policy is well known to us as is the corresponding toleration of linguistic diversity among the Swiss Cantons. Yet even in the United Kingdom and, more strikingly, in France, the language issue is not totally resolved. What accommodation can be made to written and spoken Scots, a language with its own rich literary heritage, and will French national language policy continue to ignore the existence of spoken and written Langued'oc or Breton as opposed to Langued'os?

Thus in many nations the problems of literacy and national language policy are a good deal more complex than we commonly believe, since one of the most striking features of the twentieth century has been the persistence and, indeed, resurgence of ethnic identity. To be sure, definitions of ethnicity are not invariably couched in linguistic terms (vide: the international Jewish Community), but in the vast majority of cases, ethnicity is associated with a shared culture rooted in a common spoken and often written language. Indeed, one of the great illusions shared by many nineteenth-century "progressive" thinkers was that the primordial notions of Volktum and Volksprache would be eroded in the face of growing patterns of economic and social interdependence leading, in turn, to the ultimate disappearance of nation-states and the emergence of a world common culture and language. (Doubtless many of these thinkers also held the comfortable Eurocentric view that such a world community would be rooted in western traditions.) Subsequent history has confounded such predictions, for economic and social change has been frequently associated with increasing demands by minorities for linguistic and cultural autonomy. Indeed, the cynic might contend that Europe, for example, is now in some respects a good deal less culturally unified than it was under Roman, Ottoman, or Austro-Hungarian hegemony. Ironically, from the ruins of the last two Imperia have emerged new nation-states ostensibly created with ethnic considerations in mind, states which now themselves confront the problem of seemingly troublesome minorities such as the Magyar speakers of Romanian Transylvania, the Albanians of Yugoslavia, and so on. Alongside these examples we can range a multiplicity of both "Old" and "New" nations in Africa and Asia, examination of which would lead us to conclude that multilingualism not monolingualism is the norm in the vast majority of contemporary nation-states.

ALTERNATIVE APPROACHES TO LANGUAGE POLICY

Given this situation we might tackle the issue of language and literacy policies in three ways. First, we could consider a series of "principles" that should undergird such policies. Thus in UNESCO and other publications it is often suggested that national language strategies should be rooted in the principle that all children should initially become literate in their own mother tongue. Adumbration of such a principle may rest upon some implicit or explicit theory of "natural rights," or be based upon the more pragmatic view that the transition to literacy in the "national language" is made far easier if the child has first achieved literacy in the mother tongue. Yet as I suggest later, enunciation of such *obiter dicta* turns out to be fairly vacuous in practice, for the problem with principles is that they involve "implementation" in the context of various political and economic constraints. In the ensuing discussion I shall not ignore normative or ideological issues, but I feel that they sometimes have very limited implications in the actual national language policy arena.

A second tack that might commend itself to the scholar would be to attempt some general classificatory exercise wherein multilingual states are ranked, for example, on the basis of their degree of linguistic fragmentation, level of economic development, or type of political structure, and see whether these types of variables might be predictive of various kinds of policy decision. Of course, classifications serve a useful purpose in mapping out a range of different outcomes, but anyone who seriously believes that such an exercise would have any real predictive value has a far greater belief in the efficacy of the social sciences than do I.

A third approach might be to look around for a "theory" that would help us understand various languages and literacy policies in multilingual states. Thus Laitin has recently suggested that "game theory" can be useful in explaining language and literary conflict in multilingual nations and in predicting how particular languages gain written and spoken dominance.[1] Like most forms of neo-utilitarian theory the approach rests upon a few simple assumptions concerning the relations between central and regional authority wherein the former has, for example, a powerful interest in the establishment of an official language in terms of the cost reductions resulting from eliminating the need for translation. In effect, by treating central government or local (language) groups as games players involved in transactional relationships it is possible to throw light on language policy outcomes. Thus where one group establishes linguistic hegemony "subjects in the lower classes have little to gain economically by holding on to a disenfranchised language and eventually begin to give it up." Indeed, a critical "tipping point" is reached where the pressure on minorities to switch becomes very strong and thus minority languages may disappear as an instrument of spoken or written discourse.

This kind of approach is indeed useful and, for example, could explain the virtual disappearance of Irish as a spoken and written language during the colonial and postcolonial period. Indeed, that language hardly survives (except as an entrance examination subject for the Civil Service) in spite of attempts to reinstate it, thus emphasizing Laitin's observations concerning the tipping point.

Thus in the following discussion there is an implicit acceptance of a game theory orientation. However, the approach—since it rests upon a set of *ceteris paribus* assumptions—can (like much neo-utilitarian theory) attempt to explain everything but may end up by explaining nothing except on a *post hoc* basis. It really does not help very much to say that a particular language or literacy policy was adopted since, in the final outcome, positive utilities outweighed the accompanying negative utilities, unless we have a clearer specification of the economic, social, political, and historical parameters within which these policies emerged.

Let me explain (through an example) what I mean by this rather protean statement. The East African nations of Kenya and Tanzania appear to have much in common: Both are multilingual states that comprise a multiplicity of Bantu and Nilotic speaking populations; both were subject to British colonial rule, and the language policies pursued during the colonial period had ostensible similarities. Moreover, in both nations Swahili (initially a coastal Bantu language) was and is widely used as a *lingua franca*. In Tanzania, Swahili has now been promulgated and generally accepted as the national spoken and written language, but similar attempts to establish it in Kenya are almost certain to fail. One could, I suppose, explain this difference by asserting that in game theory terms the "equilibrium" outcome in Tanzania, but not in Kenya, favors Swahili. However, this simply begs the issue, for it is clear that divergent outcomes can only be explained in terms of the relative distribution of linguistic groups, differences in national economies, and more precise variations in the nature of the colonial experience. In this kind of situation game theory suffers from the same limitations as neoclassical economics: Given certain sets of "preference functions," economists can predict market outcomes under *ceteris paribus* conditions. Yet, very properly, the economist is not concerned with the historical, social, or cultural determinants of those preference functions. I would submit that in terms of language policies it is precisely these factors that we need to investigate.

In the following pages, therefore, I shall attempt to isolate a number of those crucial factors that are really operative in national language policy decisions (the "hidden agenda" as it were), but I am also obliged to recognize that outcomes tend more often than not to be "unique" to region or nation. Unavoidably, then, I shall have to produce something like a catalogue, but in so doing will suggest that ostensibly "enlightened" policies may lead to undesirable outcomes, and that *all* decisions concerning the relation between national and local languages generate negative as well as positive consequences.

IDEOLOGY, HEGEMONY, AND PRACTICE

First, it is important to bear in mind that the basic reasons for ethnic demands for linguistic autonomy (which are often couched in cultural terms) are manifold. Doubtless in some cases pressure from minorities that their language should constitute the medium of instruction in their schools stems from a justifiable fear of loss of group identity where the latter is essentially based upon language, culture, and religious belief. Alternatively, such demands may mask more fundamental economic considerations involving conflict over the allocation of scarce national resources and uneven rates of economic development as between regions. Thus, is conflict between Serb and Croat in contemporary Yugoslavia a reflection of major cultural or linguistic differences, or is it rather a reaction to regional economic disparities? Likewise, would Basque separatism take such sharp form if very real linguistic differences were not compounded by the fact that the Basque speaking region exhibits a distinctive economic profile compared with most of the rest of contemporary Spain? Igbo attempts at secession from the Nigerian Federation in 1967, apparently fueled by linguistic, religious, and broader cultural considerations, only became a reality with the discovery of substantial oil resources off the Nigerian south-eastern littoral. One might point to more cases of this nature, but they should make us more cautious about predicting the outcomes of national language policies. For example, a government may adumbrate a general principal that major linguistic groups have a right to acquire literacy in their own languages and that these languages should become the principal media of instruction in local schools. Such a policy could be predicated on the notion that it will defuse political dissent and potential secessionist pressures. In fact, such strategies could lead to an escalation of demands since the origins of conflict might be essentially economic rather than linguistic or cultural in origin. Thus "national integration" might be better ensured through economic strategies than through "progressive" and "tolerant" literacy and language policies.

Indeed, the whole question of what constitutes an "enlightened" language policy in multilingual states is itself problematic. As noted earlier, one strand in the liberal tradition has emphasized linguistic unification and cultural assimilation as an essential prerequisite for the emergence of the "just" state. Such a strand was exemplified in some traditions of French political thought stemming from the ideals of the Revolution and partly manifested in French colonial policy. I have little brief for that colonial policy nor do I ignore the degree of cultural ethnocentricity that underlay it. Yet while we may deplore the gap between French ideals and practice we cannot summarily dismiss the view that national ideas of liberty, equality, and fraternity are never fully realizable except on the basis of common language and culture. Such an assertion would command little support today, but it seems to have been replaced by an equally extreme but ostensibly "liberal" view which emphasizes the absolute right of all linguistic minorities to achieve literacy in their own languages—all of which must be accorded coeval status. This kind of pietistic statement seems to be based on an implicit normative assumption concerning the absolute and equal worth of all cultural and linguistic traditions. The mind boggles, however, at the possible political, social, and economic outcomes if many multilingual states seriously attempted to implement policies based on such an assumption. I have used these two extreme perspectives rather to emphasize the fact that language policies in multilingual states tend to lie on some continuum between these polarities: Some nations may tend toward "assimilationist" strategies that emphasize the salience of an official national language over the claims of linguistic minorities, while in others a more tolerant attitude exists toward continued cultural and linguistic pluralism.

However, in attempting to examine some of the factors that seem to determine at what point on the scale language policies will fall, we should note that any language policy adopted in multilingual states involves cost. Normally, we think in terms of the direct costs of policy implementation, and some of these are obvious enough. Where a multilingual and multiliteracy policy is espoused we confront the issue of textbook production and specialized teacher training: Costs here must be seen in terms of the size of a linguistic group and the potential market share of consumers. Where a language might exist in as yet unwritten form high costs may be incurred in plotting the number and distribution of speakers. Moreover, dialectical variation may require the development of a "standard" form of the language and the creation of a viable orthography. One could add to this list of potential direct costs, but here we note that no government can simply ignore them particularly where linguistic enclaves are small in size. But even more important here is the issue of the "opportunity costs" of policy: The outcomes stemming from the choice of one policy option that conflict with other desired objectives.

It is tempting to provide an example of this kind of situation from the less-developed world, but I shall rather draw it from an economically developed Western nation where the long-term consequences of an historical policy decision have now had time to manifest themselves. Although at the beginning of this essay I pointed to some of the literacy/language issues that still exist in Western nations, I would venture that most of these issues, troublesome as they may seem, will reach some kind of practical accommodation. Welsh, after all, constitutes no threat to English as the "language of power," nor does Langued'oc offer itself as a national alternative to Langued'os, and both France and the United Kingdom have the economic resources to accommodate these languages of literature and tradition into national life. Indeed, in the kinds of examples which I provided some kind of solution will be reached, and in no case (even that of Belgium) does linguistic controversy threaten the continued viability and integrity of the State. The one possible exception to this situation is Canada, which provides an illustrative case study.

At the close of the Seven Years' War the maintenance of British political hegemony was paralleled by a culturally tolerant or laissez-faire attitude toward the French-speaking population. Rooted in French language, culture, and Church, the French-speaking minority was allowed to "go its own way" and was under little formal or informal pressure to speak English or to integrate itself into the broader pattern of social and economic change that transformed Canada in the nineteenth and early twentieth century. Of course, there was discrimination against French speakers, but this is only half of the story. Whether British policies were based on "indifference" or "cultural tolerance" made little difference to the outcome: By the early twentieth century French speakers constituted a disadvantaged minority with little stake in Canada, and the still possible secession of Quebec arises, in part, from historic economic imparities stemming from "pluralist" policies. However, secession, whatever it achieves in terms of cultural *amour propre*, would carry enormous economic costs for both the English- and French-speaking communities.

Since we all have the advantage of historical hindsight, what "solution" do we believe should have been adopted, bearing in mind that an alternative policy of emphasizing English as the national language in the school curriculum would have met with resentment and conceivably rebellion? Indeed, I could well imagine French colleagues observing that if France had won this colonial war then there would have been no contemporary secessionist problem since English speakers would have been given the option of learning French and assimilating themselves to French culture or would have been "advised" to migrate to the thirteen colonies. *"Pour faire l'omelette il faut casser des oeufs"*; contemporary Canada would be politically strongly integrated and linguistically unified.

The argument that this is, after all, a "colonial" example and not relevant to the position in most contemporary less-developed multilingual states misses the point. The issue is one of the relation between political hegemony and language policy, and whether the potentially dominant group consists of the colonial power or a "local" minority is beside the point. If this is contested then I would suggest that we inquire of Tamil speakers how they regard the policy of elevating "indigenous" Hindi to the status of the national language in the Republic of India, or how Yoruba or Igbo speakers in the Nigerian Federation would react to claims that Hausa (the most frequently spoken tongue) should be the medium of instruction or even a second language to be taught in the schools.

In fact, whatever language/literacy policy is adopted in multilingual states its architects are likely to be "damned if they do and damned if they don't." Whatever decisions are made will have negative as well as positive outcomes for the obvious reason that national objectives usually conflict. Culturally pluralist or assimilationist language policies all have long-term negative political or economic results, and under these circumstances policymakers can only attempt to balance a range of putative outcomes one against the other and follow that strategy which appears to generate the least number of potentially undesirable consequences. The relative "weighting" of these outcomes is, of course, very much locally conditioned and solutions are always "second best." Indeed, perhaps we might drop the term "solution" altogether and talk of the best achievable "accommodation" within a given pattern of constraints.

From this perspective, some of the most frequently intoned *obiter dicta* (that UNESCO, for example, conceives should undergird language and literacy) tend to be rather empty. We have noted earlier that it is highly unlikely that the principle that all individuals have a right to achieve literacy in their own mother tongue would be implementable in poor states that exhibit a high level of linguistic fragmentation, and particularly where the mother tongues in question do not exist in written form. To add the qualifier "so far as is possible" is evasive because such a policy usually is *not* possible.

Further, the idea that language policies should be related to the presumed "developmental needs" of children does not take us very far. Regrettably enough and to the possible dismay of child psychologists, nation-states are rarely able to make this a central principle undergirding language/literacy policy. This as we have noted is evident in situations where it is suggested that a child's mother tongue be used as a transitional medium on the assumption that literacy in a "national language" can be more easily attained if the child has first attained it in the ancestral one. This is of little help where children derive from smaller linguistic minorities with an often unwritten language. Moreover, the principle ignores the realities of social and economic change in many nations. For example, migration and increased urbanization in much of sub-Saharan Africa means that many classrooms contain children drawn from six or seven linguistic groupings, and one is unclear as to what policies are viable in such situations.

In fact when hard choices have to be made I suspect that policymakers explicitly or implicitly base their decisions on three kinds of criteria. First, economic considerations weigh heavily. I have already drawn attention to some of the direct cost considerations involved in literacy policies, though it should be noted that the situation may vary where central governments or local communities are differentially involved in the support of schools: Some options may seem more desirable if we are not obliged to pay for them!

Second, the political implications of language/literacy policy must weigh heavily in the minds of planners. Judgment here, I suspect, is very subjective, but certainly the question must be raised as to what extent the alternatives are conducive to the continued viability and integrity of the nation-state. National political elites (particularly those drawn disproportionately from a dominant linguistic group) are unlikely to subscribe to policies that in the long run might contribute to their own demise!

Finally, the social consequences of language policy cannot be ignored. All languages might be equal in the sight of God (or anthropologists) but I fear that they are not in the sight of Humanity. Within any multilingual state one language, whether indigenous or that of a formal colonial elite, constitutes the language of power and status. Literacy in that language is vital in terms of the potential mobility of individuals and groups, while other languages, even those possessed of a rich literary tradition, are largely irrelevant to processes of status attainment except at a purely local level. Any language policy, however ostensibly tolerant, must be considered in terms of its implications for social stratification if it leads to a situation where certain groups have disproportionate access to the "key" language. Indeed, the motives of some elites might be questionable in this context. It is worth remembering that the South African Bantu Education Act which constitutes one pillar of the whole system of apartheid was predicated on the ostensibly innocuous idea that African children had the right to be taught in their Bantu language within a curriculum based on their own cultural traditions. Although Afrikaans was permissible as a second language, there was obviously an attempt to diminish the extent of English instruction. Africans clearly perceived that English was the "language of power" in South Africa and very rightly concluded that this language strategy was yet another attempt to reinforce their subordinate status. In this case, the motives of the regime were clear enough, but similar outcomes could emerge from policies that are inspired by seemingly more enlightened assumptions.

THE BURDEN OF HISTORY

These, then, are some of the key issues that underlie any discussion of language/literacy policy. I alluded earlier, however, to the constraints within which options must be examined. The greatest constraint of all is obviously history, and all national language policies are "prisoners of the past." That "past" itself comprehends a multiplicity of variables, namely: the degree of linguistic fragmentation within the nation-state; the extent to which minority languages are associated with a written and literary tradition; the existence of a local *lingua franca* which may potentially offer itself as an acceptable national language; the nature of the colonial heritage and the policies pursued by the former colonial regime; or the degree to which the claims of religious orthodoxy require the teaching of a ritual scholarly language (as in Islamic states where the majority language may or may not be Arabic). Moreover, membership in a worldwide literary, scientific, and technological community mandates the variable dissemination of a major European language at least at the secondary and tertiary levels of the formal educational system.

This list of historical constraints can, I am sure, be extended, but the point is that they explain why most nation-states (particularly postcolonial polities) have been extremely conservative in their deliberations on national language policies. Only two nations have been able, for very different reasons, to "create" national languages which represent a radical breach with the past and which have been universally acceptable to their citizenry. The first is Israel where an historic liturgical language, Hebrew, has been "recreated" as a national tongue. The second is the Republic of Indonesia where Bahasa Indonesia, based on Malay, has been diffused in a linguistically complex situation where it is conceivable that opposition might have been forthcoming from numerous and politically powerful minorities, such as the Javanese. I would submit, however, that these cases are unusual and not replicable.

For the most part, multilingual states have been content to rest with their heritage while making minor and often merely rhetorical concessions to political demands. From this perspective, it is clear that there are no definitive "solutions" to national language issues. The search for general principles that should undergird policy is futile. This is not to suggest that interesting comparative observations cannot be made that cast light on the dynamics of language policy. Thus one might ask about two linguistically fragmented post-colonial states where no indigenous written tradition exists, namely Nigeria and Papua New Guinea. Why is it that in the former nation Pidgin English remains a "low status" *lingua franca* while in Papua New Guinea Melanesian Pidgin bids fair to become the national language for internal purposes? Likewise, as noted earlier, in Tanzania, Swahili has been accepted as the national language but in neighboring Kenya efforts to enshrine a similar policy will almost certainly fail. Numerous examples like this can be cited and provide a happy hunting ground for the scholar, but they only serve to emphasize the uniqueness of each case.

Finally, let me suggest that in some cases it is better to have no formal national language policy at all, or (if such a policy exists) that it would be impolitic to attempt to implement it. Once again, the experience of certain postcolonial multilingual states is instructive. The first example is that of the nations of sub-Saharan Africa.

During the colonial period the language policies of the British and French regimes differed significantly. In the former there was an attempt to utilize "major" indigenous and initially unwritten languages as the medium of instruction in primary schools, followed by a transition to English for that tiny minority of children who entered secondary institutions. Such a policy required linguistic investigations resulting in the development of standard orthographies and the printing of texts in local languages. In contrast, French educational authorities emphasized the use of the French language as the medium of instruction at all levels, and such linguistic research as took place was not related to educational outcomes (although there is evidence that Africans themselves sometimes utilized the French orthography to write in local languages).

Since independence, most African states have followed the precedents set by the colonial powers. While African elites may deplore these precedents and emphasize the salience of local languages in processes of "national reconstruction," there is precious little evidence that they will break with the colonial past. To be sure, some Francophonic countries have attempted to use selected local languages as the medium of instruction, but there is little sign of widespread success of such efforts. Conversely, one Anglophonic state (Ghana) attempted in the Nkrumah years to elevate English to the status of the formal national language to be used as the medium of instruction in the schools. Such a policy seemed to meet with little opposition and its subsequent limited success probably stems from pedagogical and resource problems.

For the most part, however, real changes in policy do not appear to have occurred. The reasons for this are clear enough: In virtually no African state would it be possible to establish an indigenous language as the national spoken and written medium without vehement opposition from other minorities. At the same time, French or English is being widely if slowly diffused in these societies. It may be "Nigerian" English or "Chadian" French but from a functional viewpoint this is of little significance. The long-term consequence of the current situation will be a massive increase in the use of these European "residues" and their ultimate recognition as the *de facto* as well as formal national languages of most African states. Concurrently, there is no evidence that such a process will lead to the disappearance of the vast majority of African languages, whether written or unwritten. They will continue to maintain their present vitality in much of the ordinary business of life. The oft-repeated assertion that current developments threaten African "cultural identity" is as vacuous as the assertion that the widespread use of Latin in medieval Europe destroyed the cultural identity of Frank or Anglo-Saxon. In the contemporary situation African governments are as much to be applauded for their pragmatism as criticized for their timidity; "let sleeping linguistic dogs lie" is their best option.

Another multilingual, postcolonial state, the Republic of India, affords an interesting contrast. Unlike those of sub-Saharan Africa, all the major Indian languages existed in written form at the time of Independence. Along with a rich and diverse indigenous literary tradition there was English, the language of the colonial regime that, as in Africa, was spoken and written only by a relatively small minority. In the event, the new leaders of India decided that the elevation of English to the formal status of the national language was incompatible with India's sense of dignity and self-respect as an independent state. One may sympathize with this view and realize that the "psychic scars" stemming from the colonial period bit deep. However, the decision to promulgate Hindi as the national language after a formal transition period resulted in political tension. For that substantial portion of the Indian population which spoke a cluster of Dravidian languages, Hindi (an Indo-European tongue) was linguistically closer to English than, for example, Tamil or

Telugu. Moreover, English was more widely diffused in the Dravidian south and was politically more "neutral" than Hindi or any other Indo-Aryan language. The language policy of the Republic was thus construed by many as an attempt to establish the political and economic hegemony of the North over the South by placing the latter at linguistic disadvantage.

The legacy of bitterness resulting from the policy is apparent and, though the threat of secession may have diminished, successive Indian Commissions and Government proclamations have been obliged to defer the formal date of transition to Hindi. Does anyone now seriously believe that Hindi will ever become the formal, let alone the *de facto*, national language of India? Pride may sustain these aspirations but, as in Africa, English (Indian English, to be sure) probably continues to diffuse at a significantly higher rate throughout the subcontinent than does Hindi. It would seem retrospectively that failure to enunciate a formal and rigid policy elevating Hindi might have had long-term positive outcomes. Perhaps a more formal recognition of the limitation of present policy will only come when the acceptance of English as a "functional" language becomes psychologically detached from its symbolic status as an instrument of former colonial overrule.

SOME CONCLUSIONS

The skeptical tone of this essay has been prompted by the rather bland and pietistic nature of some of the literature on language policy in multilingual states. In the last resort policy decisions stem from the hard realities of political and economic hegemony in such states and are everywhere determined by resource constraints. Of course, linguists, behavioral scientists, and even social philosophers like to feel that their research and writing exerts some influence on policy decisions but, in the event, it is difficult to point to linguistic policies that have stemmed from their research. Game theory, however, as Laitin suggests, does give us insights into the nature of power relationships that, in fact, influence outcomes.

Let me conclude this essay on a positive note. In the long run, language issues often tend to work themselves out in the context of social and economic change, and accommodations tend to be gradualist (or Burkean) rather than transformationist in nature. In fact, history records the continual emergence or disappearance of cultural groupings based on language. To be sure, there are examples of forced linguistic assimilation based on conquest or repressive political hegemony, but more often patterns of linguistic change are gradual and less traumatic in nature. Although in some instances notions of identity and meaning are so inextricably involved with language that groups will resist any attempts at linguistic assimilation, there are other cases where language may have a more circumscribed functionality leading to groups relinquishing their own linguistic heritage with a minimal amount of conflict. This would seem to be the case, for example, among the traditional ruling dynasties of the inter-Lacustrian Bantu who were generally of Nilotic origin but whose languages have now been replaced by those of the conquered. Conversely, attempts to resuscitate linguistic traditions in the interests of the maintenance of a "cultural heritage" are rarely successful once the tipping point has been reached. For "dead languages" are simply those that have lost functionality in the context of social and cultural change. Frequently, however, languages coexist on an "amicable" basis wherein each has a circumscribed functional domain. Thus the language of power (whether political or economic) may be taught in the schools while that of family, religion, or literature remains equally vital.

Given the changing social and economic milieu within which language and literacy has its being, the long-term consequences of language policies are always difficult to predict. At best, recognition of diversity may ensure that cherished traditions are not trampled upon, but at worst it can lead to the "freezing" of current patterns that are, in fact, already in a state of flux. Policies that lead to the latter outcome can only be acceptable to those who see humanity as composed of a cluster of linguistic and cultural "museums."

The University at Albany

5

The Textual Contract:
Literacy as Common Knowledge
and Conventional Wisdom

ALAN C. PURVES

In truth the prison into which we doom
Ourselves no prison is: and hence for me,
In sundry moods, 'twas pastime to be bound
Within the Sonnet's scanty plot of ground:
Pleas'd if some souls (for such there needs must be)
Who have felt the weight of too much liberty,
Should find brief solace there, as I have found.

— William Wordsworth

I should like to argue in this essay what may seem to many to be a commonplace, but a commonplace that often tends to be lost in the various controversies concerning literacy policy and literacy instruction such as that between process and product or between functional literacy and literacy for liberation. Wherever enacted in the world, the activities of being literate carry with them the burden of acceding to and employing a large body of common knowledge and conventional wisdom. Accession and use may be seen as entering into a contract with the world of text, an act not unlike the act which social philosophers have referred to as the social contract. We may define the textual contract as the mediation between the individual and the community that is accommodated under the heading of rules, or, more profitably, conventions (Engeström, 1987). The activity of being literate, in this sense, is a deliberate and social activity, one that takes place in the world; it should not be seen as an abstracted mental state or condition. Those who are involved in literacy education should, therefore, be aware of their social responsibility.

In making this claim, I question whether literacy is a form of liberation. Although reading and writing may be seen as liberating activities in that they can allow the imagination to explore new worlds and experiences, liberation occurs only subsequent to entry into the textual contract and thereby the mastery and provisional acceptance of conventions and the acquisition of a body of knowledge. The tension between liberation and constraint is the paradox to which Wordsworth refers in the epigraph, and is a subject to which I shall return later. Being literate is, in this respect, no more and no less than being a member of a speech community and an established culture, which is to say literacy is a specific form of communicative competence (Hymes, 1974).

In her history of writing, Gaur (1985) states that writing is information storage. From the earliest invention of writing the main function of the text was to store information, usually commercial but also governmental and later religious information, so that it could be retrieved by the writer or by some other person at a later date. Of necessity, then, written language had to be standardized so as to allow access to the information contained within the graphic code. In early civilizations, writing was done by scribes who perfected the system and made advances in the technology of writing, such as shifting from the stylus to the brush or pen. The scribes also set forth standards for penmanship, conventions of writing such as word boundaries and sentence boundaries, and even text structures and matters of morphology, grammar, and syntax for the written language. Some of the conventions they set were for efficiency, and some were for elegance. From the earliest times, therefore, the various scribal groups established a contractual arrangement for being literate, a contract that was clearly social and that clearly transformed the individual from a state of "natural" existence to a state of acting in a world defined by textuality and texts.

As a result of the development of moveable type and the availability of cheap paper, the scribal world opened up to a vast new group of people—the middle class—during the seventeenth and eighteenth centuries and simultaneously or consequently more and more people became literate. The kinds of information stored increased to include the literary arts and popular literature as well as the news of the day and advertising. Changes in the structures and forms of written language came slower, and in most societies the textual contract of prescribed text structures and standards for words, syntax, and text structures continued in constantly but slowly modified forms as different groups took on scribal responsibilities and different fields of knowledge took on their own scribal functions (Goody, 1977, 1986; Olson, 1977; Ong, 1982). In addition, the scribal traditions often prescribed standards as to how texts should be read as well as indited; to some extent these standards arose from religious practices such as a reverence for the exact wording of the text as opposed to a tolerance for individual interpretation and the piling of commentary upon commentary, but scribal practices in the reading of lay texts, such as in the reading of law in England or the *ex-*

plication de texte in France, also had their influence (Goody, 1986; Purves and Purves, 1986).

ALPHABETS AND OTHER TEXTUAL CONVENTIONS

One of the persistent aspects of text from the days of the clay pouch and the cuneiform tablet to those of the electronic message is that all texts have in common certain qualities, to which we may ascribe the term convention. Among these conventions are the use of a visual symbol system comprising marks and spaces. This system became standardized early in the history of a writing language, and as writing instruments, means of transcription, and surfaces have been developed or discarded, the conventions have become modified in more or less obvious ways. Conventions in writing emerge from the necessity for information to be retrieved by the writer or someone else at a later time or in a different place, which can be done only if the symbols have a standardized core of reference. As is the case today, much early writing was commercial and the various bills of lading had to be standard both as to the number of jars and the type of wine or oil in those jars. As time has passed, the number and types of convention in writing have increased, since the medium has come to be used for an increasing number of functions beyond the commercial and historical and as the society using writing has become more and more complex and subdivided.

We may divide the conventions into three broad categories: spatial, linguistic, and structural. The spatial characteristics range from the direction or flow of the visual display to the arrangement of segments of print or the variation in type faces to indicate aspects of meaning or structure. In Western culture the display currently runs from upper left to lower right with some minor exceptions such as warnings written on road pavements. The spatial characteristics of text are particularly notable in the relation of text to blank space. These relations act as cues for the reader, often telling the reader what sort of text is presented. The greater the proportion of white space to text, the more likely the text is to be poetry or an advertisement. In a Shakespeare play the more dense the text appears the more likely it is to be comic. Columns of text signal certain kinds of information; newspapers, for example, use column spacing and type size to indicate the distinction between news and advertisement. In some types of text, type size and color can indicate the importance of the message or the loudness of the noise represented by the letters. Other visual devices such as boldface, italics, and the like have particular referents given the place in which they are situated. In a text such as this boldface indicates a division; in the telephone directories of several societies it may indicate a commercial establishment.

In many languages linguistic conventions begin with the alphabet. It is an unknown and useless feature of oral language, but is necessary to written language and is important both for its graphic representation of the phoneme and for its order. In all alphabetic written systems the very order of letters has been standardized, and most written language systems have added other standard symbols as well to mark such conventions of written language as sentence and paragraph boundaries as well as questions, insertions, or quotations. These symbols become in themselves sources of information. Because of the consistent order of the alphabet, such works as directories and indices can be created, not to mention dictionaries. Other linguistic conventions peculiar to written language include spelling and punctuation as well as certain aspects of syntax and grammar. Written English,for example,demands the placement of modifiers near what they modify, a demand not made by the oral language with as great a degree of stringency.

Structural conventions of texts include the order and arrangement of segments of the message. Some of these may have counterparts and antecedents in oral language, but in many cases they have evolved into their own format. The recipe form is a good example of such an evolution. Although the sequence of the text resembles that of the narrative in that it is time bound and sequential, the modern recipe begins with a list of ingredients, then a sequence of necessary actions; this is not a necessary sequence, although both the what and the how are requisite, but it has become a useful one. Other structural conventions can be seen in the telephone directory with its segregation of alphabetical and occupational listings, the newspaper article with its initial summary followed by elaboration, or the scientific report with its prescribed order of presentation and its demand for an elaborate description of the experimental conditions.

Some of the more stringent structural conventions are those of literary genre; Wordsworth's sonnet is a testimony to a form that had been established for some four hundred years before he wrote, one that is still followed if not slavishly at least with due attention to its properties. Even so innovative a poet as e.e. cummings preserved certain features of the conventional sonnet so that he could make radical breaks with other features of convention and thus startle and delight his readers who were also aware of the convention. There are similar generic conventions operating with respect to prose fiction, drama, and various kinds of nonfiction. The conventions of a Gothic novel make it popular with a large number of readers, who appear to the outsider to be rereading the same book under different titles, but who derive pleasure in great part because the form is predictable. In the hands of the master, the predictability can be used to advantage, for the master can undercut the prediction and twist it to serve other ends.

As with the conventions of all sorts of texts, literary conventions in themselves serve as conveyors of information and appear to form part of the way by which the writer and the reader can meet as partners in the textual contract. They are not simply nice, they have become necessary. Both writer and readers use them to provide a context for the new information contained in the text. They provide signals as to the identity and the posture of both reader and writer.

The issue of literary convention raises a number of questions. The first is how originality and innovation occur. This issue has been treated by critics from John Livingston Lowes to Harold Bloom (1973), both of whom suggest that writers face an uneasy relationship with tradition, but that it is out of this unease that a great deal of the most creative work emerges. Lowes (1930) suggests that conventions can become stultifying if they are adhered to slavishly and that there comes a point where an innovative writer breaks with tradition in order to redirect the nature of the convention. Bloom concurs in suggesting that writers must account for tradition even if to break away from it and that the "anxiety of influence" is one of the wellsprings of art. The juvenilia of a great number of writers show them writing within an established tradition, out of which they break when they begin to "come into their own." From their own testimony writers appear to relish convention and the restriction of form in precisely the way that Wordsworth described in the epigraph to my essay.

The change of convention may be likened to the ways by which scientists appear to break out of inadequate scientific "paradigms." The psychologist Engeström (1987) suggests that the change, which is a form of learning, is prompted by the "double bind" of Bateson (1972). There is a primary contradiction between the conventional form of text and the need of the writer to express a particular set of ideas or feelings; the writer first finds a new instrument and thus creates a new model which contains latent inner contradictions that anticipate the created new form. In writing, the step may be from parody of the older form to a new form that transcends the inner complications of the parody. Such seems to have been the case with a writer like Wordsworth in *Lyrical Ballads*, which title itself is an oxymoron from which the poet needed to break out.

On a more mundane level, many teachers of writing in the United States have sought to break out of the "five-paragraph theme"; the problem with their effort is that their perception of the double bind is not shared, nor has there arrived in schools the double contradiction that is necessary for such a shift (Engeström, 1987).

THE POET, THE CHILD, AND THE INSANE

This point leads to the question as to how far a writer can bend or break the textual contract, which is the mediation between the individual and the community that is accommodated under the heading of rules, or, more profitably, conventions. Some literary works appear to have tested the limits greatly. One can think of poets like Blake, Pound, and Rimbaud; novelists like Sterne, Joyce, and Marques; playwrights like Pirandello and Stoppard, and essayists like Wolfe and Capote. Each of these in different ways pushed beyond the bounds of the established convention. Some, like Joyce in *Finnegan's Wake*, came close to being so unconventional as to be unreadable. Christopher Smart in the eighteenth century appears almost to have gone beyond the bounds of convention, as does William Blake. The work of these writers resembles the writing of the mentally ill, and studies of institutionalized writers indicate that the conventions can be pushed quite far before the writing becomes gibberish. To a certain extent, the limits of unconventional writing are established by a community of readers, who will tolerate Joyce, perhaps, but not a slum child or "Son of Sam."

As I shall observe in the last section of this essay with respect to school writing, the young child who knows some of the conventions or partially knows the conventions will make what appear as "errors" to the more mature reader and writer. It has recently been fashionable to see these naive errors as interesting steps in the struggle toward conventional literacy, governed by rules that do not quite accord with the socially accepted conventions. Teachers and researchers are charmed by "invented spellings," scribbles that superficially resemble letters or stories, persistent misreadings or mispronunciations, and interpretations of stories and poems that seem "cute." To the child these are serious attempts to become conventional, and the child does not see herself as "cute" or "charming." The child has failed in being conventional in the best sense, and must be seen as a naif who does not fully understand the nature of the textual contract. The situation of the child is paralleled by that of the second language learner who knows the target language imperfectly and who writes or speaks in what has come to be known as "interlanguage," a partially realized approximation of the conventions of the target language.

The psychotic reader or writer often reads or writes in a way that almost makes sense, almost looks like appropriate graphic representation, or almost approximates the common reading of a text. These readers and writers have been studied with particular emphasis on their penmanship and orthography, but there have also been studies of structure and sense. Psychotic writers are to some extent systematically aberrant or unconventional, but they are certainly not considered part of the literate mainstream. They have not accepted, or have abrogated, the contract. In Bateson's terms, they have not found a way out of the double bind.

To the observer, the texts produced by poets, children, or psychotics may appear similar. A poet like Dr. Seuss may go "on beyond Zebra" (perhaps because his work is known as play), but children and psychotics may not. It appears that Dr. Seuss has demonstrated that he knows the terms of the contract because he (or his publisher) has labeled his work as art, but the others have not so established themselves. Why the childish or the psychotic deviation is not accepted, but the literary is, when all seem similar, is a paradox of many cultures. There is indeed a poetic license that is not granted to children or the institutionalized unless they have proven they can abide by the Rules of the Page.

THE CONTRACTUAL AGREEMENT OF READERS AND WRITERS

It is relatively easy to establish what I have set forth so far: that a part of the textual contract sets conventions for the presentation of text; the evidence surrounds us. It is somewhat more controversial to assert that other standards and traditions that constitute the textual contract have persisted in all literate societies and form a part of that which defines a society. Scribner and Cole (1981) have shown how the development of Vai script in Liberia has brought with it a set of conventions about language, text forms, and (more importantly) ways in which texts are to be read and written. Vai texts are for communal reading and writing. These conventions with respect to Vai exist parallel to the conventions used for reading the Koran, which is also communal but sacramental, and for reading English, which is a solitary affair. The evidence I would advance for these assertions and for the implications I would draw in the subsequent parts of this essay come from the two cross-cultural studies undertaken under the auspices of the International Association for the Evaluation of Educational Achievement (IEA), one in literature and one in written composition.

The IEA Study of Literature (Purves, 1973) explored the nature of interpretive communities as national or regional phenomena by examining the preferred responses of students to literary fiction (e.g., what the students indicated was important to write about) in secondary schools in ten educational systems: Flemish-speaking and French-speaking Belgium, Chile, England, Finland, Iran, Italy, New Zealand, Sweden, and the United States. In an earlier study (Purves and Rippere, 1968), there emerged twenty core issues concerning literary texts each of which could be framed as a question. In any one country students selected certain questions from that core. The questions could be classified according to the object of concern (e.g., character, language, theme) and according to the illocutionary force of the statement (personal-reactive, analytic, classificatory, interpretive, or evaluative).

This study showed that as students progressed through secondary school, they became more consistent in their responses across texts and thus came to approach all the fiction that they read from a uniform perspective. Students in any one country tended to have increasingly similar responses as they progressed through school; the between-student variance decreased as a result of age, but more probably because of years of schooling, as we shall see. This is not to say that the different stories had no effect on the students responses, but that in each of the systems of education studied, the effect of the text was less strong on the older students than it was on the younger ones.

In terms of national differences, the results showed that there were both an international interpretive community and national communities. Aside from one or two general rejections ("Is this a proper subject for a story?") and predilections ("What happens in the story?"), students in different countries exhibited sharply different profiles of response. Two sets of questions form the coordinates on which one could plot the major differences between countries. The first coordinate could be said to be a "personal-impersonal" continuum, and the second a "form-content" continuum. Belgium and Italy are countries whose students emphasize the impersonal and the formal; students from Chile, England, and Iran emphasize the personal and the content-oriented response; and United States students are concerned with content from an impersonal point of view.

Responses to what one reads, then, are an important aspect of literacy because they place the act of reading within the larger social world of literacy activity. They depend partially on the particular text read, but more crucially on the culture of the reader, on the reader's accession to a particular form of the textual contract. Such dependency increases as people progress through the school system; students' responses become increasingly like the responses preferred by teachers and (to a lesser extent) experts (critics, curriculum makers, and teacher trainers). It would seem that the school serves as a major force in influencing how students respond to a text, and thereby serves as the conduit into the interpretive community of a particular society.

One part of literacy learning within a given society, then, is learning the terms of the textual contract as they form the large interpretive community that helps bind a society together. While learning to read, an individual learns to form a pattern of discourse about what is read, a pattern that is shaped by a culture and its conventions and traditions with respect to how the reader should act toward the text. Such appears to be true of a broad spectrum of readers in elementary and secondary school language classes as well as of the society at large (Heath, 1983; Reder 1987) and of more specialized readers in particular disciplines and occupations, as Fish (1980) and Guthrie and Kirsch (1984) suggest.

What other contractual patterns of performance are learned as an individual becomes a member of a literate society? The IEA Study of Written Composition is exploring that issue, in the writing performance of students in Chile, England, the Federal Republic of Germany, Finland, Hungary, Indonesia, Italy, Netherlands, Nigeria, New Zealand, Sweden, Thailand, the United States, and Wales. One facet of the study is an exploration of the extent to which students are taught to be members of rhetorical communities. The hypothesis underlying this exploration is that in schools students learn to write according to some conventions, independent of the structure of the language and dependent upon the literary and cultural heritage of the society. That is to say that many aspects of texts are not bound by the morphology and grammar of a particular language but by the custom and convention of the textual contract.

The IEA Study of Written Composition seeks to provide a way of examining the possibility of such differences by looking at a systematically drawn sample of writing in a number of rhetorical modes by an average school population writing in the language of instruction. It is also examining the criteria used by teachers of writing to judge student writing in each of the countries in order to see if there are systematic differences that might help define rhetorical communities.

As an initial step, a number of compositions were written by small samples of students at or near the end of secondary school in several of the countries in the study and in three countries no longer in the study (Australia, Japan, and Israel). The compositions were on the subjects "My Native Town" and "What is a Friend?", both thought to be relatively neutral topics that would not force a particular kind of pattern of organization or style on the students. If the compositions were not in English, they were translated by a literary translator and checked by bilingual teachers for their fidelity to the original. A team of researchers then examined the whole group of compositions and found that the compositions tended to differ systematically by culture of origin along a number of continua, some of which matched those of earlier researchers, particularly Carroll (1960), Glenn and Glenn (1981), Hofstede (1980), and Kaplan (1966). The continua that emerged were the following:

Personal-Impersonal: This continuum depends primarily on the frequency of references in the text to the writer's thoughts and feelings about the subject.

Ornamented-Plain: This continuum may also be defined as "figurative-literal" and depends on the frequency of use of metaphor, imagery, and other figures of speech.

Abstract-Concrete: This continuum is defined in terms of the amount of specific information and detailed references in the text as well as to the general level of abstraction.

Single-Multiple: This continuum refers to whether the text focuses on one selected aspect of the subject or tries to cover a large number of aspects of the subject.

Propositional-Appositional: This continuum, which is similar to Glenn and Glenn's abstractive-associative and to some of Kaplan's diagrams, refers to the types of connectives that hold the text together and to whether there appears to be a clear order that follows one of a number of "standard" types of development (e.g., comparison-contrast); such a composition would be propositional. An appositional composition would use few connectives besides *and* or *but,* and would often omit cohesive ties other than collocation, idioms, and repetitions.

These characteristics appear to distinguish the writing of students in different cultures; the differences are not inherent in the language but result from some form of cultural learning because the differences appeared to occur between students writing in the same language (such as English) but living in different cultures such as Australia and Scotland. Students in the United States are more propositional and less figurative than students in Australia (Takala, Purves and Buckmaster, 1982).

It is clear so far that the compositions of students in various countries can be grouped according to these dimensions. One might proceed to ask whether the styles are those desired by the educational systems of the countries. It is here that one turns to the question of criteria. In the pilot phase of the study, a number of these compositions were given to groups of teachers from the countries in the study, and they were asked to both rate and comment on the compositions. From a content analysis of the comments (followed by a factor analysis), four factors emerged (apart from mechanics, spelling, and handwriting): (1) content; (2) organization and structure; (3) style and tone; and (4) personal response to the writer and the content (Purves, 1984a). These "general merit factors" of judgment appeared in all countries, but the relative emphasis and interpretation varied systematically.

In order to check the teachers' criteria, students were asked to write a letter of advice to people younger than they who were about to attend the student-writers' schools. The letter was to suggest ways to succeed in school writing, and a content analysis of the resulting compositions showed that spelling, handwriting, grammar, and neatness were of paramount importance. There are strong national differences in perception, however, such as the relatively low emphasis on organization in Chile and on style and tone in the Netherlands. In New Zealand and Sweden, teachers appear to emphasize process more than in other countries, but in Sweden more of this emphasis concerns choice of topic than is the case in New Zealand. There are differences within other categories as well. In the Netherlands the emphasis under "Presentation" is weighted more toward grammar than in the other countries, whereas in Chile the balance tips heavily to appearance and spelling. Under "Organization" there is a strong concern in the Netherlands for using an organization set by the teachers, a condition that is of less importance in the other countries. In Sweden, teachers seem to favor simple sentences, a feature less important in the other countries. From this evidence it appears that teachers in particular countries appear to favor particular ways of preparing and presenting written discourse, or so their students see it (Takala, 1987).

The Written Composition Study suggests that students in a particular educational system (as part of entering into the textual contract) do indeed learn to become members of a rhetorical community. They learn not only how to write but also what aspects of their writing are valued by their teachers. At times there is direct instruction, at times it is implicit through the examination and grading system, but in either case the students learn that being able to write is being able to produce texts that match certain models. These models serve as criteria for students and teachers alike. If one puts these findings together with the findings of the literature study, we can see that learning literacy in a society is not merely a matter of acquiring a set of skills, but learning a set of culturally approved conventions about producing and receiving written discourse. What other conventions they learn are touched upon in other papers in this volume. Schools (as well as other institutions, such as the workplace or religious or secular communities) are the environments where the terms of the textual contract are passed on from generation to generation.

THE SOCIALLY ACCEPTABLE ACTIONS OF THE LITERATE

A great part of becoming literate is learning not only the textual conventions but also the conventional acts of a particular community and thus becoming a part of that community as it engages in the activity of literacy. Recent cognitive psychology has tended to support this view, suggesting that literacy involves the acquisition of knowledge that is arranged in schemata, or as *chunks*. Such knowledge includes semantic knowledge or content, as well as linguistic and rhetorical structures (Anderson, Spiro, and Montague, 1977: Scardamalia and Paris, 1984). The previous section of this essay suggests that this view is too limited, and that schemata should be broadened to include models of the structure and style of various types of discourse in certain situations, such as those appropriate in a social, academic, religious, or commercial context. Schemata should also be broadened to include models of the functions of different sorts of text within the society, which we may think of as the "social pragmatics" of reading and writing, and particularly as models of how to proceed in the activity of reading or writing. All of these models, as well as the schemata concerning content, are the culturally determined and common property of a society that uses written language for the storage and retrieval of information and the distribution and acquisition of meaning through written discourse.[1] The more complex the society, the more complex and manifold will be the models and schemata (Reder, 1987).

Culture may best be defined as Edward Said has defined it: "[C]ulture is used to designate not merely something to which one belongs but something that one possesses, and along with that proprietary process, culture also designates a boundary by which the concept of what is extrinsic or intrinsic to the culture comes into forceful play" (Said, 1983, p. 9). This root definition of "possession" and "being possessed" seems to apply both to those societies that operate through what might be called natural filiation (a system of intergenerational and familial relationships), and to those that operate through affiliation to some arbitrarily instituted set of relationships. Current American literate culture, for example, is a culture of affiliation, whether it be the culture of Hawthorne and Harriet Beecher Stowe, the culture of Black Studies, the culture of feminism, the culture of basal readers, or of National Writing Projects, or of "hard science."

Any culture serves to isolate its members from other cultures and any culture is elitist in some senses. As Said points out, "What is more important in culture is that it is a system of values saturating downward almost everything within its purview; yet paradoxically culture dominates from above without at the same time being available to everything and everyone that it dominates." Cultures are exclusionary by definition; people who have a culture see others as outside or beneath them; and certainly very few people transcend cultures or are full members of more than one culture, although they may be members of several subcultures, such as that of mycologists, joggers, or film aficionados as well as of the broader culture of "generally educated" Americans.

To be a member of a culture, one must possess a fair amount of knowledge, a large part of it tacit, concerning the culture: its rules, its rituals, its mores, and its heroes, gods, and demigods. This knowledge lies at the heart of "cultural literacy" (Hirsch, 1987). In a literate society, much knowledge is brought into play when people read and respond to a text that comes from the same culture. It is such knowledge that, in fact, is brought into play when they read and write as social beings within a particular community. The lack of such knowledge keeps others outside, as witness the problems of visitors to a national or disciplinary culture who suffer trifling embarrassments or serious misunderstandings.

As a person becomes literate within a culture, that person gathers and assimilates a great deal of knowledge about text forms, text functions, and procedures for reading and writing texts, all of which is represented within schemata. There is knowledge of the lexicon, both oral and in print; there is knowledge of syntactic structures and of generative rules; there is knowledge of text structures such as how stories begin and end or what a paragraph or a nursery rhyme looks like; there is knowledge of appropriate phrases and other locutions to be used in certain contexts; and there is knowledge of when and under what circumstances it is appropriate to write a particular kind of text or respond to a written text in a particular fashion. These kinds of knowledge, in addition to the knowledge about the world at large, are lodged in the mind and are called into play in different situations where reading and writing are called for. Being literate, therefore, involves a series of culturally appropriate responses that bring various storehouses of knowledge into use when the situation calls for them.

A reader in the United States, for example, appears to know that texts are to be read for a single gist (if it is a literary text the gist is hidden and moral), or for the facts and procedures they detail. The reader knows too that certain texts that come in window envelopes with a first-class stamp are bills, and others that come in window envelopes with cheaper postage are advertisements. A writer in the United States knows that a discursive composition is to be started with an anecdote or a generalization, and that a business letter should not include personal information. Each of these and more is a socially approved act within a cultural context that is part of the textual contract determined by a subgroup of United States society.

These schemata serve as models in the individual's head when the individual reads or writes, and they signal when a particular text that is being written or read meets the demands of the situation in which a literate act is called for (Purves and Purves, 1986). In addition, a literate reader knows when certain texts are to be read and when others are superfluous (such as the information printed on the inside flap of a cardboard milk carton in the United States or a ticket in the Metro in Paris), as well as when particular written forms, or procedures with regard to texts, are called for (when it is important to make a written record, for instance, or when it is important to revise, or to check surface features, or to respond to a text with more than a word or a phrase).

Possessing this complex array of knowledge, a literate individual engages in the acts of reading and writing. Such acts constitute the activities of literacy, which call into use cultural knowledge concerning the activity within a given textual contract. Successful performance depends both upon the knowledge that an individual has and the adeptness demonstrated in deploying that knowledge. Literacy, then, should not be thought of simply as a matter of an individual skill or a set of habits, but as the use of such skills and habits in a culturally appropriate manner that indicates that one knows what is required in a particular literate community, whether the narrow community of members of a discipline or a field of endeavor, or the broader community of a particular society. There are norms and conventions appropriate to the world of Paolo Freire just as to the world of the basal reader. Literacy is a communal and contractual affair involving conventions at many levels, and those who work to promote literacy should be aware that they are not simply purveyors of a skill but conservators and imparters of a set of communal standards.

THE SPECIAL NATURE OF SCHOOL LITERACY

Some of the evidence behind what I have so far advanced comes from an examination of the reading and writing of students in primary and secondary schools. There seem to be some differences between what goes on with respect to literacy training within these institutions and what goes on outside of them (Scribner and Cole, 1981; Heath, 1983), but these differences tend to be less great in a society like the United States than one like that of the Vai of Liberia. The twin domains of school reading and school writing can be seen as vehicles for acculturation into the textual contract. Kádár-Fülop (1988) describes three major functions of the school language curriculum in school, basing her argument on Weinreich (1963).

The first of these functions is the promotion of *cultural communication* so as to enable the individual to communicate with a wider circle than the home, the peers, or the village. Such a function clearly calls for the individual to learn the cultural norms of semantics, morphology, syntax, text structures, and pragmatics as well as procedural routines so as to operate within those norms and be understood. The second function is the promotion of *cultural loyalty* or the acceptance and valuing of those norms and the inculcation of a desire to have them remain. A culturally loyal literate would have certain expectations about how texts are to be written or to be read as well as what they should look like, and would expect others in the culture to follow those same norms. Because Americans had a loyalty to certain norms in the 1960s, for example, they reacted strongly when a cigarette advertisement substituted "like" for "as," and one suspects the advertiser was fully conscious of this loyalty. Today that particular loyalty has been lost, to some extent, thanks to the persistence of the advertisement.

The third function of literacy education is the development of *individuality*. Once one has learned to communicate within the culture and developed a loyalty to it, then one is able to become independent of it. Before then, deviation from those norms and values is seen as naive, illiterate, or childish (Vygotsky, 1956; Markova, 1979). For example, many teachers of English in the United States will accept a sentence fragment in a student's composition only when they know that the student is fully aware of the rule and the effect of breaking it. In some societies, particularly those of emerging nations, individuality in reading and writing does not form any part of the curriculum; in "romantic" postindustrial societies it is given great lip service but is seldom really tolerated.

The IEA studies of secondary school students in each of the cultures have shown that they are aware of the norms and standards of school writing and reading, such as the importance of handwriting, spelling, and neatness, or that texts contain a main idea and that in literary texts that main idea is hidden. They have also acquired other norms and cultural values concerning writing and the appropriate response to a text. Whether they could live up to these norms and standards when asked to write a composition or criticize a text is another matter. Probably many could, some could not, and some choose not to. The important bond they share is a general understanding and acceptance of those norms and standards. Students know, by and large, and accept as valued, more norms than they might have the skill to emulate. They know they should "watch their language," that is, even if they deviate from the norms of "Standard Written English."

As formal educational institutions, then, schools set out to make literacy learning serve both broad societal purposes and purposes specific to the subculture of schooling and the academy. School reading, for example, differs from out-of-school reading in many respects. An individual outside of school may purchase or borrow a novel, read it, and put it down. There is no demand to do anything, not even to finish the text. In school, reading a novel is a complex activity of which the act of perusing the text is but one constituent. Other acts include various demonstrations to a skeptical audience that one has read the text with something called comprehension, or appreciation, or understanding. The individual must be prepared to answer oral or written questions about the content, structure, or style of the text, must be prepared to produce some sort of reenactment of the text, or may be expected to commit part of the text to memory. In school the individual must also be prepared to read different types of text on demand, to shift subject matter and form as well as response style every hour on demand, to have the reading interrupted and continued on cue, and to read texts that may be opaque or downright incomprehensible. I remember observing a secondary school language class where I was told by the teacher that two students in the back could not read. The class was reading and discussing an obscure modern poem; the two girls in the back were reading a magazine about film stars and discussing it intelligently. They could read but they could not—or would not—do school reading.

For most cultures, the domain of school reading and the relationship of those two girls to it may be represented as involving two aspects: reading competence and reading preference—what students can do and what they should choose to do. The distinction is based primarily on the criteria used to assess these two forms of achievement. Competence is usually associated with a set of standards of performance upon which there is some consensus. Preference is usually seen as a set of desired behaviors upon which there might appear to be less consensus than with competence, but in practice the consensus may be greater, as we have seen with literary response preference. The preferences often do not appear as stated outcomes, although they may appear in some printed curricula (Purves, 1971, 1984b); as Heath (1983) observes, preference may indeed be the most important aspect of the reading curriculum.

Like school reading, school writing asks the following of the individual: (1) articulateness according to certain conventions; (2) fluency or the ready production or consumption of copious amounts of text; (3) flexibility in moving from genre to genre; and (4) appropriateness, suiting what is done to the norms of the genre and the situation. The competence aspect includes two sorts of competence: one relating to the motor acts in producing text, the other relating to the acts involved in discourse production. Again, schools focus a great deal of attention on writing preferences; not all writing activities are approved in schools (e.g., graffiti, love notes), despite the various sorts of ingenuity with language they might display. Writing in school must follow particular conventions, and the conventions appropriate in one subject are not always those in another. Students must be apprenticed to five or six literate subcommunities seriatim during the day or the week.

In both school reading and school writing, then, we can see that students are expected to learn the terms of the textual models and become literate in the large cultural community of readers and writers, but also in several specialized academic communities. As they progress through the academic world to the university, they will learn the even more specialized practices and preferences of various scholarly communities. As they go into various occupations, they will learn the conventions of literate behavior in the various institutions that make up a complex society. Vast numbers of people accept the conventions of the community and even seem to thrive comfortably within them. For them as consumers of the culture, familiarity and conventionality are comfortable. Soap operas and reruns, gothics and repetitive articles appear as welcome relief from the shocks of change in other parts of their lives; they can retreat to an orderly and predictable world of text. There are many others, however, who find such convention boring. Some of them are artists; some are teachers and academics; some are judged deviant or subnormal; all of them are the ones who test conventional wisdom and common knowledge, and prevent the conventions from becoming totally stagnant and sterile.

CHANGING THE TERMS OF THE TEXTUAL CONTRACT

Over the centuries there have been many changes in the conventions of text as well as in the approaches to reading and writing. Among these changes have been the standardization of punctuation, spelling, and letter forms brought about by the advent of movable type and by the agreement among printers and publishers that there should be consistency. The deletion of the apostrophe in the possessive form of *it* at the beginning of the nineteenth century so as to avoid confusion with the contraction of *it is* is a good example of change by consensus. Some of the most dramatic changes in this century have been the acceptance in Germany of the roman as opposed to the gothic type, the establishment of Bahasa Indonesia as the national language of literacy in a polyglot society, and the implantation of close reading of determinable meaning as the dominant form of academic interpretation in the United States. There have also been innumerable attempts at control of the contract that have failed. The most notable of these have been the failures of *L'Academie Française* to stem the anglicization of the French language and the various attempts at spelling reform in England and the United States. The terms of the textual contract very often change but seldom by fiat. The success of Bahasa occurred in part because of the elimination of other languages from the world of text. This was as deliberate an act as seems to have been the decision not to print Luther's Bible in Prussian and Saxon, thus allowing those languages to atrophy. The success of the "new criticism's objective treatment of literature" came about in part because of a textbook (Brooks and Warren's *Understanding Poetry*), but in part, too, because the type of reading matched the stringencies of multiple-choice testing that was then gaining a strong hold on the educational system.

Spelling reform has generally failed, although there have been some changes in spelling over the history of written language. Crusading reformers like George Bernard Shaw have had less effect than have the subtle reformers such as those in advertising and the neon lettering business. The change from *co-operate* to *cooperate* or *over-all* to *overall* in the United States resulted more from the activity of printers and copy editors than from any deliberate planning by lexicographers or language teachers. The government has changed the standard abbreviations of states in the past fifty years, and various businesses have modified what had been conventional openings and closings in correspondence. All of these changes have been modest and generally evolutionary.

In the past two decades, there has been a concerted attempt on the part of some interested in language education in the United States to change the terms of the textual contract as it is set forth in the schools. With respect to both reading and writing there has been a dissatisfaction with the relatively impersonal approaches to reading and interpreting texts as well as to the impersonality, selectivity, literalness, and propositional nature of the preferred rhetorical stance. To change the first there has been a call for "response to literature"; to change the second there has been an emphasis on personal or expressive writing. Both changes deal with the nature of the terms of the textual contract, but neither denies the fact of the contract. To observe the attempt, one of the few that has been consciously set forth by a reformist group in a society other than spelling reformers, leads one to speculate on whether this attempt will be doomed to failure as well. The inertia of the textual contract, and its apparent imperviousness to revolution, may prevent major changes, particularly since the society at large may not share the perception of a double bind (Engeström, 1987).

What may well have a greater effect on the textual contract is the force exerted by the technology of production and reproduction of text.

Such has been true in the past. The advent of the copying machine and carbonless forms means that it is easy to save and duplicate ephemeral writing, and so all sorts of textual materials are available to increasing numbers of people, many of whom have little need of it. We may now have documents without reading them. There is no longer a need to transform information into knowledge by reading it. It is available and external to us by virtue of being readily reproducible. The word processor has changed the very nature of writing more profoundly than have all sorts of curricular plans and pedagogical programs. With the electronic keyboard and the disc, it is possible for a writer to change text with relative ease. It is also possible for the writer to recycle whole segments of text with a push of a button. Desktop publishing has brought about revisions in the format of text so that what was difficult with hand-set or electrotype is now simple. The fact that certain scholarly journals do not exist save in the memory of computers changes the whole concept of the library and of the text. A text no longer needs to be palpable, much less immutable. All of these changes, I suspect, will alter the nature of the textual contract as much as did the advent of papyrus or the printing press.

Whether the change is revolutionary and conscious or evolutionary and unconscious is not the issue; there has been and will remain a literate contract, a mediation between the individual and society through sets of conventions that enable the two to function in a world of text and information. Although the terms and specifications of that contract will be modified, the fact of the contract cannot be abrogated as some educators have suggested. Literacy is a social activity made up of a variety of acts and operations. As Engeström citing Leontev writes, "we may well speak of the *activity of the individual* but never of *individual activity*; only actions are individual" (Engeström, 1987, p. 66). Literacy, to follow from this point, is an activity that controls the individual. The individual cannot control it. The individual participates in the contract, employing many actions that are virtually unconscious, as we have seen. Within this perspective, schools must be seen as social institutions to help children enter into and come to terms with that contractual arrangement which is literate activity in all its complexity.

The University at Albany

III

Literacy from the
Individual's Perspective

6

Literacy and Individual Consciousness

F. NYI AKINNASO

For present purposes, the term "individual consciousness" is used as a shorthand for the totality of an individual's knowledge, thoughts, beliefs, impressions, and feelings and the ways these are represented in behavior, especially in speech and writing. Individual consciousness is thus not simply a mental state but a dynamic process involving both the internalization and representation of social reality. An important aspect of social reality about which this paper is concerned is the range of values, attitudes, beliefs, and uses associated with those reading, writing, and speaking practices we have come to call literacy.

Although received notions about individual consciousness have led us to believe that only psychologists can study the subject, literacy research within the past decade has shown that it is futile to expect that the effects of literacy on individual consciousness can easily be detected through the contrived tests of the traditional psychologist. Apart from the cultural-specificity of psychological tests, there is the theoretical question about the place of human interaction and cultural processes in a theory of knowledge that defines skills and epistemic processes as "mental" in the sense that they are entirely contained within the human mind, a conception of language for which Chomsky continues to be criticized. The point I wish to make is that if individual consciousness is viewed only as a "mental" state, then we would be shutting the door to the study of human interaction and cultural processes which shape and are, in turn, shaped by individual consciousness. Indeed, it is this symbiotic relationship between mental and sociocultural processes that marks the point of departure of the sociohistorical school of psychology (Vygotsky, 1962, 1978; Cole and Scribner, 1974; Wertsch, 1985a, 1985b) and the application of the sociohistorical approach to the study of literacy (see, especially, Scribner and Cole, 1981; Langer, 1986). I accepted the invitation to address certain issues that the title of this essay entails in order to highlight certain aspects of my own experience that have some implications for the relationship between literacy and individual consciousness.

Received notions about literacy have many parts. But perhaps the most popular these days is the notion that literacy defies a monolithic definition. Rather, it is conceived of as a range of socially constructed practices, values, and competencies regarding reading and writing activities as well as certain ways of speaking. The quality and quantity of these activities are hopelessly variable, as are their effects on participants. This emic notion of literacy (see Wagner, this volume) has been elaborated in many different ways. For example, Scribner and Cole (1981) view literacy as a form of social practice, while Street (1984) and Langer (1986) propose what they call "ideological" and "sociocognitive" models, respectively, to capture the underlying cultural, ideological, and social-ecological constraints on literacy practices. In the same vein, Jenny Cook-Gumperz (1986) advocates a perspective of literacy which emphasizes its "social construction." Indeed, today, it is becoming very fashionable to pluralize literacy as a kind of protest against monolithic or "autonomous" conceptions of the subject (for example, a new institute in the Boston area is called "The Literacies Institute," thus drawing attention to this protest).

In his contribution to this volume, Alan Purves highlights another dimension of literacy practices, the idea that literate individuals within a given community do not act alone as such but participate in what he terms a "textual contract." One popular assumption about literacy acquisition implicit in these models is that a community specifies its own type and standards of literacy, sometimes through legislation but mostly by convention. But the nature of this community has not always been fully specified. In general, however, the intended scope of community is the immediate community of the learner. The emphasis on such literacy practices as "parents as reading partners" supports this view. Very shortly, I shall delineate a community that embraced literacy but whose members could neither read nor write, although my focus will be on the effects of this new mode of communication on those who became literate in the community. As I shall demonstrate shortly, the new literates had to redefine their community and expand it beyond their immediate cultural and spatiotemporal horizon.

There is yet another notion about literacy that requires further clarification—the notion that literacy is more than the act of reading and writing. In this view, literacy is given an extended definition to include ways of perceiving, thinking, speaking, evaluating, and interacting that characterize a group of individuals and set them apart from others (see especially Langer, 1986). The implication here is that "literate thinking," involves ways of perceiving the world and talking about it, a perception that may result from interacting with either text or text users. In

Purves's terminology, literate consciousness would result from participation in the textual contract or from interaction with such participants.

The underlying assumption is very clear: that literacy involves major changes in forms of perception and communication. However, while all researchers would agree to this, there is no agreement on the cognitive consequences of these changes or on their effects on individual consciousness. The arguments run in one of two directions. One sees literacy as a *causal* agent and interprets the sociocultural changes associated with changes in forms of communication in terms of epistemic changes, altered forms of representation and forms of consciousness. Advocates of this view include Goody, Havelock, McLuhan, Olson, Ong, and Stock. In three separate volumes, Goody (1977, 1986, 1987), in particular, draws upon sociohistorical data to argue vigorously in support of the equation, "writing = civilization," where civilization entails "democracy," "individualism," "rationality," "skepticism," "logic," and a range of unique cognitive operations.

The other group, typified by Eisenstein, Scribner, Cole, Finnegan, and Street, has been more cautious in interpreting the sociocultural changes associated with changes in the forms of communication. These changes are seen as resulting more in altered social and institutional practices than in the development of unique cognitive operations. To advocates of this view, then, literacy is a *facilitating* agent, promoting the deployment of preexisting cognitive capacities into certain channels that are socially and ideologically sanctioned by the user-group. Scribner and Cole are particularly careful in distinguishing between cognitive capacities and skills, arguing that the former are universal and uniform while the latter are culture-specific and variable (Cole and Scribner, 1974; Scribner and Cole, 1973, 1981). Thus, while literacy facilitates the acquisition of certain cognitive skills and operations, it does not, in itself, engender novel cognitive capacities as the "causative" argument would like us to believe (see Akinnaso, 1981, for further discussion).

Understandably, these two groups have differing views about the relationship between literacy and individual consciousness. Supporters of the "causative" argument see the development of "rationality," "skepticism," "logic," etc.; the rise of individualism, democracy, etc.; and the evolution of bureaucracy, urbanization, etc., as direct results of literacy, while supporters of the "facilitating" argument do not see a causal link. Notice, however, that neither group denies the fact that literacy alters the world we live in and the way we perceive and talk about that world.

I want to contribute to this discussion by inviting you to go along with me to Ajegunle-Idanre in southwestern Nigeria, the village in which I was born and raised in the early nineteen-forties. Located about ten miles away from the town of Idanre, Ajegunle was a small agricultural community with fewer than five hundred inhabitants in 1954 when I started going to school. I was already more than ten years old then and had seven siblings, two of whom were older than myself. The others were much younger, being between one and three years old. Father had four wives. Like others in the village, he was a farmer in cocoa, yams, plantain, and maize, while the women maintained secondary plantations for vegetable crops. We used to work on the farm for several weeks, sometimes months, at a stretch before ever going to the town where Father owned what looked to us then like a mansion.

Father had several cocoa plantations scattered in different locations within a radius of about ten miles, the nearest to the village being about three miles. Plantations for other crops were located in appropriate places within this area, but usually away from the cocoa farms. Except for cocoa, farming was by shifting cultivation, meaning that a new plot was cultivated for new seedlings after each harvest season. Our routine was fairly regular. Typically, we would wake up early in the morning, usually around 5:00 A.M. There was no clock in the house (and no one could read a clock, anyway) but Father knew when it was time to wake up. The crowing of the cock and the activities of certain birds or rodents were good indicators. Father would ensure that everyone got up from bed and would assist us in preparing for the day's work. An important aspect of this preparation was walking us to the farm on which we were going to work for the day. We usually arrived at the farm between 7:00 and 8:30 A.M., depending on distance from the village, and would work until about 12:00 noon before the first day's meal. Time was determined either by the nature of some shadow or, sometimes, by Father's intuition. We usually closed for the day's work between 4:00 and 5:00 P.M. Our next meal was dinner, which was served around 7:00 P.M.

Father was a devoted worshipper of *ifa*, the Yoruba god of divination. Although he did not learn to divine by himself, he owned the divination apparatus which he inherited from his father, who was a professional diviner. There was an annual festival in our home that usually took place in the month of January. The festival was a combination of ancestor worship, thanksgiving for the passing season, and renewed devotion to *ifa*. Professional diviners were always invited to conduct the festival, which lasted seven days. A key feature of the festival was divination for each member of the family in order to find out what was in store for each person for the new year, and what to do in order to ensure the promised blessing or avert evil, depending on the diviner's predictions. Shortly after I was born, it was predicted during one such divination session that I was going to be a diviner. A few years later, it was also predicted that Father should beware of *esin alejo*, "the religion of strangers," which might divert my life course from divination.

As it turned out, this prediction "came to pass" as Father converted to Christianity around 1948, although without forsaking the worship of *ifa*. By 1950, most elders in the village had partially converted to Christianity. Because there was no church in the village, villagers had to go to the town every other Sunday for worship.

A few years later, a branch of the Cooperative Union for cocoa farmers was established in the village. Partly because he often had a very high annual yield of cocoa and partly because of his perceived stature in the village, Father was appointed the first Treasurer of the Union. Of all members of the executive of the Union, only the Secretary was literate in the sense of being able to read and write and do simple calculations. Two other adults had learned how to read simple messages in Yoruba and sign their names. One of them, who was a devoted Jehova witness, could read and possibly write in English.

The above events—conversion to Christianity and Father's appointment as Treasurer of the Union—provided Father with major encounters with literate activities. He had a copy of the Bible, the catechism, and the hymn book, which he could not read. He often kept other farmers' sales invoices, lots of cash, and the books of account of the Union for some hours or days before returning them to the safe. And for a few years, the Union operated from a wing of our house in the village. During this time, the Union's safe was kept in a corner of Father's bedroom.

There was another event that increased the encounter with literate activities: membership in church associations, which met every other Sunday in the town. These associations and the Cooperative Union institutionalized a specific scribal function, that of record keeping. Each association appointed a record-keeper or secretary, locally known as *akowe* (a-ko-iwe [Nominalizer + Write + Book]), "one who writes." In no time, traditional neighborhood and townwide associations began to appoint secretaries to keep records of their deliberations. The secretaries were often younger people, often pupils of local primary schools, whose parents had earlier converted to Christianity and sent them to school. Scribal functions expanded rapidly in Idanre in the nineteen-fifties from recording minutes of meetings to keeping records of commercial transactions, especially preparation of sales agreements, and list making, especially lists of names of donors and their donations during major ceremonies such as marriages and funerals, records that became very important in updating one's reciprocal obligations.

About this time, an adult literacy campaign was accorded priority in the agenda of the Idanre local government, then known as Native Authority, the lowest tier in the colonial government establishment. The adult literacy campaign in Idanre was, of course, part of the local chapter of the mass literacy campaigns that resulted from a series of Colonial Development and Welfare Acts and from policy enactments by the Advisory Committee on Education in the Colonies in the nineteen-forties and fifties (see Foster, 1971, for a review). The campaign, which started as a component of more general community development programs, soon enlisted the participation of the Cooperative Union which, in no time, began to require its members to learn how to sign their names, instead of merely thumbprinting, for money or equipment received or loaned from the Union. Because signing was mandatory for Treasurers of local branches, Father had to learn how to sign his name and recognize his signature.

There were, then, three major factors that prompted the demand for literacy in Ajegunle village, all three factors being external to the local, social system. First, there was Christianity, an external religion of the Book. Associated with this religion was the first set of books in many village households, namely, the Bible, the catechism, and the hymn book. The Sunday school and the regular primary school also came as direct results of missionary activities. Second, there was an external political system, the colonial administration, that relied on a literate bureaucracy whose effects were locally felt in the administration of the Idanre Native Authority, later known as the Idanre Local Government, which promoted the adult literacy campaigns. Third, there was the external economy of cash crop management associated with the adoption of cocoa and coffee. An important aspect of this new economy was record keeping, especially sales invoices and receipts, which became necessary because farmers were not immediately paid for the crops they sold. The Cooperative Union institutionalized the new management practices, while also enlisting the participation of the farmers.

Although there was neither a church nor a school in Ajegunle village in the fifties, the above factors prompted and increased the demand for literacy, thus preparing the way for sending me and a few other children in the village to school. The first direct impact on us was partial separation from village life, when I had to live with my grandmother ten miles away in the town, returning to the farm only on weekends and vacations. Little did Father (or I, for that matter) realize that we were going to be permanently separated. For, as it turned out later, my quest for advanced literacy had to have a spatial dimension. First, after primary education, I went to the boarding house for high school training in the only school just established in the town. Every further advancement beyond that took me several miles away from home until I finally made it to the University of California at Berkeley for graduate training. Moreover, the more I trained, the further away from home I went in search of a job.

While in primary school and, to some extent, in high school, there was a very close relationship between me and my father, especially during weekends and vacations. One of my favorite assignments was to assist him and his friends in calculating their cocoa sales, based on invoices they had obtained from the Cooperative Union. I could observe that the accuracy in sales records that literacy afforded was of particular interest to cocoa farmers in Ajegunle village at that time. Although they were nonliterate themselves, they carefully kept their invoices and were always delighted to know that someone else who did not know when those invoices were written could read them accurately. This "magic" was not lost on Father who, in addition to being Treasurer of the village branch of the Cooperative Union, was also a member of several village, town, and church associations and therefore encountered literacy in various contexts. Nor were Father's remarks lost on me when I first assisted him in calculating his sales for the year, based on the invoices he had carefully preserved. He said in Idanre dialect (of Yoruba): "*Ye o! Oyibo ku u se!*" The closest expression to this in English would be something like, "What ho! The White Man works wonders!!"

Father and I did not always agree on the calculations. There was a particular occasion I would never forget, not just because Father was right, but because of what he said. I missed the calculation by fifty pounds (sterling) or so because I forgot to "carry" some figure from one row to another. I first insisted that I was right (not having realized my mistake) and queried father as to why he was so sure that I was wrong. Then he brought out several small bags filled with pebbles. The pebbles were of three different sizes. Each of the biggest ones stood for one hundred pounds and the smallest ones for one shilling. Pebbles of intermediate size stood for ten or five pounds each, depending on how father wanted it. These were the basic tools father used in his calculations, and he was usually correct (at least to the pound). So, on this occasion, he was correct and his words to me were: "*Wa a ka'we si un; Wa a lo sul'oba gan an do i bo ye e yeke yeke.*" "You will read (study) more; you will even go overseas so that you can be a master of what you learn." The underlying assumption here was that I needed more training in order to avoid the kind of mistake I had made with my calculations.

Of course, at this stage in my life, I still believed that Father knew almost everything. After all, it was only a few years back, during my first day at school, when Father disputed my age with the headmaster.

The headmaster had insisted that I was only six years old, his arguments being that I looked small and, after all, six years was the statutory age of enrollment. To prove his point, he made my father watch a simple experiment that was widely used in many primary schools at that time. He ordered me to stretch my right arm over my head until my hand touched my left ear. Since my hand could barely touch the ear, I was pronounced no more than six years old. Father did not agree. In no time, he started his own calculations by counting the number of yam harvests he had had since I was born. He also remembered that I was born shortly before the Ogun festival. By his calculation, I was twice as old as the headmaster had suggested. In the long run, a compromise was reached: The headmaster put me down for eight years old, having convinced Father that it was to my advantage to be younger on paper. (I later found out that the younger you are on paper, the more years of service you would have and, subsequently, the more pension you would earn after retirement.)

Perhaps because of his close contact with invoices and books of account, books (as defined below) and any piece of paper, for that matter, were very important, almost sacred, to Father. He already knew that you could store and retrieve knowledge from books. The absence of a bookstore in town also added to their sacred quality. You had to go somewhere else to get them. In local terms, it was like going in search of a knowledgeable diviner. Indeed, the importance of books to my people is vividly captured in local vocabulary about literacy and literate activities. Thus, as you can see, the base word in the following terms is *iwe* "book":

ka'we	ka count	+ iwe + book		"read"
ko'we	ko scratch	+ iwe + book		"write"
koowe	ko learn	+ iwe + book		"learn, study"
akowe	a -er	+ ko + scratch	+ iwe + book	"writer, secretary, stenographer, literate person, etc."
omo ile iwe	ile house	+ iwe + book		"school"
omo ile iwe	omo child	+ ile + house	+ iwe + book	"pupil/student"

The word *iwe* itself is a highly generalized lexicon, covering anything from a scrap of paper to a dictionary or an encyclopedia. Invoices and letters are also *iwe*. Indeed, so basic is the word *iwe* in local usage that primary and secondary school diplomas are curiously referred to as *iwe meefa* "six books" and *iwe meewa* "ten books," respectively (I have yet to discover the logic behind the numbers). Interestingly, however, the word for teacher is not a derivative of *iwe*. Rather, it derives from the word *ko* (note the high tone) "to learn" (*iko*, noun, "learning"). Thus a teacher is known as *oluko* (o + ni + iko) "one who owns learning." It would appear that the word *ko* (without the high tone) as opposed to *ko* derives from the vocabulary of learning associated with traditional knowledge such as *ifa* divination. Thus the phrase *ko'fa* (ko + ifa [learn + ifa]) "to learn ifa" is analogous to *koowe* (ko + iwe [learn + book]) "to learn or study."

To go back to Father, books, and me, it is important to note that the nearest bookstore was the CMS (Church Missionary Society) bookstore, located ten miles away, in Akure, then the Divisional Headquarters of the colonial administration. While in primary school, Father always went with me to Akure to purchase necessary books and stationery for the new school year. Our purchases were often based on a booklist I had brought home from school at the end of the preceding school year. Father always allowed me to buy books outside the list once I or (sometimes) the bookseller convinced him that they would add to my knowledge. Indeed, after I was promoted to Primary Six, Father voluntarily gave me extra money to buy any additional books I wanted, partly because I took first position in the promotional examination and partly because I was going to be preparing for the Primary School Leaving Certificate, a major achievement by local standards.

With some of the extra money, I bought various books, three of which I can now remember as a book on letter writing and simplified editions of *Tales of the Arabian Nights* and Shakespeare's *The Tempest*, the latter two being recommended by the bookseller. But perhaps the most spectacular purchases for me then were postage stamps. I had learned in school about letter writing (which was why I bought the book on letter writing) and pen pals. I had also come in contact with Langfield's and Lennard's Catalogs and known that I could order clothes and shoes from England. I had also learned a curious word in school, the word "hobby." I had chosen photography as my hobby, partly because a professional photographer was, at that time, a tenant in our family house in town. With the book on letter writing, Langfield's Catalog, postage stamps, and additional funds from my mother, I could order a camera from England. Well, I did, but my first order was returned with a note that I was required to send a "money order" and not cash. Actually, I read that requirement somewhere in the catalog, but I thought that a money order meant an order backed up with money (i.e., cash)! Anyway, I went back to the post office to straighten that out and my camera arrived some two months later.

By this time, when I was literate enough to order a camera from England, I had become a local celebrity in our village. I had successfully communicated with the White Man in his own language through the medium of *iwe*. My father took pride in telling his friends about my accomplishments. I myself began to feel important and self-confident. My participation in local affairs increased tremendously as I became an "authority" in preparing sales agreements, reading invoices of cocoa sales and calculating necessary sums, recording minutes of meetings of local associations, explaining to local farmers how to use insecticides, writing letters and keeping records on various issues for local villagers, and so on. More importantly, I was occasionally invited to the executive meeting of the local branch of the Cooperative Union to be the "eye" of nonliterate members. In fact, my attendance at these meetings became frequent (especially during vacations) after audit reports indicated that the Secretary of the Union had cheated and embezzled some funds. When I first read the report (of course I had to translate from English to the local dialect) to Father and a small group of friends (who were also members of the Union), they were very appreciative. It was as if I discovered the fraud myself. The farmers later banded together and protested to the Head Office of the Union in town, calling for the replacement of the Secretary, and they won. The Secretary was replaced at the end of the farming season.

From these early beginnings, my involvement with literacy and literacy education grew into teaching in the local high school (after my high school diploma), at a Nigerian university (after a college degree) and in various other universities in Nigeria and the United States after the doctorate. Many readers can now begin to fill in much of the remaining detail in this autobiographical account, especially since I became a member of their professional group, circulating my vita, which contains a great deal of what I have been doing since I left college. For the remainder of this essay, I want to concentrate on how I acquired literacy in a nonliterate environment and the influence it has had on me and people in my immediate environment at the early stages of my literacy education.

First of all, it has to be noted that I had no reading partner at home. There was no one to read to me and almost no one to read to. In the absence of domestic literacy, much of my learning in the early years took place in school. Our teachers were painstaking and instruction was highly repetitive at the beginning. Moreover, homework was minimal, perhaps in the realization that there would be no one to assist us at home. I was already leaving primary school by the time the next person in my family went to school.

I can recall vividly now that after mastering the Yoruba alphabet and learning how to read, I was eager to find someone to read to. Fortunately one Sunday evening, Father requested that I read the Bible to him. He had listened to a sermon in church about Paul, the apostle, visiting a governor. He wanted me to read that story to him. I searched in vain for the passage. Father could not understand why I could not pick out the story from the Bible, thus questioning my claim to readership. Without exactly succeeding in convincing him that it was difficult to locate a passage you never read before (especially when there were no prompts or clues), I elected to read the creation story from Genesis that I had read in school. In no time, father fired another query: Why couldn't I read the story in our dialect? I told him the Bible was not written in our dialect, but in the dialect of Yoruba we learn at school. Then another question: What did the Bible say about *Oodua (Oduduwa)*, the ancestral founder of Yorubaland? I told him that the Bible does not contain stories about the Yoruba people. And yet another question: How could a creation story leave out *Oodua* and the Yoruba people? The only response I could give then was that the writers of the Bible probably did not know about the Yoruba people. I wish I had the anthropological insight at that time to tell him that every culture has its own creation myth and that the story in Genesis is just one of such myths.

We probably had three or four Bible reading sessions thereafter. But soon after the initial reading trials, my desire to read the Bible to Father waned considerably, largely because the medium of instruction in school had now switched completely to English. I wanted to read in English but there was no one in my family to read to in English. I needed an outlet and reinforcement for my learning. In retrospect, it is not unlikely that this need was partly accountable for what was considered an abnormal behavior that nearly led to my withdrawal from school: I was told that I began to speak English in my dreams. When my grandmother first noticed this behavior, she was hysterical. I was prevented from going to school the following morning. Instead, she took me to the family diviner. The complaint was that I was communicating with my "colleagues" in the other world, which meant that I might soon die, like three other siblings before me. Fortunately, however, Father came to town that weekend and convinced grandmother that my "English dreams" were an extension of my school experience. Father could relate to the *sheme-sheme* (Grandmother's expression for my strange English language) because he had interacted with literate people in the Cooperative Union. He knew that *sheme-sheme* was their language and that the Secretary of the Union and I had spoken such language before. And, fortunately too, as I now recall, my "English dreams" did not last long enough to give Grandmother continued concern.

I eventually resorted to writing letters to pen pals in the United States, England, and Australia. The Langfield Catalog orders also provided me with a necessary outlet. And I loved reading. But my reading was limited to whatever books I owned because there was neither a library in my primary school nor a bookstore in town. There was a library in town within the premises of the local government offices, but children could not go there, let alone borrow a book.

I had a friend and classmate in primary school who came from a different village but was living with his aunt one block or so away from my grandmother's house, where I stayed during the greater part of my primary school years. My friend and I shared similar interests in reading, but his family could not afford to buy extra books for him. I shared my *Tempest* and *Arabian Nights* with him. He loved both of them as we shared our impressions about the stories. We both agreed to buy other Shakespearean plays, most of which were listed on the back cover of *The Tempest*. We approached my mother for extra money to buy some important books we thought might make us pass well in school and she obliged. I can now remember that my friend and I both rode on the same bicycle to Akure where we bought several books, including a map of the world and several simplified editions of Shakespeare's plays, including *Hamlet*, *King Lear*, and *Romeo and Juliet*.

For me, the most outstanding purchase this time was the world map, because it enabled me to locate the countries of my pen pals. My world suddenly enlarged. I was no longer a small village boy, but one who "knows" the world! My pen pals gave me that feeling, too. They were real people, unlike Prospero and King Lear (not to mention Ariel, the spirit) that I read about in books. I felt as though I really knew my pen pals and that they knew me. They encouraged me to write and to write better. My American pen pal even sent a dictionary to me, but I could not use it because the spellings confused me. Nevertheless, I found in these pen pals and the Langfield Catalogs (which I received regularly from England for several years) a literate community, the kind of community that my immediate environment could not provide. Thus, my ability to read and write had transformed me beyond my immediate environment.

I want to use this metaphor of transformation as a launching pad for my discussion of the relationship between literacy and individual consciousness. But let me warn at the outset that I am not making any universal claims, although I might be raising certain issues of some general nature. There are, basically, four major areas of experience where the impact of literacy has been most noticeable: (1) language (and speech), (2) thought, (3) religion (and culture), and (4) social organization, including the organization of the polity and the economy (see especially Goody and Watt, 1963; Akinnaso, 1981; Goody, 1977, 1986, 1987). Partly because of differences in disciplinary and theoretical orientations, we tend to isolate these areas of experience in our discussion of the effects, consequences, or implications of literacy as if they belong to different compartments in our consciousness. The nature of schooling, writing, and "scientific" enquiry further socializes us into talking about experience in bits and pieces. The segmentation of experience is further reinforced by the linear nature of language: Sounds and letters are produced in chains. Although individual consciousness is about the totality of being, rather than bits and pieces, I will follow tradition by highlighting certain aspects of my own consciousness that have been most seriously affected by literacy.

Although I acquired literacy in three languages, namely, English, Yoruba, and to some extent Latin, I would say that I acquired only one literacy—alphabetic literacy—for at least two reasons. First, except for a few additional diacritical marks to indicate phonetic and phonological distinctions in Yoruba, the three languages make use of the same alphabet. Second, my formal training in Latin and Yoruba was very short, the former being provided only as a school subject and the latter being provided for one or two years or so only in keeping with the transitional bilingual education policy where the increasing use of English was matched with the decreasing use of the local vernacular. During our own time, the vernacular was meant to disappear in high school (except during indigenous language lessons); you were seriously punished for "speaking in the vernacular."

As indicated in the Bible-reading episode above, I first learned to read in a dialect of Yoruba other than my own. I failed to master the spoken version of this new dialect partly because, at age twelve, I had developed deep-rooted phonological and discourse habits, and partly because there was no one to talk to in this strange dialect once I left the school premises. Interestingly, however, I had no difficulty with the written version of this new dialect in part because both writing and the new dialect of Yoruba were, for me, two inseparable aspects of the same "strange" experience. Learning to write the alphabets was part of learning the new dialect, and learning the new dialect was learning the language of the school. I confronted this experience with all my attention.

My encounter with difficulties with written language began when we switched to English. Then I began to make "grammatical" mistakes, errors that I could never make in my own dialect of Yoruba. The need to avoid such mistakes, to learn how to construct "correct" sentences, was part of the motivation for my love of reading. Although the sentences I was required to write in school were not exactly in the books I read, I had a feeling that reading them would improve my performance. Even if they did not affect my performance directly, the books prepared me for high school English if only in the sense that I had no difficulty relating to such notions as "sentence" and "paragraph" when they were later introduced. They were all in the books I had read.

However, I soon learned, especially in high school, that my language problem was not limited to English language lessons alone. I had to use English and construct correct sentences for other school subjects as well. Language, then, became the major preoccupation, at least as far as I was concerned. And this was no mean preoccupation. Imagine the plight of a nonliterate farmer's son from a small, local village, confronted with a new dialect of his language that he *must* learn, after age twelve. Imagine his plight when he had to switch to another, unrelated, language at age fourteen, just as the new dialect was being mastered. Imagine the poor boy as he said after the teacher:

Exercise 1		*Exercise 2*	
Singular	*Plural*	*Present*	*Past*
cat	cats	talk	talked
man	men	sleep	slept
child	children	go	went
sheep	sheep	hit	hit

Notice the unpredictability of these morphological markers and imagine the plight of the farmer's son as he tried to cope with the irregularities. The problem was compounded by the fact that Yoruba is an isolating language, essentially lacking in morphological complexities. The result is that the Yoruba schoolchild is least prepared for the grammatical and semantic importance of morphological markers. Worse still, in those days, the child had to learn this strange language in a situation where his out-of-school experience provided no verbal reinforcement.

But while these appeared to be factors most unfavorable to learning, I was fascinated by the challenge. One of the books we used in school in those days was *Student Companion*, which contained enormous amounts of data and exercises on English grammar. I read the entire book over and over again. The cumulative result was a keen sensitivity to language, a sensitivity that prepared me for "*amo, amas, amat . . .*" when I later encountered Latin in high school. With hindsight, I can now relate meaningfully to the popular claim that literacy raises one's consciousness about language. Indeed, since language is the major medium for literacy, it is not too much to expect that certain differences will emerge over time between "literate" and "oral" language within the same speech community (Akinnaso, 1982a, 1988), just as significant differences have developed between "ritual" and "conversational" language in nonliterate societies (Akinnaso, 1982b, 1985; Sherzer, 1983).

Whatever the degree of discontinuity between home and school language, however, my own experience shows that it is not insurmountable. But a keen sensitivity, especially on the part of the learner, to the differences between the nature and uses of speech and writing is very crucial to bridging the discontinuity. While the onus of knowing what was necessary to know was essentially on me, given the nonliterate environment in which I learned, I must acknowledge that there were several people who contributed to my sensitivity. There was my father who encouraged and supported my quest for reading; there was the bookseller who drew my attention to Shakespeare's plays; there were the pen pals and the Langfield Catalogs; and, as I will show later, there were also two teachers who lived in our house in town.

While I became very sensitive to language and certainly developed more metalinguistic awareness than my nonliterate colleagues in the village, language was not necessarily the most significant aspect of my consciousness affected by literacy, especially in regard to my relationship with people around me. Rather, it was what I and my friends used to talk about and how we talked about them. I had two very close friends when I was in primary school. One (B), male, was my classmate in primary school, the same boy who shared my books and the bicycle ride to Akure. My other close friend was (F), female, a cousin. F never went to school and, therefore, was in the village whenever I went back there on weekends and vacations. Since she lived only two houses away from mine, we sort of grew up together, and I continued my pre-school close relationship with her. I was always eager to see her whenever I went back to the village. However, once she fed me, in about five minutes or so, with details of local events that happened while I was away in school in the city, there was little else to talk about. At first, after I learned to read well, I would tell her stories from my books. But I soon stopped doing that when I noticed that she could not respond. She knew neither Prospero nor Ariel and she could not relate to the story of Ali Baba and the forty thieves because their exploits did not happen in the village. Moreover, they were very different from the tortoise exploits and other folktales she knew.

In contrast, B and I would share the same stories with excitement, talk about the characters, and, on many occasions, refer to the appropriate pages in the books to explore interesting points of detail. While my conversations with F were always in the Idanre dialect of Yoruba, my conversations with B often involved extensive codeswitching: one, two, or all of the Idanre dialects, standard Yoruba, and English would be used, depending on topic and context. It soon became very evident from my interaction with B and F that I was living in two separate worlds and that B and F were symbols of the two. B knew and was part of my literate world, whereas F knew and was part of my nonliterate world. I soon learned that I needed to keep both worlds separate in my daily interactions with people around me. I had to select the appropriate audience for my "book" stories just as I had to choose appropriately between speaking in English (which was considered an overt symbol of literacy) and speaking in (which dialect of) Yoruba. Because of his encounter with literate activities, while being nonliterate himself, Father provided me with some sort of bridge (certainly not a very strong one) between both worlds. A clear example of this mediating role was his intervention during the "English dreams" episode. All the writing that I did for Father was done in either standard Yoruba or English, depending on topic and audience. However, after the Bible reading encounter, I began to read such writing back to Father in the Idanre dialect as often as possible.

Admittedly, nonliterate bilinguals are also faced with the problem of matching language choice with audience and topic. The peculiar problem for me was that English had superseded my native tongue as the medium in which much of my knowledge was being acquired. While this is not a literacy issue *per se*, the point is that much of this knowledge came from books when reading became my preferred way of knowing. At first, I did not pay much attention to the differences between my book and nonbook knowledge. However, differences began to emerge and became more and more significant as my literacy advanced. My readings of George Orwell's *Animal Farm* provide a useful illustration. I use the word *readings* (in the plural) advisedly because I read *Animal Farm* at least four times. I first read the simplified edition in primary school. It was no more than a story about pigs and it was not substantially different from the folktales I knew even before I went to school. At that stage, the story blended well with my experience, although I knew then that my nonliterate friends did not know the story.

The story was substantially richer when I read it again in high school. This time, we read the full, rather than an abridged, edition. The teacher was a Scot whose dialect of English differed significantly from that of my previous teachers. Since he was my first white teacher and the first white that I encountered at close range, I thought that all white men spoke that way. In any case, the issue here was that he introduced to my consciousness the second level of meaning that *Animal Farm* was all about. The word "satire" came to my vocabulary, as well as a hazy connection between the story and the idea of revolution. I did not know the full meaning of satire and the connection between the animals' actions and the nature of rebellion or revolution, however, until my third reading of *Animal Farm*. At this time, I had just completed high school training and was preparing myself for the London GCE (General Certificate of Education). I was now on my own, as it were, and started reflecting on all my readings to date. Then I began to make connections I failed to make before. I began to "read" beyond the story. This new notion of reading characterized my approach to my studies when I eventually went to the university. Thus, when I encountered *Animal Farm* again, it was easy for me to go beyond the story to reading critical commentaries and discussing (an important literacy event!) *Animal Farm*. This critical attitude was sharpened later in that year by my encounter with Beckett's *Waiting for Godot* and Kafka's *Metamorphosis*, neither of which makes much sense if read literally.

The critical attitude that I began to develop in high school had grave consequences for my relationship with Father and others in the village. I made the first mistake when I began to question Father about the need for the annual *ifa* festival. I began to ask direct questions about the art of divination. I cannot recall now whether my intention was to question the authenticity of divination, but I do remember that Father read that meaning into my questions. Since I could not show up for the festival at the end of that year (I was writing the GCE examinations in Akure), Father concluded that I had rebelled against him and our tradition. To complicate matters, villagers began to complain to Father that I was no longer as helpful as before because I was becoming more and more unreachable.

On the instigation of his friends, Father invited me to the village after I informed him of my admission to the university. He and his friends took turns to praise me for my achievement and for what I had done for them, imploring me to continue in that way. One of them even expressed the group's optimism that I would become the Secretary of the Cooperative Union someday. I immediately recognized the discourse strategy, a strategy that could be described as "praise before you blame." When an errant boy is being called to order by a group of elders, they usually begin by praising him before he is told about his errors or wrongdoings. And I was right; by the end of the meeting, each of them had stressed the uselessness of any literacy that has no direct benefits for the recipient's village. Each of them had told me that the god of divination brought me to the world and has been guiding me since birth. Father did not send me to school to question the origins of my being! One of them even added that the Secretary of the Union who went to school before me (I am sure the farmers did not know that he had only primary education) never once questioned the validity of our customs. Although Father was never as harsh as some of his friends on this occasion, it was clear that some tension had developed between us. The "usefulness" of my literacy had been called to question.

Of course, Father did not buy the idea of my becoming Secretary of the Union, as he later confided in me, but he wanted me to be close to the people and not raise doubts about our tradition. But by now I had developed certain habits which were not congruent with those prevalent in our tradition. I had developed a critical attitude and a sense of detachment or aloofness. I needed and valued privacy in order to carry out my studies. At first, Father thought that these were mere idiosyncrasies and he took steps to correct me; but my actions were later corroborated by those of two new tenants in our house in the city. The tenants were teachers who had just been transferred to teach in the local primary schools. One of them was, in fact, assigned to my primary school. These two teachers reinforced Father's encounter with literacy and, especially, talk about literacy. They assured Father that I was a very good student and that I needed every assistance from him to be able to continue to do well. Father was skeptical of their comments and, typically, demanded to know how they could evaluate me when they never taught me. One of them replied that they had looked up my records in the primary school and had also heard good reports about me from my high school teachers. The testimony and advice of these teachers and the fact that I won a government scholarship for university education persuaded Father to finally "let me go." For me, it was only partial freedom, because Father kept making sure that I did not forsake my roots. He kept consulting a diviner during every major transition I had to make, even until I went to graduate school.

Father's gratification eventually came when I graduated from college and took a teaching position in the local high school where I had graduated a few years back. To crown it all, I bought a car, through a combined loan from the high school where I was teaching and the village branch of the Cooperative Union, the latter loan being granted in Father's name. My sphere of operation now shifted from the village to the city, as I joined the small group of educated elite in the city. Since my degree was in English, I was invited by politicians and even the king of Idanreland to prepare "welcome addresses" for visiting eminent politicians and to draft petitions on behalf of the king or local government.

By this time, the bush path leading to Ajegunle village had been widened into a manageable motorway and I was able to commute as frequently as needed to resume my old scribal duties. But it turned out that I was not seriously needed for these functions any more because many younger children, including my own siblings, had been sent to school and had assumed those scribal duties. Nevertheless, a rousing reception was held for me during my first visit in my new car. At the end of the reception, a new role was assigned to me. The village had been involved in a boundary dispute with a neighboring village for some time. The dispute centered on the encroachment of farmers in one village on the farming land of the other, a dispute aggravated by the adoption of such perennial crops as cocoa and coffee that made it difficult, if not impossible, for encroaching farmers to move their crops as they would move a yam plantation the following planting season. Thus, arable land, especially near a stream or river (where water could be obtained easily for spraying insecticides on cocoa), became a prized possession. My duty was to use my political connections in the city to ensure a favorable settlement, since the matter had now gone up to the local government level. Thus, my village duties shifted from scribal to political functions.

While pursuing this new assignment, a delegation of cocoa farmers from the village, including Father, approached me. They wanted me to join them in negotiating the upgrade of the village branch of the Cooperative Union to a weighing station so that farmers would no longer have to take their cocoa to the city for weighing. Apart from saving costs, the upgrade meant higher ranking for the village branch of the Union. I obliged, but the obligation did not end there. I later took the delegation in my car to Ibadan, some 150 miles away, to submit the application to the headquarters of the Cooperative Union and also meet the head of the cocoa "examiners," as they were called. His duty was to interview the Secretary, Treasurer, and President of the branch seeking upgrade and examine their books. It turned out that the person to see was a colleague in the university and a good friend of mine. Instead of an interview, he took us all out to lunch. We got a positive response on the spot! The farmers were elated. *Akowe* (writer, literate person, etc.) has done it again!

By now, I am sure, I have raised issues that are much beyond mere reading and writing. True, I have highlighted certain practical uses of literacy for me, Ajegunle villagers, and even the townspeople, but I have gone beyond to touch on certain habits of speaking, of thinking, of organizing work, all of which are related to reading and writing practices. I have also highlighted certain aspects of the interaction among literacy, the villagers, and me. A clear distinction can now be made between my conceptions of literacy and those of Ajegunle villagers. Certainly, the obvious uses of literacy for Ajegunle villagers did not include the range of features—skepticism, logic, rationality, and even individualism (which seems to follow from the act of reading and writing)—expected in early Goody (Goody and Watt, 1963; Goody, 1977) and others who seek to find causal relations between literacy and these features. Rather, literacy for them was an empirical tool, a sharpened hoe, and what Meggit (1968, p. 307) described as "the exercise of shrewdness in the struggle to get ahead in life" in his account of the uses of literacy among upland Melanesians. It was surely in exercise of this shrewdness that Ajegunle villagers changed my function in the village from scribal to political, from a recorder to a negotiator. By this time, they had come to associate literacy not only with scribal functions but also with the new patterns of social organization in the local government, a microcosm of which was provided by the village branch of the Cooperative Union.

I must stress, of course, that they did not put all their faith in this new political setup. After all, the first literate person they ever interacted with at close range was the first Secretary of the village branch of the Union who committed fraud. It was an event that quickly dissolved into village discourse, producing the memorable phrase, still heard in the village till today: *Akowe yi'we* (secretary + change + book), "the secretary changed books," meaning the secretary altered the records. Thus, while (hopefully) trusting that I would follow up the boundary dispute with officials of the local government, the villagers did not forget to send a delegation to the king, the head of the traditional social organization they knew and still valued. If redress did not come from the literate bureaucrats, it might come from the king.

In contrast to villagers' conceptions about literacy, by the time I completed college, literacy had come to mean, for me, a way of life, a way of knowing, a way of talking, and a way of doing. It gave me pleasure and stimulation. It widened my horizon. More importantly, literacy made me engage in thinking as a deliberate, planned activity. The observation and description of regularities and irregularities in patterning became a conscious activity. Certainly, literacy had practical benefits, but I already took those for granted. What Ajegunle farmers considered to be the primary functions of literacy were almost its secondary functions for me. I began to hold conceptions about literacy that tended toward those of early Goody (Akinnaso, 1981). It was only recently, after I began to study literacy empirically, as an object in itself, that I began to question some of the assumptions we academics hold about literacy (Akinnaso, 1982a, 1982b, 1985), conceptions that derive largely from our own academic practice (Street, 1984).

This essay draws attention to the need for more investigation into the choices that people make among the various uses of literacy, and to the fact that nonliterate people do in fact make their own choices too. It is not only the literate whose consciousness is impacted by literacy. Nonliterates are also affected. They have their own conceptions about literacy and they are aware of the impact of literacy on their lives and their environment. They sometimes change their conceptions and uses of literacy just as literacy changes the structure of knowledge and the patterns of social relations in their society.

One interesting thing about Ajegunle villagers, however, is that they never once attempted to use literacy for ritual purposes. No one ever asked me to write down the esoteric chants of *ifa* divination, nor did Father ever ask me to write down the list of sacrificial items prescribed by our family diviner. Surely, Father and the diviners in the village knew that this could be done. The resistance to the intrusion of literacy into the ritual domain may well have resulted from the association of literacy with Christian religion and the need to keep this religion away from "polluting" their own. (True, most village elders had converted to Christianity, but the conversion was, and remains, only partial; local traditions continue to be maintained side by side with selected Christian practices.) Literacy was, therefore, consciously restricted to secular action. But contrast this with the ritual importance of writing among coastal Melanesians who also until lately were totally nonliterate:

> [They] displayed a curiously (yet practically understandable) attitude towards literacy. They took writing to be merely one more of those inherently ambiguous modes of communication with the supernatural with which they were already familiar. From this point of view, the virtue of writing lay in men's ability to manipulate it as an entity in a defined ritual fashion so that they could get a grip on the mission god and force from him his secrets. . . . Writing was rarely treated as a straightforward technique of secular action. (Meggitt, 1968, p. 302)

These variations in the attitudes toward literacy and its uses call for a shift of attention away from the search for universal or ideal types to more detailed investigation into literacy practices and actual choices in specific societies. Such case studies are needed in order to enhance our knowledge of the relationship between literacy and individual consciousness.

The University at Albany

7

Becoming Literate in a Multiethnic Society

BERNARDO M. FERDMAN

We are frequently reminded by public service announcements on television and radio that being literate can change one's life. Life is better if one can read and write, these ads tell us. At first, it would seem that there can be little that is controversial about this message. But there is less agreement about exactly what constitutes literacy and how best to achieve it. The television ads do not analyze the nature of the personal changes brought about by literacy, nor do they suggest how becoming and being literate is a process that can vary across individuals and groups, and is shaped and given meaning by society. Literacy, I believe—and in this I concur with the ads—touches us at our core, in that part of our selves that connects with the social world around us. It provides an important medium by which the person interacts with the human environment. For this reason, a consideration of the relationship of literacy and culture must be a fundamental component of any analysis of literacy and the individual.

While a number of writers (e.g., Akinnaso, 1982, 1985; Goody, 1977, 1982; Goody and Watt, 1963; Ong, 1982, Said, 1983; Scribner and Cole, 1981) have debated and discussed the connections of literacy to culture and mind, few have directly addressed the implications of cultural diversity for the processes of becoming and being literate. In this essay I discuss, from a social-psychological perspective, the relationship between literacy and the individual in a multiethnic society like the United States. More precisely, I explore some of the ways in which a person's identity as a member of an ethnocultural group is intertwined with the meaning and consequences of becoming and being literate. Cultural identity, I argue, at once derives from and modulates the symbolic and practical significance of literacy for both individuals and groups.

The goal of the essay is to provide a theoretical framework for thinking about the way literacy and culture influence each other at the level of the individual. After placing the issue in context, I elaborate and refine the construct of cultural identity and suggest how it can be useful in understanding the processes of literacy education and acquisition.

Given great disparities in educational achievement among ethnic groups in the United States, questions about the relationship between literacy and cultural identity are driven by a desire to understand better the status of ethnic minorities and to find improved ways for schools to serve their members. At the same time, examination of this question can help to highlight more clearly the ways in which literacy is a multi-faceted and multilayered construct. A look at literacy education and ac-quisition in the context of an ethnically diverse society forces us to go beyond viewing these as simply the transmission and internalization of a set of cognitive functions or skills, and to consider both the content and the symbolic aspects of what it is that is taught and learned. In doing so, we are also confronted with the need to clarify our underlying assumptions and values about the nature of such a society.

THE ROLE OF VALUES

How ethnic disparities in school performance should be addressed by educators has been a source of controversy and debate.[1] "Equal oppor-tunity" is the ultimate goal, but there is not agreement on what this is or on how to arrive there. Discussion of the relationship of literacy and cul-ture takes place in the midst of other worries about individual and col-lective rights: To what extent do groups in a multiethnic society have a right to define and to maintain distinctive identities, and to what extent do these rights complement or conflict with each other? A much-pro-claimed value in the United States is that its citizens should have equal access to opportunity without barriers or advantages based on ethnicity, race, or gender. In one version of this value, individual merit and ac-complishment are seen as the only legitimate sources of social and eco-nomic success. The educational system is promoted in this regard as "the great equalizer"—as the institution that can and should provide cit-izens with the tools they need to be productive members of society. In this view, which emphasizes the similarities among people, fairness means measuring each individual by the same yardstick. It also means that all individuals must generally be treated in a similar manner. To do otherwise would be to perpetuate inequities.[2] Another way to think about equal opportunity, however, is to emphasize the differences be-tween people, in particular those differences rooted in culture and there-fore in group memberships. In this alternative view of equal opportu-nity, fairness involves choosing a yardstick appropriate to the person and group. To ignore group membership is to deny an important part of the individual. Indeed, treating everyone the same can result in the very inequities that are to be avoided.

An underlying source of disagreement may have to do with divergent views about the proper nature of the relationship between culturally diverse ethnic groups in the society: Should each group pursue its own way and be free to maintain its own heritage, norms and values; should one group's culture be emphasized; or should some new "American" blend, comprised of something of each group, be developed? Depending on one's views, ethnic disparities in school achievement would be dealt with differently. Views that emphasize acculturation or the "melting pot" ideal would consider it more fair for the same measure to be used for all individuals, regardless of group membership. If value is placed on cultural pluralism, however, individual merit needs to be defined in a culturally relativistic way that takes group membership into account. To the extent that the maintenance and development of distinctive ethnic cultures are valued, these must be given consideration in the educational system. Literacy has become an important focus for this debate. Because schools are viewed as the institution most responsible for literacy education in this society, these conflicting values affect thinking and policy, and thus the way in which children become literate.

PERSPECTIVES ON INDIVIDUALS AND GROUPS

Beyond requiring reflection on our values regarding intergroup relations, a look at literacy in a multiethnic context demands examination of the relationship of the individual to the group. If, in shaping individual development, the educational system and society at large are to pay attention to group-based diversity—whether the goal is to strengthen it or to reduce it—then we need a more focused understanding of the psychological concomitants of ethnic differences. Certainly, in spite of commonalities within ethnic groups, a good deal of within-group variance will also be present, especially in a heterogeneous society (Ferdman and Hakuta, 1985). Consequently, from a social-psychological perspective, we need to understand better the relationships between collective and individual experience and behavior. It is at the intersection of the group and individual levels of analysis that we must conduct such an exploration.

At least in part, the degree of within-group diversity—both real and perceived—may be a function of the predominant values regarding the type of ethnic relations desired in the society. Each model mentioned earlier—pluralism, assimilation, or amalgamation—carries with it particular assumptions about the degree to which individual behavior and identity follow from those of the group as a whole. For example, a pluralist may consider it legitimate to interpret individual behavior in light of group patterns, while an assimilationist would prefer to focus on individual-level traits.

In turn, beliefs about the nature of the relationship of individual and group may affect which perspective on ethnic relations is adopted. For example, someone who sees groups as simply collections of similar individuals may be more likely to favor a "melting pot" approach, since this will not be seen as restricting individual freedom of choice. A melting pot vision of society allows plenty of room for individual differences, all the more so because they are preferably not correlated with group membership. In contrast, those who view the group level as primary—as giving definition and meaning to the individual—should tend to prefer pluralism, because they will see individual freedom present only when the groups people belong to are allowed to flourish. In a pluralistic perspective, the denial and washing away of group boundaries ultimately eliminates personal freedom.

LITERACY AND CULTURE

Ethnic diversity, by its very nature, demands attention to the role of culture in the individual's transactions with the social world. Monica Heller (1987) provides a useful perspective on the type of culture that distinguishes an ethnic group:

> [For members of an ethnic group] shared experience forms the basis of a shared way of looking at the world; through interaction they jointly construct ways of making sense of experience. These ways of making sense of experience, these beliefs, assumptions, and expectations about the world and how it works underlie what we think of as culture. However culture is not only a set of beliefs and values that constitute our normal, everyday view of the world; it also includes our normal, everyday ways of behaving. (p. 184)

So, in this view, culture includes both specific behavioral characteristics typifying a group and the underlying views of social reality that guide those behaviors. This latter part is what Triandis (1972) termed "subjective culture": "a group's characteristic way of perceiving its social environment" (p. viii). These definitions of culture suggest that how a person views social reality is mediated by collective representations of that reality.

In a society tending toward homogeneity, it is easy to think of literacy simply in terms of specific skills and activities. Once a person acquires the requisite skills, she also acquires the quality of mind known as literacy, together with the right to be labeled a literate person. In such an environment, literacy is experienced as a characteristic inhering in the individual.

In a multiethnic context, however, the cultural framing of literacy becomes more obvious. De Castell and Luke (1983) convincingly argue that "[b]eing 'literate' has always referred to having mastery over the processes by means of which culturally significant information is coded" (p. 373).Because culture exists as a product of social interaction and organization, de Castell and Luke ask us to view literacy as acquiring meaning only in the social context of particular communities. Alan Purves (this volume) properly points out the ways in which being literate involves mastering conventional wisdom and common knowledge and, in so doing, entering into a kind of "textual contract." For the present argument, what is important is that what is "common" and what is "conventional" are defined in reference to a group—to a particular community at a given point in time. It is this reference point that constitutes culture and determines what will be construed as literacy. In a culturally heterogeneous society, literacy ceases to be a characteristic inhering solely in the individual. It becomes an active and interactive process that is constantly defined and redefined, negotiated and renegotiated, as the individual transacts with socioculturally fluid surroundings. As Scribner (1986) put it, "literacy is . . . a *social* achievement. . . . [It] is an outcome of cultural transmission. . . . Literacy has neither a static nor a universal essence" (pp. 8-9). Because culture itself is in flux, so are the very definition of literacy and what constitutes "being literate," as well as its consequences (see, e.g., Cook-Gumperz, 1986).

Literacy then, in large part, involves facility in manipulating the symbols that codify and represent the values, beliefs, and norms of the culture, the same symbols that incorporate the culture's representations of reality. Because the processes referred to by de Castell and Luke are themselves part of the culture, to be defined as literate a person must carry out this manipulation in a culturally appropriate manner. "The enterprise of defining literacy," Scribner (1986) reminds us, ". . . becomes one of assessing what counts as literacy in some given social context" (p. 9). For example, the skills necessary to be considered literate in a society that employs pictographic writing can be quite different from those necessary in a society that uses an alphabetic system. Similarly, literacy in a supermarket shopper might be defined in terms of the ability to negotiate varieties of text printed on a number of different surfaces in a multitude of typefaces, with little emphasis on handling writing instruments or proper spelling; in contrast, literacy in a secretary or clerk might well include appropriate use of spelling and punctuation and the ability to decode many types of handwritten documents. In each of these situations—food shopping or secretarial work—the particular distribution of skills may also vary from culture to culture.

In addition to being skilled in use of the methods of representation—such as the alphabet, writing implements, books, and so on—the literate person must be familiar with a particular configuration of meanings in context, so as to appropriately comprehend the content of what is encoded and decoded. Becoming literate means not only developing mastery over processes, but also mastery over symbols—the ways in which cultural values, beliefs, and norms are represented. Being literate implies actively maintaining contact with collective symbols and the processes by which they are represented. Thus, literacy goes beyond transactions with a printed or written page, and extends into the ability to comprehend and to manipulate the symbols—the words and concepts—that it contains, and to do so in a culturally prescribed manner.

The school is a particularly crucial institution for mediating the process by which the individual becomes literate and for reflecting societal views of what constitutes literacy. Roth (1984) put it this way:

> Social/cultural control is tied directly to the structure of knowledge and to the manner in which knowledge is presented in the schooling context. Schools, acting as agents for the culture, control the extent to which personal knowledge may enter into the public knowledge of school curriculum; they thus have a direct influence upon cultural continuity and change. In selecting what to teach and how it is to be taught and evaluated, schools reaffirm what the culture values as knowledge. . . .
>
> Because literacy provides a powerful means for individuals to make a personal tie to society in general, literacy acquisition, particularly reading instruction, holds implications for cultural transmission, that is, for how knowledge is transferred, reproduced, and transformed. The prime focus of 1st grade is to establish reading literacy so that the 'knowledge' our culture sees as significant may be maintained. (p. 303)[3]

Roth's analysis certainly holds for a homogeneous society in which the schools indeed are "agents for the culture." To apply to a multicultural society, however, her view must be expanded to consider the relationship of the culture(s) represented by the school and those of its pupils.

In a multicultural environment, the individual who is becoming literate may be faced with an array of alternative methods and contents, representing different views of literacy. The value placed on behaviors that are construed as literate in the context of one group will not be equivalent to the value given them by a different culture. For example, penmanship might be much more valued by Chinese—who must spend long hours learning the appropriate brush-strokes for each pictogram and who generally value the aesthetic qualities of text—than by Americans—who might emphasize primarily the content. In a religious Christian community, it is likely that time spent reading the Bible is considered to be well spent, while among secular intellectuals reading newspapers may be more important. Whereas those raised in upper-class New England may place a premium on being familiar with the classics of U.S. literature, Mid-Western farmers may be more concerned with their ability to read the latest commodity exchange tables and the manuals for their machinery. U.S. educators tend to see creative writing by children as a valued activity, and this perspective is incorporated into school curricula; this may appear strange in countries where students are encouraged to learn and copy the work of great thinkers rather than to produce original work.

As part of their formal schooling, children will encounter the behavior preferences of the educational system, the school, and teachers. These preferences have in turn been shaped by the sociocultural environment of the school and its agents. Other messages will be conveyed through interactions with family and peers, the media, and even the various segments of the educational system. Whether or not these messages are congruent with each other should in part depend on the degree of cultural heterogeneity represented by the messengers. In educating their pupils toward literacy, schools will vary in the degree to which they incorporate the cultural views of the ethnic groups to which their pupils belong. To the extent that schools tend to reflect the dominant culture, pupils from the dominant ethnic group are more likely to find consistency between the various construals of literacy than are ethnic minority students. In either case, because literacy education tends to be left primarily to the school, children become literate in the cultural image represented by their school.

So it is that literacy education can constitute a profound form of socialization. A person who becomes literate does so in the context of a particular definition of what is involved in literate behavior. This person is, as Purves (this volume) and others (e.g., Heath, 1986; Wallace, 1986) remind us, trained to internalize the behaviors appropriate to a functional member of a specific social community. In the case of a majority child attending majority schools, this is essentially transparent, in that neither educator nor pupil need consciously attend to the ways in which they are engaged in a process of cultural transmission. In the case of minority group members, however, the process may be less smooth, depending on the extent to which their group's standards for cultural significance differ from the dominant group norms. For members of cultural minorities, the potential conflicts will be greater, as will the salience of group membership.

The processes and symbols involved in literacy education will mean something different depending on what reference group the individual uses to interpret them. Thus, at the individual level, whether deliberately or not, the process of becoming and being literate involves becoming and being identified with a particular culture. It is the relationship of the individual to the group that forms the basis for cultural identity.

CULTURAL IDENTITY

From a social-psychological perspective we are most concerned with the mutual influence of the individual and his social environment. Cultural identity is an idea that can help to conceptualize these links. In this section, I delineate the related but distinct constructs of group and individual cultural identity. By its very nature, culture is only meaningful with reference to the group, yet is enacted by individuals, so it is a central concept in understanding how the person and the collective are connected. To understand how literacy and cultural identity interact, we must be clear on what is meant by cultural identity.

The Group Level

An ethnic group's identity involves a shared sense of the cultural features that help to define and to characterize the group. These group attributes are important not just for their functional value, but also as symbols. For example, for many Puerto Ricans in the United States, the Spanish language is not just a means of communication; it also represents their identification as Latinos and their differences from the majority culture. Even if Spanish reading and writing ability is absent, the desire to conserve some degree of Spanish-speaking ability may reflect a desire to maintain distinctiveness from the surrounding society (see Ball, Giles, and Hewstone, 1984; Hakuta, Ferdman, and Diaz, 1987). Group cultural identity has to do both with the particular features of the ethnic group and with the significance that is attached to these features in a societal context. A group's cultural identity will play an important role in the nature and outcome of intergroup comparisons that it makes and thus in the way it comes to evaluate itself (see Ferdman, 1987; Montero, 1987; Tajfel and Turner, 1986). When a group perceives that its cultural features compare favorably with those of other groups, it should come to hold more positive images of itself. If, on the other hand, features central to the group's cultural identity are viewed negatively in the society, the group will probably incorporate a negative component into its self-evaluation.

Kochman (1987) makes a useful distinction between emblematic and nonemblematic ethnic indicators. "Emblematic indicators are those racial and cultural features that serve an identity function or otherwise mark and maintain social boundaries" (p. 220) between the in-group and the out-group. These are features that in-group and/or out-group members will tend to think of as "ethnic." Nonemblematic indicators are those cultural patterns that do not serve such functions, and of which in-group and out-group members may or may not be aware.[4] As defined here, then, cultural identity at the group level involves those features of the group that are widely perceived as emblematic by the in-group. While outsiders may consider particular features as characteristic of most group members, thereby rendering them emblematic in Kochman's sense, these features would not necessarily form part of the group's collective cultural identity, unless the in-group internalized this external point of view or had otherwise also incorporated these features into its self-image.

Smolicz (1981) uses the concept of core values in a similar way, although in a more restrictive sense than intended here. According to him, core values "generally represent the heartland of the ideological system and act as identifying values which are symbolic of the group and its members" (p. 75). What is important in defining the centrality of a cultural feature is not the particular type of value or characteristic. Rather, "whenever people feel that there is a direct link between their identity as a group and what they regard as the most crucial and distinguishing element of their culture, the element concerned becomes a core value" (pp. 76-77).[5] As elaborated here, an ethnic group's cultural identity is based on such core values, but also extends beyond them to include other features and values that the group generally perceives itself as possessing and that help it to maintain its character as a group.

The Individual Level

In conceptualizing cultural identity at the group level, I have assumed a certain degree of uniformity within the group. However, although members of the same ethnic group will tend to demonstrate shared cultural features (this is in part what defines their common ethnicity), variation within groups will also be present. Individual members of ethnic groups will vary both in the extent of their identification with the group and in the degree to which their behavior is based on the group's cultural norms (e.g., Boekestijn, 1988; Ferdman and Hakuta, 1985). In a multiethnic society in which members of different groups are in various degrees of contact with each other, a variety of options may be available to individuals regarding how to relate not only to other groups but also to their own. Ethnic group members will express their choices in part through the behaviors they demonstrate in different types of situations. Especially in the case of minority group members or immigrants, the extent to which an individual follows the group's typical cultural pattern may be an indication of the degree of that person's psychological assimilation or acculturation (Berry, 1986; Graves, 1967). Jones (1988) points out how such variation may also reflect minority group members' perceptions regarding the instrumentality of particular behaviors in different contexts, such that an individual may behave in accordance with the group's cultural patterns in some situations but not in others. The distinction between the group and the individual level is important, in part because, as Berry (1986) puts it, "not every individual participates to the same extent in the general acculturation being experienced by his group" (p. 38; see also Berry, 1983), and, conversely, because some individual group members may acculturate more rapidly than the group as a whole. Thus, over time, acculturation processes may affect both what the cultural features are at the group level (cf. Taylor and McKirnan, 1984) and whether or not particular individuals demonstrate them in their behavior (cf. Berry, 1986). In addition, contextual factors may influence whether individuals are likely to behave in line with the group's cultural identity. Because of this intragroup variation, to render cultural identity useful as a psychological construct we must transpose it to the individual level. Beyond behavioral differences, we should expect within-group diversity in the degree to which particular features are seen as central to the group's identity.

At the individual level, then, cultural identity has to do with the person's sense of what constitutes membership in an ethnic group to which he or she belongs. Each person will have a particular image of the behaviors and values that characterize the group's culture. The term is distinguished here from the related and broader social-psychological concept of social identity, as well as from ethnic identity. Tajfel and Turner (1986) define social identity as consisting "of those aspects of an individual's self-image that derive from the social categories to which he perceives himself as belonging" (p. 16). Social identity incorporates both the person's knowledge of membership in particular social categories and the value and feelings attached to those memberships. Ethnic identity can be defined as the portion of an individual's social identity that is associated with membership in an ethnic group.[6] Cultural identity, while clearly linked closely both to ethnic and to social identity, is neither equivalent to them nor coterminous. While both ethnic and cultural identity help the individual to answer the question, "who am I?" cultural identity is the component that associates particular cultural features with group members. Social identity and ethnic identity deal with the symbolic aspects of social categorization—the boundary between the in-group and the out-group—and the associated affect. A particular individual, for example, may base her social identity primarily on gender, while her sister may focus more sharply on her Polish background. Thus, the first sister's ethnic identity as a Polish-American would be somewhat less strong than that of the second sister (see Babad, Birnbaum, and Benne, 1983). Cultural identity as defined here is a more specific construct. Cultural identity involves the perceived bases for a person's ethnic categorization—that which is inside the boundary—and the person's feelings about this content. The second sister's cultural identity includes the perception that being Polish generally implies being strongly Catholic and maintaining close family ties. It also incorporates her feelings about these features: She is somewhat ambivalent about the first and she feels quite positively about the second. Cultural identity thus includes the individual's internalized view of the cultural features characterizing his or her group, together with the value and effect that the person gives those features.

Paralleling the distinction made here between cultural and ethnic identity, Keefe and Padilla (1987) discuss the difference between the processes of acculturation and ethnic identification. Acculturation involves changes in the cultural patterns shown by groups when they come into contact with one another. In ethnic identification, in contrast, "the particular assemblage of cultural traits becomes less important than the attitudes of members towards the people and culture of in-group versus out-group as well as members' self-identification" (Keefe and Padilla, 1987, p. 41). Thus, an individual may maintain a strong identification with a particular group while adopting new cultural traits. Similarly, Herman (1977), in studying the nature of Jewish identity, suggested that its analysis at the individual level must address both "(1) the nature of the individual's relationship to the Jewish group as a membership group; and (2) the individual's perception of the attributes of the Jewish group, his feeling about them, and the extent to which its norms are adopted by him as a source of reference" (p. 39). The first component involves aspects of the person's ethnic affiliation—in the present terms, both ethnic and social identity—while the second has to do with the ways in which that affiliation is represented—that is, what I refer to as cultural identity.

Two people may perceive their identification as members in a particular group to be just as central to their ethnic identity, yet define its meaning quite differently. For example, for one Jew the primary features of being Jewish involve following the religious laws and becoming learned in the Bible and in the Talmud, while for another, religious observance is secondary or nonexistent—more emphasis is placed on Jewish values and on supporting the State of Israel (cf. Herman, 1977). Yet both claim an equally strong connection to the Jewish people. Similarly, Puerto Ricans living in New York and in Puerto Rico, while sharing an ethnic identification, will have divergent experiences and ways of looking at the world, with resulting differences in their cultural identities. For one, the experience of minority status and ethnic distinctiveness in an urban environment will play a relatively more central role, while for the other the Spanish language and living on the island will be relatively more important (cf. Flores, 1985; Ginorio, 1987).

Thus, cultural identity involves those parts of the self—those behaviors, beliefs, values, and norms—that a person considers to define him or her socially as a member of a particular ethnic group, and the value placed on those features in relation to those of other groups. Changes in those features would imply a shift in the person's way of thinking about him- or herself in a social context. Via his or her cultural identity, the individual answers the question: "What is the appropriate way for someone such as me to interpret and to behave in the world?" While at the group level, a collective set of emblematic cultural features that comprise the group's cultural identity may exist, at the individual level what is relevant is the person's particular perspective on the collective view. Individual members of an ethnic group will vary in the extent to which they perceive particular attributes as central to their cultural identity and in the value they give these attributes. In addition, they will vary in the degree to which they see themselves as representing these attributes.

Status and power differentials between groups may play a role in the cultural identity individuals come to hold. In a multiethnic society, it is the minority group member that is typically identified in group terms, while members of the dominant group will be more likely to see themselves and to be seen by others in individual terms, "or at least as not belonging to any particular category" (Deschamps, 1982, p. 89; see also Tajfel, 1978). Some researchers (e.g., Guillaumin, 1972) have suggested that minority groups tend to have complex views of the majority and not just of their own group, whereas the majority tends to see the minority as a deindividuated mass. Thus, we might expect that members of minority groups will be particularly aware of their attributes as being associated with group membership and thus as forming part of their cultural identity. Members of the dominant group, in contrast, because they may be less accustomed to thinking of themselves in group terms, may be less conscious of the cultural sources for behavior. For them, identity may be construed primarily at the individual level and not be perceived as connected to the group's features. One implication of this is that minority group members are able to choose (and sometimes are forced) to adopt the dominant ("mainstream") perspective to interpret social reality.

CULTURAL IDENTITY AND LITERACY

Because literacy is a culturally defined construct, it follows that it should have close links to cultural identity. At the societal level, it is clear that literacy education involves not just the imparting of particular skills, but also the transmission of values (de Castell and Luke, 1983). Kádár-Fülop (1988) points to the development of "language loyalty"—the encouragement of positive attitudes toward the language—as an important function for literacy education. De Castell and Luke (1983, 1987) forcefully show how literacy campaigns are carried out in the context of particular social agendas. In an ethnically diverse society, these values are not necessarily shared across groups. Indeed, de Castell and Luke (1987) write that:

> [I]f literacy campaigns are seen primarily as attempts to forge or to impose a common cultural tradition, and only secondarily as attempts to disseminate competence at reading and writing, then we ought to reconsider the alleged current crises not as failures in the mass transmission of reading and writing but as failures of a far more fundamental kind: failures in the mass inculcation and perpetuation of a desired sociocultural tradition. (p. 428)

From a social-psychological perspective, the question becomes one of describing the individual, interpersonal, and intergroup processes by which such failures (or successes) may come about.

The concept of cultural identity permits such an elaboration. The idea that cultural symbols have affective significance for the individual suggests that the process of becoming and being literate will tap into these feelings. When there is a mismatch between the definition and significance of literacy as they are represented in a person's identity and in the learning situation, the individual is faced with making a choice that has implications for his or her acquisition of reading and writing skills, as well as for his or her relationship to particular texts and the symbols they contain. The student must either adopt the perspective of the school, at the risk of developing a negative component to his or her cultural identity, or else resist these externally imposed activities and meanings, at the risk of becoming alienated from the school. Whereas for majority children, the school's perspective is likely to parallel whatever cultural identity they have, this is less likely the case for members of ethnic minorities.

Henry Giroux (1987) points out how individuals' "stories, memories, narratives, and readings of the world are inextricably related to wider social and cultural formations and categories" (p. 177). In the context of literacy education, the issue has to do with what is experienced by the student as "owned" and what is experienced as "not owned" by his or her group. To which texts and to which writing tasks does the student engage in a relation of "us" or "ours" and to which as "they" or "theirs"? When a child perceives a writing task or a text and its symbolic contents as belonging to and reaffirming his or her cultural identity, it is more likely that he or she will become engaged and that individual meaning will be transmitted or derived. In contrast, those tasks and symbols that serve to deny or to devalue aspects of the individual's cultural identity, or even those that are neutral in relation to it, may be approached differently and with less personal involvement. For example, reading in a group setting and analyzing texts is an important component of Jewish religious practice. An Orthodox Jewish child who perceives these activities as important components of his cultural identity may become more involved in similar tasks at school because they are linked to his sense of who he is. A child who, for cultural reasons, is accustomed to reading aloud, with a group, may approach reading assignments at school differently from a classmate who thinks of reading as something that is done alone and silently. Another student, who believes that reading books assigned at school is not "something my people do," will probably be less likely to complete such assignments; the very same child may be very adept, however, at reading other materials, such as comic books.

Matute-Bianchi's (1986) research among Mexican-descent and Japanese-American high school students and Trueba's (1984) work in the Mexican-American barrio show that what is important in shaping the attitudes toward school-related activities of ethnic minority group members is their perceptions of themselves and others in a social context and of the value of their education in relation to those social perceptions. In the California high school that she studied, Matute-Bianchi was able to distinguish five subgroups among the students of Mexican descent on the basis of how they identified themselves ethnically and which behavior patterns they perceived to go along with these labels. For some of the groups (the "Mexicans" and the "Mexican-Americans") success in school was not viewed as incompatible with their cultural identity. As they learned the dominant culture of the school, these students did not believe that they had to give up what they considered important about their identity as Mexicans. In contrast, for other groups (the "Chicanos") maintaining their identity involved engaging in behaviors serving to reduce the chances for academic success:

> Chicanos and Cholos . . . appear to resist certain features of the school culture, especially the behavioral and normative patterns required for

school achievement. These norms, assumptions, and codes of conduct are associated with being white or gringo or quaddie or 'rich honkie.' To adopt these cultural features—that is, to participate in class discussions, to carry books from class to class, to ask the teacher for help in front of others, to expend effort to do well in school—are efforts that are viewed derisively, condescendingly, and mockingly by other Chicanos. Hence, to adopt such features presents these students with a forced-choice dilemma. They must choose between doing well in school or being a Chicano. (Matute-Bianchi, 1986, pp. 253-254)

The Japanese-Americans who were interviewed were all successful students. They, in contrast to their peers of Mexican descent, did not see components of their ethnicity reflected in their identities as students. Thus, they did not see a need to behave differently, in the school context, from the ways members of the dominant culture behaved. This was the case even for students who outside of school participated in activities—such as praying at a Buddhist temple—explicitly linked to their Japanese identity.

Trueba similarly found that the families he studied perceived a clear relationship between literacy in English and acculturation. As he put it:

Posing as illiterate in some contexts was equivalent to keeping one's own identity as 'cholo,' i.e. as marginal in school and involved with peers in other activities. In the home, however, dedication to books and relative facility to deal with text signaled eagerness to make it in the Anglo world, and that had a price, because it required some adjustment in peer reference groups and in social activities. (Trueba, 1984, p. 33)

Thus, we may expect that those people who wish to become more acculturated will be more likely to engage in activities that will help them to acquire English literacy.

Two personal examples are in order here. As a child, I delighted in reading anything I could get my hands on. But one of my favorite types of stories as an eight- and nine-year-old were *midrashim*, myths and legends based on the Bible. If given to me, I was just as likely to read Norse legends; however, these did not have the same impact on me and I did not see them in the same light. Because of my Jewish identity, my relationship to King David or to Abraham was a more personal and significant one than my connection with Thor. The Biblical stories, because they touched on my cultural identity, had practical and symbolic meanings that went beyond the story and extended into helping me to learn more about myself—my group—in a social context, and into giving me conceptual tools with which to interact with other group members. Similarly, when I want to read a Latin American author, I will do so in Spanish, my native tongue, rather than in an English translation. My choice is not based solely on a desire to read the original, but also to reaffirm my connection with Latin American symbols and texts. In spite of what is ostensibly similar content, I experience the images and meanings differently in the two languages.

These examples highlight the ways in which personal meaning is derived from broader social meanings. However, the relationship of reading and cultural identity may not be just a function of the symbolic content of the text. The significance of the text itself and the context in which it is read may indeed be at least as, if not more, relevant. So, for example, if reading the *New York Times* contributes in an important way to my cultural identity, I will relate differently to that text than someone who approaches it as an outsider. Similarly, reading the *New York Times* every day will have a different meaning when I do it in New York from when I do it in Paris. While in both cases the activity may be similarly related to my cultural identity, in the latter case it may be seen as a more obvious statement of where I stand in relation to my social environment.

In a study relevant to this issue, Hakuta and I (Hakuta, Ferdman, and Diaz, 1987) conducted a study of Puerto Rican elementary school children and their parents in New Haven, Connecticut. We found some indication that reading Spanish newspapers reflected the degree of identification with Puerto Rican culture, rather than solely language proficiency. At intermediate levels of English ability, twice as many of those respondents who planned to return to Puerto Rico as compared with those planning to stay in New Haven reported that they regularly read *El Vocero*, a Spanish-language daily newspaper flown in from the island.

I have argued so far that cultural identity mediates the process of becoming literate as well as the types of literate behavior in which a person subsequently engages. At this point, it becomes possible to formulate more precise questions that will be useful as a guide to further thinking and research about the ways in which cultural identity affects how and whether an individual becomes literate as a result of schooling:

(a) How is literacy defined in the individual's group and what is its significance? What behaviors are included in this definition?

(b) What significance do particular texts have for the individual's cultural identity?

(c) How do the particular pedagogical approach, the texts that are used, and the purpose of literacy as communicated by the school relate to the learner's motives and sense of identity (and more subtly, what messages does a reading and writing curriculum communicate about the value of the learner's culture?) and

(d) What relationship does the learner perceive between the tasks assigned in school and his or her cultural identity? Must the learner change the nature of the self-concept in order to do what is asked?

Attention to these questions by researchers and educators may help us to understand better the ways in which the meaning of literacy for individuals is influenced by their sense of themselves as cultural beings. In turn, such understanding should be useful in better serving members of a heterogeneous society as they acquire literacy.

Until now, the discussion has focused on the implications of cultural identity for literacy development. The relationship, however, is better seen as bidirectional. Not only will cultural identity mediate the acquisition and expression of literacy, but also, literacy education will influence and mold the individual's cultural identity. Modifying the means by which the person interacts with others across time and space (i.e., making the person "literate") will eventually require the person to redefine (or reaffirm) his or her view of the self in a social context. A clear example is that of the immigrant who seeks—or is forced—to acculturate not only by learning a new language but also by adopting a whole new set of symbols and meanings. I was struck one November by a picture in the *New York Times* showing newly arrived Vietnamese immigrant children in school dressed up like Pilgrims and Indians, in "celebration" of the Thanksgiving holiday. Clearly, they were being asked as a condition of citizenship to take as their own a new set of cultural icons and referents. The school was teaching the children not only to understand the images and associations evoked by Thanksgiving, but also to do so from the perspective of the dominant culture. In a more subtle, but not less powerful, way, the reading and writing activities that children are asked to engage in at school, to the extent that they are accepted, will ultimately affect no only the children's sense of who they are, but the ways in which they can figure it out.

Literacy education, as de Castell and Luke (1987) so forcefully argue, can never be content-free. By providing the individual with the symbolic material with which to understand and transact with the social environment, and requiring him or her to do so in particular modalities, the range of possibilities for the person is channeled and narrowed. Certainly, this is a significant part of socialization. The problem may arise for ethnic minority group members who as a result must dissociate from those aspects of themselves that would otherwise serve to provide them with a positive sense of identity in the social environment.

Linguists and psychologists (e.g., Erickson, 1984; Guiora, 1985; McEvedy, 1986) have pointed to the cognitive aspects of this channeling process, as it occurs in learning a first or second language. Guiora and his colleagues (1985), for example, found that children who spoke languages with greater gender loadings (Hebrew) developed gender identity sooner than those speaking languages with little (English) or no gender loading (Finnish). McEvedy (1986) points out how the concept of *we* is very general in English, but much more fine-tuned among the Pitjantjatjarra of Australia, who employ different pronouns depending on exactly who is in the situation and how distant they are from the speaker. These arguments suggest that, for example, a French child who is educated in English and grows up without learning the French language will have a different experience of gender and of interpersonal relationships from a child educated in French, as a result of the use of different linguistic markers in the two languages.

The issue, however, extends beyond this into the meanings that become attached to various symbolic representations as they relate to the person's sense of his or her integration into a cultural group and of the group's place in society—into what Erickson (1984) refers to as the "politics of social identity." Erickson summarizes Scollon and Scollon's (1981) work among Alaskan natives in this context:

> In their interpretation, Alaskan native teenagers come to see the acquisition of Western written literacy as a kind of metaphoric adoption of a new ethnic group identity. To become literate in school terms would be to disaffiliate symbolically from their parents and other members of the Alaskan native village, a few of whom are 'literate' in traditional knowledge and skill, such as that involved in hunting, and many of whom are marginally literate in school-like practices of literacy. Caught in ambivalence between multiple cultural worlds, Alaskan native youth resist adopting the complete system of school-defined literacy, and then suffer the consequences of marginal acquisition. They do not belong fully to the old ways or to the new. (Erickson, 1984, p. 539)

We might ask what happens to those Alaskan natives who do fully adopt "school-defined literacy." Their cultural identity, also, should be fundamentally altered. Indeed, after becoming and being literate in this way, and using the materials they now have access to, because they are mostly generated by other ethnic groups, these Alaskans will have perspectives on their own ethnic group that are probably quite different from those held by the traditional Alaskans.

It would appear, then, that the impact of literacy education as a socialization agent on individuals' cultural identity can be either destructive or constructive. When the person loses the capability to derive and create meaning in a culturally significant way, he or she becomes less, not more, literate. To the extent that successful learning—as defined from the school's point of view—forces the ethnic minority child to become disconnected from what is personally significant, his or her ability to construct a positive and coherent cultural identity will be weakened. I do not wish to argue, however, that children must learn only about the heritage and products of their own culture. Indeed, the opposite is true. James Banks (1977, 1981, 1987) presents a useful view of multiethnic education that aims toward inclusion rather than exclusion. He recommends providing all students with "cultural and ethnic alternatives" (Banks, 1977, p. 8) in such a way that they learn both about their own culture and those of others. One goal of this approach is to prevent minority group members from feeling that they must become alienated from their identity to do well. By explicitly incorporating into schooling a culture-sensitive approach, students can be allowed to discover how what they are learning relates to their ethnic identity; as they learn, they will then be able to better articulate their cultural identity. This process can occur not only as they discover what is their own; it is also facilitated through contrast, as they discover what belongs to others.

Literacy education, when it acknowledges the role of cultural identity, may serve to enhance self-esteem as it derives from a sense of self in a social context. If individuals can acquire the tools by which they can better define their cultural identity, for example by comparing it with a range of possibilities, then learning about a range of cultural products can be enriching. To do this, the individual who is becoming literate must be encouraged to consider the relationship of what is learned to the self and to the group, by calling attention to the ways in which alternative perspectives on the methods and contents of literacy are possible. When this is done, it may result in an environment that is more empowering (Cummings, 1986) for members of dominated groups. Rather than aiming for a curriculum that avoids discussions of ethnicity, the goal should be to facilitate the process by which students are permitted to discover and explore the ethnic connections that do exist.

As pointed out earlier, the process by which literacy education shapes individuals' cultural identity takes place in an intergroup context. Because the definition of becoming and being literate at the societal level in part has to do with defining group boundaries and status, in a

multiethnic society it is likely that the debate over literacy reflects vari-
ant values regarding the proper place of the society's component
groups. The current debate over cultural literacy (Hirsch, 1987) may be
interpreted in this light: The controversy is about the issue of what
should constitute cultural identity at the national level, and what should
be the nature of the relationship of minority and dominant groups in the
society. In terms of the present discussion, the problem with Hirsch's
recommendations does not lie in the idea that Americans should be
more familiar with a variety of terms and ideas. Rather, it lies in the implication that the meaning and significance of the terms included are absolute. Hirsch's view that writing and reading skills are culture-bound
makes good sense. The issue in regard to cultural identity, however, is
that of the relevance of the content for the reader or writer. What does a
particular concept symbolize in relation to the individual's sense of self
as group member and in relation to the state of intergroup relations in
the society? In literacy education, attention must be given not only to
teaching lists of important facts, but to developing individual skills in
exploring the relationship of these facts to the self. Students must be encouraged to discover and decide for themselves—in the context of their
cultural identity—what information and what values are conveyed.
What is it that makes a particular fact important and *for whom*? For example, the value attached to the concept *Crusades*, and even what is described about it, will probably be quite different for a Jewish, a Christian, and a Moslem individual. Thus, in the United States, the drive to
educate all students about a set of "facts" in the name of literacy education can be seen by minorities as a thinly veiled excuse for the imposition of a particular type of cultural identity. This way of pushing one
version of equality may simply serve to allow the dominant group to
maintain its position while still holding on to democratic and meritocratic values.

CONCLUSION

I have argued that cultural diversity plays an important role in influencing the relationship of literacy and the individual. People's perceptions
of themselves in relationship to their ethnic group and the larger society—as reflected in what I have called cultural identity—can change
and in turn be changed by the process of becoming and being literate.
As the United States debates alternative visions of positive ethnic relations, those advocating the goal of extending literacy to all members of
the society might well incorporate a view of all individuals as cultural
beings. If this is done, perhaps more sensitive and articulated models of
literacy acquisition can be developed, models that better take into ac-

count the social context in which literacy is defined and expressed. When everyone—minority and majority alike—is encouraged to develop a clear and strong cultural identity we may well see a society, not of excessive uniformity and constraint at the individual level or undue divisiveness at the group level, as some might suggest, but rather a society which would permit a full range of individual variation, choice, and flexibility, while at the same time recognizing the importance group identifications hold for individuals. In such an environment, perhaps literacy can indeed become a universal characteristic.

The University at Albany

8

Literacy and the
Betterment of Individual Life

DONALD A. BIGGS

Arguments about the values of literacy for improving personal lives have been very heated and very dogmatic. All too often, they have been debates about the negative personal and social outcomes that result from reading "dirty," "unpatriotic," and/or "ungodlike" books. The history of censorship is in many ways based on theories about two different kinds of literacy: Good literacy which leads to the betterment of personal lives, and bad literacy which leads to the worsening of personal lives. It seems to follow that society needs to protect people from bad literacy, and encourage good literacy. The perplexing question is, who is to say what is good and what is bad literacy? The antagonists disagree about definitions, propositions, and assumptions regarding both literacy and the good life, and there is no amount of facts, data, or logic that will convert either party. One might describe these debates as "dogma eat dogma." The debates seldom reach any consensus because the antagonists assume that it is possible to answer unequivocally the question of how literacy contributes to "the good life." The purpose of this essay is to examine this question from an individual's perspective, so no attempt will be made to provide uncontroversial answers. Instead, my task will be to raise questions about various constructions of literacy, their assumptive frameworks, and their values.

The essay discusses personal and "lay theories" of literacy and the good life as presented in professional articles and literature in the humanities and social sciences. The assumption is that personal theories of literacy somehow influence the ways that different individuals will anticipate the effects of literacy experiences, and influence the extent of their involvement in particular literacy programs. Much of the difference in individual behavior in regard to literacy is governed by those individuals' different theories about how literacy will improve or better their personal lives.

This essay uses a constructivist approach (Watzlawick, 1984) and the Philosophy of Constructive Alternativism (Kelly, 1963) to examine differences in personal theories of literacy and the good life. Personal theories about literacy are important cognitive factors that affect expectations and ultimately the actions of persons. These theories determine perceptions of the meaning of literacy experiences. The constructivist approach assumes that individuals don't discover the reality of "good" or "bad" literacy or even the so-called facts about literacy; instead they construct personal meanings regarding the significance of literacy experiences through a perceptual/cognitive process that includes "lay theories" and constructs, as well as their personal hypotheses about how literacy can better their personal lives.

Debates about literacy and the good life can be framed by way of different theoretical and cultural perspectives. Very often these perspectives will be those of academic disciplines, professions, or cultural and/or ethnic groups. Such viewpoints usually represent normative, shared-construct propositions endorsed by a particular group. Economists, anthropologists, or representatives of ethnic groups describe their collective theorizing or thinking about literacy and the good life. Other essays in this book provide examples of the views of various disciplines, professions, and ethnic groups regarding the question of how literacy contributes to the improvement of individual lives. This essay, however, uses the concept of "lay theories" or *personal* theories to describe individual perspectives, values, and attitudes about literacy and the good life (Furnham, 1988). I propose a two-fold typology for describing personal theories of literacy and the good life: (1) Literacy as individualism; and (2) Literacy as cultural wisdom. The typology may be useful for understanding differences in what individuals consider to be meaningful literacy experiences and differences in how they behave or respond to literacy activities.

Personal theories of literacy include those of teachers, parents, professionals, and the students who are involved in literacy activities. I treat them as relatively stable cognitive structures and processes that are important factors in determining how individuals view the meaningfulness of literacy experiences and how they respond to these experiences (Dann, 1986). Lay theories include prototypical definitions for both literacy and the good life (Rosch, 1973; Rosch and Mervis, 1975) and assumptions about the factors or modalities in literacy that promote changes of improvements in personal lives. The concept of prototypes as applied to lay theories of literacy suggests that the definitions used in these theories may be viewed as "fuzzy sets" (or natural categories with loosely defined boundaries) in which the defining characteristics and experiences are probabilistically related to each other. If personal definitions of literacy and the good life are treated as natural categories of human thought rather than formal discrete abstract categories, the expectation is that individual differences in lay theories reflect "degrees of overlap" rather than distinct categorical differences.

Lay theories of literacy and the good life also include assumptions about the ways literacy experiences promote meaningful and "good" changes in personal lives. However, the theories differ regarding their views of both the modalities in literacy experiences which promote personal changes and the nature of the desired changes. Those who espouse individualistic theories of literacy and the good life seem to emphasize consciousness raising, changes in self-structure, and changes in personal traits, while those who espouse cultural-wisdom views of literacy seem to emphasize improved social skills, advances in wisdom, and improved cultural or ego identity functions.

Lay theories about literacy and the improvement of individual lives allow individuals to make sense of literacy experiences, to attribute praise, blame, and responsibility, and to make their relationships to literacy stable, orderly, and predictable (Furnham, 1988). These lay theories are one cognitive factor that can influence the successful achievement of the goals of a literacy program. Dann (1986) describes four features of lay theories of education and/or schooling that may be generalized to apply to lay theories of literacy and the good life: (1) They are relatively stable cognitive structures; (2) They are often implicit; (3) They have a structure and quasi-logical base; and (4) They are one important factor determining behavior.

This essay also employs Kelly's Person-Scientist metaphor (1963) to describe how individual lay theories about literacy and the good life influence behavior. Kelly's model is used to describe how individuals employ lay theories to generate personal hypotheses or predictions about the relevance of literacy experiences for improving their personal lives. The assumption is that individuals understand literacy experiences by actively constructing meanings that organize and frame perceptions and experiences, and that their psychological processes are channeled or directed by the way in which they anticipate events. Individuals use personal theories of literacy to generate hypotheses about what others will do and also about what they think others expect them to do. Having generated hypotheses about literacy, individuals seek information to evaluate their validity.

Personal hypotheses about literacy and the good life are evaluated in terms of their effectiveness in anticipating future events. Individuals' personal theories of literacy are used to generate such hypotheses that in turn influence motivation and achievements through a mechanism which Bandura (1963) labels as cognitive control. Elements of cognitive control include, besides a person's theories, the complexity of their perceptions and the complexity of their self-knowledge. Because individuals' theories about how literacy experiences will affect their lives can influence their motivation and because individuals tend to confirm their personal hypotheses, it might be argued that a person's theory about literacy and the good life is a major factor in creating the supposed "realities" of different literacy programs that are often the subject of quantitative comparisons and moral and intellectual judgments.

Lay theories about literacy and the good life, I think, can be divided into two groups. There are those who hold the individualistic perspective that literacy is a form of liberation or consciousness raising and believe that individuals should be free to make autonomous choices about literacy experiences. For them, literacy is a personal condition that involves taking charge of one's development. John Stuart Mill in his treatise *On Liberty* argues that society has no right to withhold knowledge: Individuals benefit from both correct and incorrect knowledge, becoming either more knowledgeable about the nature of truth or more aware of errors in faulty or incorrect beliefs. The values of literacy experiences are assessed in terms of their contributions to higher levels of conscious awareness and to free choices of personal beliefs. With this theory, however, come puzzling issues regarding the criteria for assessing the ways literacy experiences promote optimal individual development. Very often, adherents assume that only individuals are in a position to determine which literacy experiences will better their personal lives, and that human freedom is a *sine qua non* for good literacy experiences. The values which underlie these lay theories of literacy are most likely principles of autonomy and self-direction.

A second group of lay theories about literacy and the good life comes from a cultural or collectivistic perspective, arguing that literacy promotes the development of cultural wisdom and a sense of identity within a community (Hirsch, 1987). This position implies that cultural groups have a responsibility to establish standards, based on their consensual values for literacy experiences. Indeed, a representative for a group may find it necessary to curtail the availability of certain literacy experiences because they might adversely affect or undermine the values of the community. For example, it can be argued that the persecutors of Socrates and Jesus were not particularly evil people, for they undoubtedly thought their actions served the values of their community. Their behaviors should be judged in reference to their commitment to maintaining their respective cultural beliefs and values. The values underlying such cultural theories of literacy and the good life are most likely principles of loyalty, social responsibility, and identity commitment. Cultural theories of literacy presume that good literacy experiences provide goals that engender purpose for individual lives, and also provide guidance for those individuals in determining the nature of worthwhile personal goals.

Individualistic theories of literacy include viewpoints that emphasize personal needs and desires, as well as perspectives based on self-actualization or individual development models of maturity and health. The *cultural* perspectives emphasize the importance of convention and commitment to social/political principles such as the Social Contract or Bill of Rights. In this essay I shall refer to individualistic and cultural theories of literacy as a typology, though I recognize that within these types are a number of different perspectives. This kind of typology of theories of literacy is similar to Furnham and Lewis's (1986) categorization of lay economic beliefs along two dimensions: individualistic-collectivistic and tough-minded/tender-minded.

Lay theories of literacy involve obvious differences in cognitive content, which can be described by a dimension like individualism and cultural wisdom. However, they can also involve different cognitive structures or ways of thinking about literacy and the good life. Perry (1970) uses the concept of cognitive structure to refer to the assumptions and expectancies that people hold about the origins of knowledge and values. He classifies cognitive structures as Duality, Multiplicity, and Relativism. Individuals with Dualistic views about knowledge assume that literacy experiences are either right or wrong, are good or bad, and that answers exist, authorities know them, and good literacy experiences teach what authorities have found to be right and correct. Individuals with Multiplistic views about knowledge assume that there is a diversity of reasonable opinions held by knowledgeable authorities about literacy and the good life. Since authorities do not agree, there can be no definitive judgments about the values of particular literacy experiences. Everybody's opinions about literacy are matters of personal taste and preference. Individuals with Relativistic views about knowledge assume that different opinions on literacy and the good life can be evaluated by analyzing and comparing the empirical and rational evidence that supports them. Some opinions about literacy and the good life are better than others because they are more logical and are based on empirical evidence. Perry's model suggests that individuals who hold either to individualistic or cultural theories of literacy will use different criteria for evaluating hypotheses about literacy, depending on whether they assume that truth and values are dualistic, or if they assume that truth and values are matters of opinion or taste, or if they assume that standards of truth and value are open to tests of evidence. This essay examines the content of literacy theories but cautions the reader that the impact of lay theories of literacy may be affected by differences in cognitive structure.

LAY THEORIES OF LITERACY

Literacy as Individualism

The *individualistic* perspective on literacy reflects the humanistic tradition of the Enlightenment with its emphasis on rationality and reasoning. Individuals are apt to choose this view of literacy because it is part of the world view of modernity with its focus on empiricism, pragmatism, and faith in the rationality of the individual (Shils, 1981). Literacy is understood to be a mechanism for advancing human freedom and opportunity as well as for improving the human condition. The individualistic view of literacy assumes that individuals establish goals for literacy based on enlightened self-knowledge. The standards for evaluating literacy are usually phenomenological and reflect differences in personal perspectives. Literacy is judged solely in terms of personal meaningfulness. People are assumed to be in the best position to know what they want, and often their verbal statements of needs and goals are accepted at face value.

An individualistic perspective on literacy is described by Freire (1987), who differentiates between a literate person as subject and a literate person as object. For him, literacy can be viewed as either an activity that a person does or an activity that happens to a person. He argues that literacy involves the experiences of participating and intervening in the historical process, the acquisition of democratic experiences, and the awakening of critical awareness or consciousness. From this perspective, literacy is a form of increased personal awareness that enables people to reflect on themselves, their responsibilities, their role in the culture, and to reflect on their power of reflection. For it is in developing this latter power that literacy programs foster real increases in capacity for making responsible choices in the culture. Similarly, Akinnaso's essay in this volume argues that literacy involves changes in individual consciousness, or particular ways of perceiving and talking about the person's phenomenal world. Literacy includes radical changes in perception, cognition, and awareness of personal responsibility for meaning.

The concept of functional literacy can be viewed from an individualistic perspective (see Freire, 1969; Bhola, 1979). The acquisition of literacy skills can be considered part of fundamental social changes and can even be viewed as an experiment in human liberation. For instance, the

1975 International Symposium for Literacy (Bhola, 1979) considered literacy to include the provision of the conditions for the acquisition of a critical consciousness of the contradictions in the society in which a person lives. Consequently, literacy is assumed to stimulate individual initiative by increasing a person's participation in the creation of action projects that influence the world, transform it, and define the aims of authentic human development.

Individualistic theories about literacy include two types of psychological theories of personal development (Baltes, 1987; Chandler, 1987; Kohlberg and Mayer, 1972). First, in maturational or functional views of literacy, individuals can be described along a developmental sequence using a stage of literacy which is equated with particular, normative, age-related tasks. Second, in cognitive developmental views of literacy, the stages or levels of literacy used to describe individuals are equated with age-related qualitative differences in modes of thinking or problem-solving. The cognitive-development model of literacy involves a hierarchically organized dimension of thought structures within an invariant sequence in which each stage builds on a previous stage of reasoning and prepares the way for the next stage. In maturational theories of literacy, valuable literacy experiences will provide for the successful achievement of well-defined literacy tasks. In cognitive developmental views of literacy, valuable experiences provide stimulation, enrichment, and optimal exposure to higher levels of reasoning (Kohlberg, 1969; Kohlberg, Boyd, and Levine, 1985; Kohlberg and Mayer, 1972).

Individualistic theories about literacy include those which emphasize the role of literacy in developing moral virtues. These theories assume that literacy experiences need to expose people to the virtues of good character and the values of adopting good habits. The assumption is that literacy should develop people of moral character who will choose the real "goods" rather than apparent "goods" in their personal lives. Moral virtues are viewed as character traits that play an important role in determining how people live their lives. Consequently, good literacy experiences develop moral virtues that will contribute to the pursuit of happiness by putting real goods in the right order, by limiting desires, and by encouraging individuals to put aside things they want if they get in the way of obtaining things they need (Adler, 1978). From this perspective, a truly literate person desires only that which is really good for him/herself and nothing else.

Children's stories and literature often play a key role in moral literacy because they describe the importance of developing moral virtues and good habits. Stories provide accounts of the values of choosing to emulate a virtuous hero or heroine. Or the stories tell of the ominous outcomes for those who choose to lead "easy lives" that reflect bad habits and vices. For instance, *The Shoemaker's Present: or How a Boy Became Obedient* (author unknown) tells the story of young Thomas and his parents' desire to raise him to be a good person. However, Thomas exhibited a stubborn and decided disposition that was difficult for them to subdue (a vice). He would scream when he didn't get what he wanted, and "to all intents and purposes Tommy Smith was in a fair way to growing up to be a very wicked young man" (p. 8). Still, Tommy Smith was not a bad boy in every respect, because he had some virtues: He did not tell lies, steal, or use bad language, and he worked readily and hard at whatever he was told to do—when the work pleased him. It was his temper, not his will, that was at fault for his bad behavior. Tommy was led to see the evil of his vices (stubbornness) when he had a strange encounter with an old shoemaker who made him "magic" shoes that controlled his personal freedom to do as he wished. As a result of his experiences with the magic shoes, Tommy learned personal habits of obedience and character virtues. Only then, when he knew what was right, did he develop the habit of acting obediently without stopping to think whether it was pleasant or not. He learned the habit of being obedient to parents and teachers who were wiser than himself—rather than following whims and fancies. The reader is left with very few doubts about the virtues of being "obedient" to adults.

Behavioristic views or technical models of literacy provide other examples of individualistic perspectives on literacy. These approaches usually involve the application of scientifically derived principles of human technology to the alteration of literacy behaviors and the achievement of personal literacy goals. Individuals with a behavioral theory of literacy help people identify and operationally define their literacy goals and set up relevant programs to achieving them. The emphasis in behavioral approaches is on the uses of effective literacy activities, procedures, and techniques. These approaches reflect a strong faith in human reasoning, the methods of science, and the rationality of individuals. This scientific-humanistic view of human nature defines literacy in terms of effective methods of achieving individually determined literacy goals. Officials responsible for literacy programs are expected to accept these personal goals and then provide experiences to facilitate the achievement of them. (A troublesome aspect of this theory of literacy is the absence of room for prescriptive judgments about the values of literacy experiences that are independent of individual views. Even if an individual's goals for literacy are questionable, that is, people with a behavioristic perspective may not challenge them. This view of literacy has little to offer to the unguided who ask, "How will my participation in a literacy program contribute to a more meaningful life?" Woolfolk and Richardson, 1984, contains a critical discussion of the major assumptions in behavior therapy.)

Individualistic theories of literacy assume that the experience of autonomy, including the freedom to judge how literacy will affect your personal life, is important in becoming a literate person. Individuals are encouraged to make autonomous choices about literacy in accordance with their individual perspectives.

Literacy as Cultural Wisdom

The cultural perspective on literacy assumes that literacy experiences improve the quality of individual lives by providing access to traditions, cultural wisdom, and observations of the actual ways that people have faced important tasks of human existence (Hirsch, 1987; Purves, this volume). Cultural literacy provides a rich resource for developing both a sense of identity and a sense of intimacy. Purves suggests, "Wherever enacted in the world, the activities of being literate carry with them the burden of acceding to and employing a large body of common knowledge and conventional wisdom." Moreover, he argues that being literate is a deliberate and social activity that takes place in the real world. To be literate is to be a member of a special community and an established culture that can provide meaning to one's personal existence. Literacy, viewed from a cultural perspective, involves access to cultural wisdom, effective interpersonal communication skills, and a sense of loyalty, commitment, and identification with the goals of a cultural group. Such wisdom is an important resource of a culture that provides meaningful definitions for reality and identifies the values of various modes of thinking, as well as criteria for making judgments about what should be personally meaningful (Baltes, 1987).

Cultural theories of literacy may be based on prescriptive judgments about the skills that define role competence. The assumption is that literacy skills allow you to function in a role and to access the wisdom of that culture. In this case, a functionally illiterate person is defined as lacking skills: ability to read a newspaper article, decipher a warning on a medicine bottle, or write a note to a physician, lawyer, or teacher. For example, Davidson and Koppenhauer (1988) define adolescent literacy in terms of the percentage of the thirteen-year-olds in the United States who have or lack reading or writing skills necessary to perform successfully in school. Many people are classified as illiterate because they cannot read for specific information, draw generalizations from a text, or make complex connections between their own ideas and those in a text. Similarly, Richmond (1986) defines functional literacy as minimal basic reading, writing, and arithmetic skills that people need on an everyday basis to solve problems in their lives.

Kelly (1963) proposes a theory of role behavior that has implications for cultural theories of literacy. He emphasizes the development of effective role skills, arguing that individuals play effective social roles in a society when they understand how others associated with them in various tasks think. Using a constructivist perspective, Kelly proposes that people who wish to play effective roles in social processes must be capable of construing other people's outlooks, including those of people who view the world differently from the way they do. This means that they must not only understand the personal outlooks of others, but they also must be able to anticipate what others will do and to anticipate what others think that they themselves will do. Culturally literate individuals are able to predict what others will do and can adjust their behaviors appropriately. Furthermore, if the others are also able to anticipate what the individuals might do, they can adapt *their* behaviors. "In order for people to get along harmoniously they must have some understanding of the other" (Kelly, 1963, p. 99). However, this does not mean that people need to understand things in the same ways. For Kelly, empathy and perspective-taking skills are important factors in cultural literacy and in role competence.

In his model, Kelly (1963) defines role as "a psychological process based upon the role player's construction of aspects of the construct systems of those with whom he attempts to join in a social enterprise" (p. 97). For him, a role is a pattern of behavior that arises from a person's outlook rather than from his functional skills. Effective role behaviors can therefore be predicted better from knowledge of the person's perspective-taking skills than from knowledge of his/her functional skills. When one plays a role, one behaves according to what one believes others think as well as what one thinks others will approve or disapprove. From a constructivist perspective, cultural literacy is more than functional skills or even cultural like-mindedness; it is empathy, understanding, and respect for others.

Ferdman (this volume) proposes a theory of cultural literacy which focuses on a person's cultural identity and how it interacts with and provides meaning and significance for making decisions about the good life. For him, cultural identity includes those parts of the self that the person considers to define him/herself as a member of a particular ethnic group. The assumption is that a person's sense of cultural identity needs to be challenged through cultural literacy experiences to become more cognitively complex. As a consequence of the challenge, they will be better able to play responsible roles in society as a whole as well as in their particular cultural subgroup. If cultural literacy promotes the resolution of cultural identity issues, then one outcome of literacy experiences should be a person with clearly delineated and integrated definitions of meaningful goals, values, and beliefs. Cultural literacy experiences are more apt to promote the development of a person's sense of identity when there are opportunities to explore and consider different cultural beliefs, as well as time to reflect upon the meanings of such beliefs for their personal sense of identity and their commitments (Erikson, 1968, 1974).

Lay theories of cultural literacy may emphasize personal awareness, understanding, and competence regarding conventions of "the world of text" as they define both the culturally literate person and the substance of cultural literacy (Purves, this volume). Purves uses the concept of a social contract to describe how a cultural model of "the world of text" and standards of literacy can be established. Although pluralistic societies do include divergent and sometimes warring cultural perspectives on literacy, the epistemological and ethical issue for those responsible for literacy programs may not involve determining which perspective is "correct" or "good," but how to develop a community model of literacy free from dogmatic certitude.

Standards for cultural literacy regarding "the world of text" can be defined from an emic or etic perspective (Wagner, this volume). Emic views of literacy focus on a single cultural system, and the contents of literacy are defined and evaluated from one cultural perspective. In such cases, cultural literacy may be defined in reference to a particular ethnic group or even to narrowly defined vocational or professional fields. If cultural literacy is defined from an etic perspective, in contrast, the focus is on clarifying assumptions about literacy and then developing propositions about principles of cultural literacy that are independent of any particular cultural system. Hirsch (1987) argues that the classical literate culture may be considered an etic perspective because this view reflects "the most democratic culture in our land: it excludes nobody; it cuts across generations and social groups and classes, it is not usually one's first culture, but it should be everyone's second, existing as it does beyond the narrow spheres of family, neighborhood and region" (p. 21).

Umberto Eco (1988), describes an "etic" theory of cultural literacy which proposes that literate persons are capable of complex thinking that involves their integrating and organizing information and knowledge about their cultural heritage. From this perspective, cultural literacy includes both individual differences in cultural knowledge and differences in complexity of thinking about that cultural knowledge (see Streufert and Streufert, 1978, for a discussion of cognitive complexity). Eco describes literacy as "a semiotic endeavor by which, with every type of signs from the kabbalistic list of the seventy-two names of God to the new Batman comics, we try to recapture our personal as well as our collective history. Only by knowing critically where we are coming from, can we know where we are going and why" (p. 26). Similarly, Erikson (1974) wrote that "our past must serve us not as an anthology from which to call apt phrases for current needs, but as a stage for observing, in all their tantalizing complexity, the actual ways in which men have faced the ancient problems of the human race" (p. 15).

One important example of an etic cultural theory of literacy is reflected in the Greek tradition of logos or discourse. Cultural literacy for the Greeks was more than knowledge of written words or books, it was understanding and appreciating ideas, seeking truth, and learning to harmoniously blend your intellectual, emotional, and physical competencies. Edith Hamilton (1942) describes the Greek way:

> The Greeks were intellectualists; they had a passion for using their minds. The fact shines through even in their use of language. Our word for school comes from the Greek word for leisure. Of course, reasoned the Greek, given leisure a man will employ it in thinking and finding out about things. Leisure and the pursuit of knowledge, the connection was inevitable to a Greek. In our ears, philosophy has an austere if not dreary sound. The word is Greek, but it had not that sound in the original. The Greeks meant by it, the endeavor to understand everything there is, and they called it what they felt it to be, the love of knowledge; how charming is divine philosophy. (p. 26)

For Hamilton, the whole direction of the Greek mind was from antiquity toward modernity or development. To be Greek was "to be completely civilized without having lost in the process anything of value" (p. 73). Pericles said of the Athenians that they are "lovers of beauty without having lost the taste for simplicity, and lovers of wisdom without loss of manly vigor" (p. 73). The Greek sense of cultural literacy encompassed freedom to think about the world as he/she pleased, to reject tradition, to search for truth. Goodness and truth were the basic values. Ignorance was held to be responsible for evil. Indeed, the Greeks assumed that cultural literacy was living the "Good Life."

LAY THEORIES ABOUT LITERACY AND THE GOOD LIFE

In this essay individual differences in lay theories of literacy have been described along a dimension from "individualistic" to "cultural wisdom." People who have individualistic beliefs about literacy assume that individuals are in the best position to determine what literacy experiences will improve their personal lives. Clearly, humans are viewed as rational beings who are capable of making their own decisions about literacy; restraints are destructive. People with a cultural wisdom view of literacy argue that literacy is a cultural phenomenon which allows individuals to access a particular world view, a set of meanings, and a body of common knowledge and conventional wisdom (Purves, this volume). Thus, it follows that individuals with a cultural view of literacy assume that communities need to develop standards for judging literacy. Moreover, they argue that persons with individualistic views of literacy cannot abdicate this role by allowing individuals to indiscriminately establish the criteria for becoming members of the literate community, nor can they allow individuals to establish forms of literacy that are antagonistic to the values of the community. The conflict between those who hold to theories of literacy as "individualism" and those who hold to theories of literacy as "cultural wisdom" is evident in the public outcry regarding Salmon Rushdie's book, *Satanic Verses* (see Appignanesi and Maitland, 1989). Clearly the Ayatollah Khomeini's position on this book was that it posed a real threat to the Muslim cultural tradition, and because of this threat to the Shiite Muslim view of the good life, the book and the author needed to be censored. In contrast, members of the literary community argued that Salmon Rushdie's work should not be censored by any cultural group. Individuals should be allowed to decide the value of the book for themselves.

Both cultural and individualistic theories of literacy have assumed that literacy experiences should include character education and should provide an appreciation of moral and intellectual virtues that will lead individuals to choose to live the good life. Literacy texts have often been used to provide functional literacy instruction and to shape virtues of character. In the United States after the Civil War, the McGuffey series was used in the public schools to provide both literacy-skills training and character education. In Great Britain, the Society for Promoting Christian Knowledge published children's stories that combined literacy skills and moral or ethical literacy.

In the *Third Eclectic Reader* (McGuffey, 1907), the author instructed teachers on the importance of constant drill: "Whenever a word is imperfectly enunciated, the teacher should call attention to the sounds composing the spoken word" (p. 5). Then, the use of the dash was explained by the following example: "The truth has power—such is God's will—to make us better" (p. 12). The text of this reader has a lesson that describes the fate of truants who tell lies. Instead of coming from school on time, a boy named James met some idle boys at the water and was led by them to hire a boat. The wind blew and none of them knew how to manage the boat.

> A large wave upset the boat and they were all thrown into the water. Think of James Brown the truant at this time!
> He was far from home, known by no one. His parents were ignorant of his danger. He was struggling in the water on the point of being drowned. (p. 29)

The moral of the story is portrayed in "somewhat ominous" terms—children who don't follow rules may suffer terrible personal outcomes.

An example from another culture of how stories are used for character education or literacy about moral virtues can be found in the Wayang or Javanese shadow plays, particularly the Mahabarata and Ramayana cycles (Mulyono, 1981). The philosophy of the Wayang is not limited "to the depiction of the struggle between good and evil in which evil is vanquished, but is tightly interwoven with a limitless number of human problems not easy to call good or evil" (p. 16). The Wayang presents puzzling ethical dilemmas that are part of the human condition of real people.

The Wayang stories describe the inevitability of making moral choices in an imperfect world, and they provide a dialectical view of human nature. "The Wayang teaches that contradictions in life are not overcome; they may only be understood and thereby accepted and borne well" (McVey, 1986, p. 21). The stories do not describe the triumph of good over evil, for justice and nobility are never exclusive properties of one side or another in a moral conflict. Uncertainty, ambivalence, and the necessity of making imperfect choices are viewed as inevitable conditions of human existence. The Wayang puppets, whether they are knights, gods, or clowns, represent different "ways of knowing" the world and different orders of meaning. The central point of the stories involves the clash between the different worlds of meaning, and the plays are always presented in terms of different levels of meaning or time.

The puppetmaster (Dalang) will use clowns to make remarks on contemporary issues and problems of relevance to the community (see Van Ness and Prawirohardjo, 1985). The clown figure is presented as both the lowest of the low and as a god. The stories teach moral virtues, such as, don't judge people by their outside appearances. People who appear to be peasants, poor and outwardly coarse, may turn out to be divine, wise, and of a high station. There is the Wayang story of the younger brother (Kumbakarna) of King Rahwana who became very angry at the King because he had declared a national emergency and conscripted citizens to go to war against the apes. However, in spite of his personal opinion that the war was wrong, he behaved as a knight and went to war to defend his country. The point seems to be that he thought it was better to die in battle than to live in luxury under a foreign king and be guarded by an army of apes—right or wrong, my country. In the Tripama it is said:

> There's another example that's fitting, the great knight of the land of Alengka Sang Kumbakarna was his name. Though an ogre in his looks, excellence was in his arm in all things. In the war of Alengka, he begged his brother to make peace for the good of the land. To hear the truth was not King Dasamuka's wish; the foe was mere apes, that's all.

The hero (Kumbakarna) goes to war against the apes and dies a horrible death such that his cries of pain even disturbed the natural order itself. The messages of this story are, first, from an ordinary point of view, the hero's choice to fight for his country even though he disagreed with the war against the apes was right, and it was a pity he died so completely in vain. Second, however, from a spiritual point of view, the hero should not be allowed to enter paradise because he took the side of arrogance and greed. He should be sentenced to wander aimlessly after death until the gods choose to end his sufferings.

The Wayang and the McGuffey readers both contain stories designed to provide literacy about moral virtues. The Wayang presents morality in a highly realistic way with subtle and puzzling differences between good and evil. In contrast, the McGuffey reader presents morality as clear-cut unambiguous "moral" lessons. The good are always pictured as very certain about the differences between good and evil in the McGuffey stories, while the central moral message of the Wayang is more uncertain, less dogmatic, and more tolerant. McVey (1986) describes the Wayang Controversy in Indonesian Communism and the deeply felt differences between the philosophical view of Marxism and that of the classical shadow play. The Wayang teaches that contradictions are not overcome but simply understood and borne. Moreover, the Wayang stories convey the idea that peasants may be more important than kings and that the outwardly coarse may be divine.

In comparing the Wayang and the McGuffey Readers, John Burrough's (1902) comments on literary values seem particularly salient: "One great danger of schools, colleges, libraries is that they tend to kill or to overlay this elemental quality in a man—to make the poet speak from his culture instead of his heart" (p. 6). He argues that literature "should not preach" but that great literature is moral without having a moral. The writer should work with ethical ideas but not for them. Life is not to be seen through the eyes of a single author, and literature needs to provide perceptions of relativity. However, these perceptions do not necessarily lead to literary license where moral and immoral are not distinguishable. Burroughs states clearly:

> To suppress or ignore the world of vice and sin is not to be moral; to portray it is not to be immoral. But to gloat over it, to dwell fondly upon it, to return to it, to exaggerate it, to roll it under the tongue as a sweet morsel—that is to be immoral; and to treat it as time and nature do or as the great artists do, as affording contrasts and difficulty and disturbing but not destroying the balance of life, is within the scope of the moral. (p. 148)

Although literacy experiences often can deal effectively with morality or ways of thinking about the good life, a problem arises when literature does not respect those who agree or disagree with the substance of particular moral arguments or when morality is presented in simplistic, dogmatic terms. Kekes (1986) argues that if a moral tradition is sound, there will be many more forms of good lives than a single life can take. A sound moral tradition is pluralistic and provides for guidance about commitment and moral conflicts. These moral conflicts are considered an inevitable part of life within a pluralistic moral tradition.

Theories of literacy and the good life that emphasize character development may focus on promoting the intellectual virtues of rationality, logic, and intellectual reasoning (Adler, 1985). Literacy experiences are judged as good when they increase awareness and appreciation for the virtues of rationality and thought in improving personal lives. Intellectual literacy teaches individuals to recognize rational and reasonable arguments and positions and thereby helps them to make better personal decisions.

In order to evaluate the contributions of intellectual literacy to improving individual lives, criteria are needed to judge the intellectual qualities of literacy experiences. Literacy about intellectual virtues contributes to the good life when there are no major rational errors of logic or fact. Erroneous information and/or illogical arguments are assumed to adversely influence the quality of intellectual literacy. Adler, in *Ten Philosophical Mistakes* (1985), presents a model for evaluating the intellectual content of literacy experiences. He discusses an intellectual mistake made by those who present morals, values, and ethics as no more than expressions of personal preferences and who conclude that standards for living the good life are just "matters of opinion." A second kind of intellectual mistake is made by those who discuss absolute and universal standards of right and wrong as determined solely by authorities. Individuals who are led to believe in either of these two mistaken views about morals are equally dogmatic. The first are unable to support their subjective and relativistic view of morality, and the second are unable to support their dogmatic views by rational arguments and evidence.

Intellectual theories of literacy also include an appreciation for the virtue of truthfulness. The question is not whether literacy experiences represent the "truth" or not. Rather, literacy experiences should not intend to mislead or be untruthful. Truth and truthfulness are not identical intellectual criteria to be used in judging literacy. Those literacy experiences which are not truthful do not contribute to the betterment of individual lives because the rationale for individual decisions about the good life is intellectually flawed. Bok's treatise on lying (1978) warns against those representatives of a society who are not truthful or who intend to mislead:

> The fact that the "whole truth" can never be reached in its entirety should not, therefore, be a stumbling block in the much more limited inquiry into questions of truth-telling and falsehood. It is possible to go beyond the notion that epistemology is somehow prior to ethics. The two nourish one another.

CONCLUSIONS

This essay provides a framework for discussing individual differences in personal or lay theories of literacy and the good life. These personal perspectives function as cognitive controls on how people interpret the meaning of literacy and judge the relevance of literacy experiences. Subsequently they influence behaviors and feelings about literacy. Individuals use personal or lay theories of literacy and the good life to generate hypotheses, predictions, and expectations about the values of specific literacy activities, activities that are then evaluated using concepts of the "good life." Individuals will judge literacy experiences as positive and/or relevant when they think those experiences will advance their achievement of their view of a good life.

The essay presents a two-fold typology of lay theories of literacy and the good life. Individualistic theories view literacy as a mode of changing personal phenomenological experiences. Since meaning is personal and is determined by individuals, literacy is viewed as a subjective experience that promotes individuals' ability to deal meaningfully with their personal lives. Effective or good literacy experiences must affect perceptual and cognitive processes of individuals or they will not be personally meaningful.

Those who hold to cultural theories of literacy emphasize the importance of introducing individuals to the best of the past and providing opportunities for them to reflect upon different cultural world views and ways of finding meaning. Cultural literacy provides an opportunity to consider a variety of personal perspectives and world views that are part of a society's cultural tradition. Good cultural-literacy experiences provide opportunities for both reflection and actions about the central values of a society.

Although two perspectives on literacy have been described in this essay, it is clear that individuals make different assumptions about how these two perspectives are similar or different from each other. The differences between the constructions of literacy as individualism and as cultural wisdom can be exaggerated or minimized. An exaggeration of the differences between the two perspectives may be found with those who treat them in a categorical and dogmatic fashion. This assumption can be called alpha bias. In many cases of alpha bias, individuals become involved in hostile encounters and try to impose their wills on each other. In the case of beta bias, adherents often fail to understand and differentiate the contributions of individualistic and cultural perspectives on literacy. As a consequence, they do not seriously evaluate the values of these different theories of literacy and may adopt one or the other perspective as a matter of convenience or taste. In cases of either alpha or beta bias, literacy programs are often narrowly defined and dogmatically defended (see Hare-Mustin and Maracek, 1988, for a discussion of alpha and beta biases in gender theories).

Literacy programs are programs in the real world and they demand that participants make commitments to a particular view of literacy as well as to specific activities to accomplish their goals. Freire (1987) suggests that such commitments can be described as either radical or sectarian. Radical commitments are critical, loving, humble, and communicative and are therefore positive stances. Individuals who make radical commitments do not deny others the right to choose, nor do they try to impose their own choices. They discuss their respective positions but respect others' prerogatives to judge for themselves that which is correct.

In contrast, those participants who make sectarian commitments regarding the relationship of literacy to individual life will tend to disrespect the choices of others and will try to impose their own choices on everyone else. Sectarianism is described as predominately emotional and uncritical, arrogant, antidialogical, and thus anticommunicative.

Sectarianism is a reactionary stance whether it is taken by an adherent to individualistic or to cultural theories of literacy. Sectarians of literacy do not think that people should think for themselves.

The University at Albany

IV

THE DILEMMA
OF THE SCHOOL

9
Literacy in the Elementary Classroom

SEAN A. WALMSLEY

INTRODUCTION

At no time in recent history has the content and mission of the elementary school been under such scrutiny as it has been in the past few years. One of the major criticisms has come from Graves (1978) who observed that elementary schools were negligent in teaching writing, and what little time they spent on writing was focused on mechanics (e.g., spelling, handwriting, grammar) to the detriment of composing. Another criticism has come from those who feel that the focus on reading skills, and the use of basal reading series to teach them, takes too narrow a view of literacy: literacy, in their view, has to include the reading of literature. The notion that the elementary reading curriculum should either entirely or substantially consist of "real" (i.e., trade) books is not a new one—Jeannette Veatch had been promoting it in the 1950s (Veatch, 1986), and authorities in children's literature (e.g., Huck, 1977) had always assumed that real literature was the proper content of elementary reading instruction. Two quite separate movements gave rise to the recent criticism. One movement with an "academic" and somewhat conservative view of literature has prompted studies of children's literary knowledge at the end of high school that have reported extremely disappointing findings (e.g., Ravitch and Finn, 1987); this has led educators to ask what kinds of literary experiences children had in the elementary years, and to recommend a "beefing up" of the literature curriculum in both elementary and secondary schools. The other has come from educators such as Holdaway (1979), Goodman (1986), and Cambourne (1988) who advocate "naturalistic" approaches to learning how to read, in which "real" reading of literature plays a central role. This latter movement has recently been termed "whole language."

A third assault on the elementary reading curriculum has come from those who feel that it has become "contentless"—caused in large measure, according to Hirsch (1987), by the domination in elementary schools of the "content-neutral" ideas of Rousseau and Dewey. In 1985, Ravitch pointed out not only how poorly elementary schools covered literature, but also how poor in content the social studies curriculum had become:

> The dearth of literature in the elementary school may go far toward explaining some of the problems encountered by secondary-school teachers, who complain that children don't like to read, don't read well, and can't apply what they read to their own lives. . . . The children of this regime arrive in junior high schools and secondary schools knowing *how*, but not *why* or *what*. They have been miseducated; they have been taught to read without learning to love reading; they have been taught social studies as a package of skills rather than as a window on the varieties of human experience in other times and places. (pp. 78-79)

A similar situation exists in geographical knowledge. In 1985, Gilbert M. Grosvenor, President of the National Geographic Society, wrote an editorial in the National Geographic in which he lamented the current lack of geographical knowledge among schoolchildren. Grosvenor quoted a study that compared college students' knowledge of geography in 1984 with that of 1950:

> In what country is the Amazon River mainly found? In 1950, 78 percent correctly named Brazil; in 1984, 27 percent did. In what country is the city of Manila located? In 1950, 84 percent knew it was the Philippines; in 1984, 27 percent. In 1984, how many could name three countries in Africa between the Sahara and South Africa? Out of 30 countries—30!—what percentage of students could name three? Eighty percent? Fifty percent? No, seven percent—and 69 percent could not name even one. . . . In fairness to the students, 71 percent said they had no geography courses in elementary school, nor had 65 percent in junior high school, nor 73 percent in high school. Geography, once required in most schools, is now being covered—perhaps I should say buried—in social studies and history, assuming that it is being taught at all. (p. 20)

Finally, according to the latest *Report Card on Science* (Mullis and Jenkins, 1988), scientific knowledge amongst both secondary and elementary students is reported not to be strong; indeed science achievement amongst nine-, thirteen-, and seventeen-year-olds is lower now—the data were collected in 1986—than in 1969.

Taken as a whole, these criticisms strike at the heart of the traditional elementary literacy curriculum, raising difficult questions about its mission and its materials. Elementary schools may have done little to accommodate Graves's (1978) criticism about the lack of attention to writing, but writing has "gotten onto the agenda" of the elementary teaching profession; to some extent, criticisms about the lack of literature in elementary school have also hit their mark, especially when the State of California mandated the teaching of literature for its elementary schools and for the country's major basal reader publishing companies. The problem is that there is a limit to what can be added to the elementary curriculum without something having to be excluded. There may have been enough slack to allow writing to be added without displacing anything, but adding literature leaves no additional room; if properly implemented, it may well displace writing. To suggest that history, geography, and science be fully restored to the elementary school to ensure that students are "literate" in these areas leaves few options other than increasing the school day (or year), or making significant inroads into the reading, writing, or literature curriculum. An understandable complaint of elementary school teachers is that they are already being asked to do too much, and that the new demands are simply unreasonable and unrealistic.[1]

There are several kinds of responses we can make to those who are pressing for reform. We could argue that elementary schools properly focus on the teaching of reading and writing skills, and that content knowledge is properly the domain of secondary schools (in other words, we admit that children don't know enough history, geography, literature, and science, but it isn't the responsibility of elementary schools—our job is to prepare children for content areas by teaching basic reading, writing, and study skills). Alternatively, we could simply relabel existing practices and claim to be already doing what the reformers have proposed (many elementary teachers have done this to "process-writing"). Or, most likely, we meet each new demand as it comes along. Thus we would first strengthen our writing program, then our literature program, and then the content areas, responding to each crisis as it occurs. Eventually, however, we have to face the problem of too much to cover in too little time.

The response I want to suggest that elementary educators take—and it is the major focus of this essay—is to take advantage of the opportunity that has been presented to rethink literacy in the elementary school. There comes a point at which tinkering with the system no longer works: What is needed is a fresh perspective, one in which we step back and look at the elementary curriculum as a whole, to envision how literacy instruction fits into the larger mission of elementary education.

The essay is organized in three major sections. First, I want to discuss competing views on what the elementary literacy curriculum should comprise. This involves an examination of educational ideologies and instructional philosophies as they relate to different conceptions of the purpose and definition of elementary reading and writing. From the perspective of these different conceptions of elementary language arts, on what grounds are existing practices deemed to be inadequate?

Second, I want to propose a framework for the elementary school language arts curriculum that addresses not only the integration of reading and writing but also the relationship between these language arts elements and literary, historical, geographical, and scientific knowledge.

Third, I want to discuss the practical problems that schools and teachers encounter when they attempt to put these ideas into practice. How are they to choose between competing views and translate principles into daily classroom routines?

COMPETING VIEWS ON THE ELEMENTARY LANGUAGE ARTS CURRICULUM

The three 'R's, reading, writing, and arithmetic, have always been the major focus of the elementary school curriculum, and teaching children the basic skills of decoding and comprehending, computation and tables, spelling, grammar, and handwriting have always been important activities in elementary classrooms. Introducing children to the study of literature, history, geography, and science has typically been a secondary focus. While the central mission of elementary schools has rarely been in question, the definition of what it means to be literate, and the methods and materials by which literacy and content area knowledge is to be accomplished, have been continually debated.

To be able to understand what one reads and to communicate effectively in writing seem on the surface to be such obvious definitions of literacy that no one would think to challenge them. Indeed, at this broad level of abstraction, there is little to argue with. A closer examination, however, reveals some marked differences in definitions of literacy that stem from different assumptions about the purpose of education in general, reading and writing in particular.

Drawing mainly on the work of Kohlberg and Mayer (1972) and Freire (1970), I have suggested that examining educational ideologies helps to explain these differences (Walmsley, 1981). There seem to me to be four major educational ideologies. The dominant ideology—what Kohlberg and Mayer call "cultural transmission"—has as its general aim the transmission from one generation to the next the attitudes, skills, and knowledge deemed appropriate for succeeding generations to acquire. According to Kohlberg and Mayer, this ideology has two branches. One branch has an "academic" perspective. It defines literacy in terms of a student's ability to read and understand both classical and modern literature, and to be articulate and sophisticated in written expression. The other branch is "utilitarian"; from a utilitarian perspective, literacy is a survival skill in a complex technological society—it is the ability to read and write functionally in order to participate successfully in everyday life (on the job, at home, and in leisure activities). I have suggested a third branch, what I now call a "literacy skills" perspective: It represents a diluted version of the academic perspective, and is differentiated from the utilitarian perspective in that its goal is mastery of school-related literacy tasks rather than those of the outside world. Essentially, it recognizes that most students' ambitions are somewhat less than academic, and it aims to ensure that students can at least become competent in basic reading and writing skills, as measured by standardized tests of reading and writing achievement. Unlike the academic and utilitarian perspectives, the literacy skills perspective appears to be neutral with respect to knowledge. It focuses on the means for gaining access to knowledge (i.e., reading) and for communicating knowledge (i.e., writing) but is not terribly concerned with the knowledge itself; knowledge is something one can access once the reading and writing skills have been sufficiently well developed—indeed, acquiring knowledge is the reason for learning how to read and write.

In secondary school, the academic perspective undergirds the literacy program for college-bound honors students, while the literacy skills and utilitarian perspectives undergird the literacy program for general education students and vocational students respectively. In elementary school, students are considered too young to be tracked into vocational education, but they are tracked into high and low reading groups that are precursors to the honors and general tracks in secondary school. There is little evidence, however, of an academic perspective in most public elementary schools outside of "gifted and talented" programs;[2] it does not appear to be the case that good readers in high reading groups are taught with an academic perspective while poor readers' instruction derives from a literacy skills perspective, despite major differences in the literary experiences of both groups. Most elementary schools appear to have a literacy skills perspective that attempts to lay the foundation for all elementary students so they can pursue academic or vocational learning in secondary school.

Literacy skills teaching in elementary school is typically carried out using separate approaches for the teaching of reading and writing. In about 90 percent of classrooms in elementary school (Shannon, 1983), reading is taught with a basal reader, and supplementary materials (e.g., practice worksheets, programs for teaching specific skills such as phonics, comprehension, and vocabulary). It is harder to characterize the teaching of writing, but from what little evidence there is (Graves, 1978; Petty and Finn, 1981; Beach, 1988), writing instruction consists primarily of teaching spelling, handwriting (at least K-3), and language (i.e., grammar, punctuation, capitalization) with commercial materials. Composing is typically taught by assigning topics for writing, then correcting them for mechanical and organizational errors.

There are also "counter-cultural" ideologies, ones that challenge the dominance of the academic and utilitarian perspectives. These views have different assumptions about the nature and purpose of literacy, and they imply quite different practices for literacy instruction.

For example, a "romantic" ideology stresses the development of an individual's "autonomy" or "ownership of self" (Spring, 1975); it defines literacy in terms of reading and writing for enjoyment, and using both reading and writing to contribute to one's own development. The goal of reading from a romantic perspective is largely to be determined by the reader or writer rather than the teacher, and the student is expected to participate in deciding the means for attaining these goals. A critical component of a romantic view of reading is that it emphasizes the reader's construction of meaning in the act of reading (e.g., Rosenblatt, 1949), and the writer's choice of topic and "voice" in composing (e.g., Graves, 1983). It also emphasizes the role of reading and writing in an individual's search for identity (Freire and Macedo, 1987). The role of the teacher is to provide a nurturing "child-centered" environment in which the child can best develop ownership and voice in both reading and writing. The knowledge and skills to be gained through a romantic approach are ultimately no different from other ideologies, but the assumption is that such knowledge and skills will be best acquired "naturally" (i.e., by using them in authentic settings, with real texts—that is, not contrived or artificial—and by treating reading and writing development as processes to be acquired in a manner similar to developing oral language). The teaching approach developed by Ashton-Warner (1963), and refined by recent educators such as Holdaway (1979), Goodman (1986), Graves (1983), Atwell (1987), and Cambourne (1988) clearly articulate romantic approaches to literacy development in the elementary school.

A "cognitive-developmental" ideology, derived mainly from the work of Piaget (1969) and Kohlberg and Mayer (1972), stresses the intellectual growth that results from interactions between readers and texts;

from a cognitive-developmental perspective, literacy is defined in terms of increasingly sophisticated problem-solving abilities (e.g., the ability to synthesize, analyze, differentiate, hypothesize, and so on). The goal of cognitive developmental literacy instruction is to promote intellectual growth. In this perspective, comprehending an author's message or bringing one's own meaning to the text are important not so much for what is gained in the particular interaction between a reader and a text, but rather for the interaction's contribution to the "development of new cognitive structures that allow the student to progress toward the understanding of increasingly complex reading materials" (Walmsley, 1981; p. 83). Similarly, writing is seen primarily as solving rhetorical challenges—how to communicate ideas about topics to audiences for particular purposes. Moffett's (1967) notion of a progression from "recording" to "reporting" to "generalizing" to "theorizing," that is, being able to operate on text at increasing levels of abstraction, is one way of thinking about cognitive-developmental reading and writing. Critical components of a cognitive-developmental approach include knowledge about content, and the increasingly sophisticated operations that can be performed on that knowledge. Perry (1970) has focused on the changing stances towards knowledge itself—a shift from absolutist toward relativistic stances. Chall (1983) draws on Perry's work to articulate her stages of reading development, which emphasize the cognitive-developmental nature of reading, especially in the upper elementary and middle schools. For example, her Stage 3 *(Reading for Learning the New)* is defined as "Reading . . . to learn new ideas, to gain new knowledge, to experience new feelings, to learn new attitudes; generally from one viewpoint" (p. 86); Stage 4 *(Multiple Viewpoints)* is defined as "Reading widely from a broad range of complex materials, both expository and narrative, with a variety of viewpoints" (p. 87). Bereiter (1972) has proposed stages of writing development that closely parallel both Perry's and Chall's schemes for reading. If a cognitive-developmental approach attempts to nourish, as Kohlberg and Mayer (1972) state, "the child's natural interaction with a developing society or environment" (p. 454), then Rosenblatt's "transactional approach" (Rosenblatt, 1978) has much in common with a cognitive-developmental philosophy.

What would be the essential elements of cognitive-developmental literacy instruction? First, teachers would have to provide genuine opportunities for readers and writers to interact with texts of sufficient difficulty and challenge so that intellectual growth might occur. Second, students would need to be exposed to a variety of topics (through reading, writing, direct experience, and listening) so that their knowledge base could be built and extended. Third, workshops in which teachers and students worked through comprehension and composition problems would need to be held.

Finally, an "emancipatory" ideology, which stems from the work of Freire (1970), defines literacy in terms of its function as a social and political change agent. Freire refers to literacy as a mechanism for people to "name their world" and to transform the relationship between oppressed and oppressors: "Literacy allows the oppressed to emerge from a 'culture of silence' and transform the relation between them and their oppressors not merely to change places with their oppressors but also to restore the humanity of both groups" (p. 28). While Freire's work has mostly been with adults, there are nonetheless implications of his work for elementary school. First, although the predominantly white, upper-middle class society portrayed in early basal readers has given way to a more balanced and realistic view of the world in current materials, there are still many stereotypes presented to children in their texts (e.g., Anyon, 1979): an emancipatory approach raises both teachers' and students' consciousness of these biases. Second, it might be argued that poor readers and writers themselves are an oppressed group, particularly if one takes the view that once they are labeled poor achievers, they are assigned to a group whose literacy activities are restricted and whose expectations become permanently lowered. An emancipatory approach to poor readers and writers would help them challenge rather than accept their status as inadequate literacy users. The pedagogical approach to emancipatory literacy involves an interaction (or dialectic, in Freire's terms) between readers, writers, and problems posed in texts as a major instructional activity, with the development of the reader's capacity for expression (in both speech and writing) being an important goal, since it is through the medium of dialogue that social and political transformation are expected to occur. The content of materials used in the emancipatory approach intentionally reflects the social and political issues that readers need to address (Walmsley, 1981; p. 85).

ON WHAT GROUNDS ARE TRADITIONAL APPROACHES TO LITERACY INSTRUCTION INADEQUATE?

Despite a growing awareness of the need to improve the quality of writing and literature experiences, the vast majority of elementary classroom teachers in America's public schools still focus most of their language arts time on teaching children reading skills, and they do so with commercial basal reader series. Similarly, writing instruction is still largely what it was when Graves described it for the Ford Foundation in 1978—teachers assign topics, children write on them, hand them in, have them corrected, and "do them over" if there are sufficient numbers of grammatical and spelling errors to warrant it. Spelling instruction with a commercial spelling series still occupies more time in the elementary language arts curriculum (typically twenty minutes a day) than composing does. The reading of literature (either to children, with them, or on their own) still occupies a very small percentage of the language arts curriculum—essentially, literature is what elementary children are expected to read at home, or to do when their "work" is done. It would appear that the dominant educational ideology in elementary schools takes a "literacy skills" perspective, one that is strongly criticized by proponents of the other ideologies.

From a cultural transmission perspective, what has happened in elementary schools is a gradual watering down of the Victorian notion of a "well-educated" student, one who has been schooled in classical literature and classical history, taught Latin and Greek, and thoroughly drilled in grammar, spelling, and penmanship. Especially disturbing is the "dumbing-down" of textbooks used for English Literature, for Science, and for Social Studies (even the term Social Studies is for some evidence that the subjects of History and Geography have been relegated to an inferior status). While admitting that Victorian methods of instruction should give way to more humanistic approaches, critics such as Hirsch, Bennett, and Ravitch are adamant about the importance of "classical" knowledge even in the elementary curriculum. For example, Hirsch (1987) writes: "To miss the opportunity of teaching young (and older) children the traditional materials of literate culture is a tragically wasteful mistake that deprives them of information they would continue to find useful in later life. The inevitable effect of this fundamental educational mistake has been a gradual disintegration of cultural memory, causing a gradual decline in our ability to communicate" (p. 113).

Bennett (1988), laying out the principles and procedures for his James Madison Elementary School, castigates "English programs that spurn serious literature in favor of bland basal readers and skill workbooks" (p. 4) and proposes a list of recommended books that "emphasizes classics of children's literature—in part because they are so often missing from elementary school instruction" (p. 7).

Ravitch (1985) remarks:

> I was equally astonished to discover the contempt with which the elementary social studies consultant viewed history and geography. Like others who don't like history and never took a good history course, this educational expert associated history with "memorization and parroting of facts" rather than problem solving. As every good historian knows, history is problem solving. The writer of history asks: What happened? How do we know it happened? Why did it happen?

Why did people respond as they did? History is about issues and controversies, about heroes and villains; it is about people struggling to improve their lives and about the ways people have devised to enslave others or to free themselves. History is the substance that students use to exercise the skills of problem solving, inquiry and thinking. . . . Education is debased when the curriculum is stripped of its content and when skills, free of any cultural, literary, or historic context, are all that is taught. (pp. 78-79)

From a utilitarian perspective, what schools are doing is inappropriate because they are not preparing students for the "real" world they will be entering upon graduation. Although most of the critics (e.g., Northcutt, 1975) have taken secondary schools' curricula to task, Venezky (1987) singles out elementary schools for criticism:

The primary emphasis of elementary reading programs . . . continues to be on the comprehension and enjoyment of fine literature. Direct instruction on those skills and strategies that would lead to finding an entry in a tax table, or to summarizing information in an article on economics rarely occurs. The results of this long standing emphasis on fiction are inadequate for present-day literacy demands. . . . (p. 44)

From a romantic perspective, the current state of affairs in elementary schools is unsatisfactory for a variety of reasons. First, elementary literacy instruction is not child-centered: It neither takes into account developmental needs of emergent readers and writers, nor the need for children to read books that interest them and write about topics of their own choice, nor even values that readers themselves bring to the act of reading. Second, literacy is traditionally defined in terms of a set of prerequisite subskills to be taught in a strict sequence, using direct instruction as the primary pedagogy, to build up a whole by teaching the component parts. From a romantic perspective, the parts are built up by teaching the whole. Especially objectionable is the use of short, vocabulary- and syntax-controlled passages that comprise the reading material with which children learn to read: real text (e.g., full-length books, poetry, environmental print) should be the material with which children learn to read. Third, traditional approaches treat the acquisition of reading and writing abilities as completely different from the acquisition of oral language competence: While the latter typically is acquired "naturally" through meaningful interactions between (mostly) parents and children, the former has to be formally "taught." From a romantic perspective, reading, writing, and oral language all can be acquired in a natural, wholistic manner.

From a cognitive-developmental perspective, traditional approaches are unsatisfactory because they fail to provide children with enough intellectual challenges through which to acquire new mental structures. Elementary reading materials have had complex ideas and complex syntax systematically removed from them: This may make the material easier to decode, but it also denies students the very opportunities they need in order to 'work through' problems of meaning and form. Especially objectionable to cognitive-developmentalists is the removal of conflict from history books, and the censoring of literary works, for it is in the working through of such conflicts in history and literature that the processes of assimilation and accommodation are able to operate. Equally troubling is the lack of sustained reading of a variety of fiction and nonfiction in elementary school, especially in grades three through six; such reading provides students with the knowledge base they need in order to operate abstractly during the onset of formal operational thinking.

Finally, from an emancipatory perspective, elementary literacy programs are unsatisfactory because they perpetuate traditional stereotypes about minorities, and through practices such as ability grouping and differentiated curricula, train poor readers and writers to accept their status and low self-expectations.

A FRAMEWORK FOR LITERACY INSTRUCTION

We clearly have not arrived at any consensus about what the elementary language arts curriculum should consist of, and given the fundamental differences among the various educational ideologies, it may be unreasonable to think that a consensus can ever be achieved. This is not to say that there is not considerable unease amongst teachers about how they define language arts, and how they assign time to the various components; they often feel guilty that they do not do more writing, or more literature, but they don't know how to incorporate them within an already crowded schedule, and they often are very unsure about how they should be taught (Walmsley and Walp, 1989). The issue is not easy to resolve: When we try to define an elementary language arts curriculum, we have to bear in mind a number of factors, including the developmental needs of kindergartners at one end, and sixth graders at the other; what our end goals are (e.g., mastery of minimum competency tests, coverage of a particular set of skills lessons, enjoyment of reading, coverage of particular works of literature, etc.); and what aspects of language arts are to be given what emphasis (e.g., how much time should be spent reading aloud, how much on the basal, etc.). Within each of these, decisions have to be made about which skills are to be covered (if they are to be "covered" at all), what kinds of books are to be read, and

what teaching strategies should be employed. Publishers of basal reading series rarely deal with these issues explicitly, and while they claim
that basals do not represent the entire language arts curriculum, these
basals nonetheless provide more than enough activities to consume the
entire time available for language arts, and are typically used as a substitute for the language arts curriculum. At the same time, those who
have proposed curricula for aspects of language arts not covered by the
basal series (especially writing and literature) have done so generally
without regard for how the various elements are to be organized within
a classroom (especially one that uses a basal series), nor for the changing
developmental needs across the grades.

While it may not be possible to construct a program that incorporates all the educational philosophies described above, I would like to
propose some principles for elementary literacy instruction that at least
takes seriously each of the ideologies' criticisms of the "literacy skills"
philosophy.

The first principle involves shifting the focus from reading and
writing as the ends of the elementary curriculum to defining them as
means. Means to what? Reading and writing are the primary means by
which students gain access to, enlarge, and communicate *knowledge*
(Walmsley and Walp, 1990). Knowledge needs to be defined broadly: It
certainly includes knowledge of literature, of history, of geography, of
science, of culture, even self-knowledge. This is not to suggest that acquiring skill in the process of accessing knowledge is unimportant; it is
to argue, however, that the knowledge itself is more important, and it
should be made a primary rather than a peripheral goal of elementary
education. With the notable exception of the literacy skills ideology,
which is essentially content-free, the ideologies presented above all emphasize knowledge, though they do so in quite different ways. Indeed
there is no easy definition of what knowledge elementary students
should be exposed to, or expected to learn. What is important here is to
redefine the relationship between language processes such as reading
and writing and the ends they serve. In so doing, opportunities present
themselves for restructuring the elementary curriculum so as to promote both the acquisition of worthwhile knowledge (however knowledge is to be defined) and the development of reading and writing proficiency without having to add content instruction to a curriculum
already overburdened by a reading and writing skills curriculum.

The second principle is *balance*—balance between the various components of language arts, between teaching and learning activities
within these components, between language arts and content areas, and
balance across grade levels. Balance between the various components of

language arts involves thinking about the relative time and attention to be devoted to reading, writing, speaking, listening, and drama. In a typical literacy skills approach, too much language arts time is focused on reading, and not nearly enough on writing. Opportunities for speaking and drama seem particularly limited, often being reserved for special occasions such as project reports or school "productions" for parents.

Within the reading and writing components, tremendous imbalances exist between the teaching of reading skills and reading of full-length literature, and between composing and editing aspects of writing. In general, far too much time is devoted to specific reading skills instruction, and not nearly enough to the reading of full-length literature. Even when literature is used, there is often a lack of balance in the kinds of materials read—current realistic fiction seems to be the dominant genre of elementary schools' literature programs, where any substantial amount of literature is read at all (Walmsley and Walp, 1989). One wonders how well students are prepared for the largely classical literary diet they will encounter in secondary school (Applebee, 1989), or the mostly nonfiction materials in the workplace beyond formal schooling (Venezky, 1987). In writing programs, composing typically is given a fraction of the time devoted to editing (e.g., spelling, grammar, punctuation/capitalization, and handwriting). Where spelling instruction occupies more than 20 percent of the time devoted to language arts—and it frequently does—there is a serious imbalance between the components of writing instruction.

As far as teaching and learning activities are concerned, the question of a balance between direct instruction in the subskills of reading and writing, and the student's own engagement in sustained reading and writing activities, is very relevant. It is often assumed, erroneously, that sustained reading and writing do not lead to learning—only direct instruction does. Cambourne's (1988) model for learning gives equal emphasis to teacher demonstrations and students' use of language; his approach is a good example of how a balance can be achieved between these competing views.

There are many reasons why language arts instruction has taken up an increasingly larger percentage of the elementary school day, thereby squeezing out content areas such as science and social studies:[3] It should come as no surprise that elementary students lack knowledge of history, geography, and science given the amount of time these subjects are allocated, let alone how well they are taught or what materials are used to teach them. But in so doing, the language arts program is now severely out of balance with other important subject areas—science and social studies are given far too little attention compared to reading.

Finally, the curriculum needs to be balanced across the grades, such that the kinds of reading and writing experiences that students engage in are developmentally appropriate and cumulative. Given the lack of coordination across the grade levels (the scope and sequence of a basal reader series is, according to Tyson-Bernstein (1988), more a result of state and local textbook adoption committees' whims than careful analyses of developmental needs), students' literacy experiences are at best haphazard encounters with literature and composing—even an outstanding language arts program at one or two grades may not be able to compensate for the dearth of literacy experiences in the others. What is developmentally appropriate for emergent readers and writers may not be appropriate for students entering the stage of formal operational thinking, yet frequently similar activities are suggested for both. Whether beginning readers and writers need intensive "decoding" instruction is open to question (see Chall, 1983; Goodman, 1986; Holdaway, 1979), but where is the justification for continuing intensive reading skills instruction in the upper grades at the expense of wide reading? Is it really appropriate that fourth graders read only a handful of books a year, while spending ninety minutes a day "refining" their reading skills?

The question raised by the principle of balance is this: How does one fit it all in? Unless the school day or the school year is to be extended (and there are many education critics who think it should), there is no alternative but to rethink how we allocate time to the various components of the curriculum and what we do with that time. To address the question of how to fit it all in, I need to propose two more principles. The first is borrowed from Sizer's (1985) proposal for restructuring secondary education—less is more. We have stuffed so much into the elementary language arts curriculum that we are now unable to cover it all at even a surface level. There are several approaches to putting the "less is more" principle to work. One would be to divide the number of hours of instruction by the number of subject areas, weighting them according to their relative importance at a particular grade level, then reorganizing instruction within those content areas according to how much time is now available. If this resulted in reducing reading instruction from ninety to forty-five minutes a day, the reading curriculum would have to be trimmed accordingly. The basal reader could be compacted (i.e., stripped of any unnecessary exercises, stories that neither entertained nor informed), or alternated (i.e., used on a rotating basis, with shared reading of single works or independent reading of trade books). Instead of teaching students twenty different comprehension "skills" (getting the main idea, following the author's sequence, recognizing bias, etc.), teachers could concentrate on improving students' general understanding of what they read, and their ability to communicate that understanding. Duplication across the various components of language arts could be eliminated. There would be no need for separate literature and reading basals; no need for language arts exercises in a spelling book. There is so much waste and duplication in most elementary language arts curricula that it would not be difficult to reduce the average program by 50 percent without any appreciable loss in content and skill coverage.

Several problems still remain, however. The first is that even a 50 percent reduction of curriculum leaves the various components intact, so that instead of a separate spelling program that takes twenty minutes a day, we might have a separate spelling program that takes ten minutes a day, the proportion of time devoted to spelling within the language arts curriculum staying constant. The second is that the language arts curriculum may still largely represent a literacy skills ideology, even though it may have become much more efficient, with time freed up for the teaching of other subject areas. The third is that simply reallocating time to various components doesn't address the main thrust of the "less is more" principle, which is that students should be covering less but exploring what they cover in more depth. While eliminating waste and duplication is essential for opening up time, it does not by itself fully address the criticisms raised earlier.

The second principle for fitting it all in is *integration*. A typical language arts program consists of a basal reader, with supplementary books for teaching phonics, vocabulary, comprehension, spelling, grammar (language), and handwriting. Often, in the intermediate grades, there is a literature series used alongside the basal reader. There are several ways to integrate these various activities. One approach is to decide on two sets of reading and writing skills. The first set generally applies across all grade levels, and is differentiated only by the textual complexity of the materials being read, or the rhetorical complexity of the writing task. For example, "understanding what is read," "knowing the meanings of words in context," "applying word attack strategies to words encountered during reading," "using proper punctuation," are literacy skills that apply across all grade levels. The second set is specific to a given grade level. For example, teaching specific literary terms such as "onomatopoeia," or punctuation rules such as quotation marks, could be assigned to a specific grade level. Such an approach would provide a rational basis for the choice of particular materials. It would also provide a mechanism for integrating the various components of language arts: If quotation marks were being studied, they could be learned in the context of books or other reading material currently being read as well as in the context of writing. In this approach, the language arts curriculum is still driven by skills instruction, but all elements of the program including reading literature and composing are drawn into the service of skills teaching and are not treated as separate entities.

Another approach, a detailed example of which is given in Walmsley and Walp (1990), involves integrating language arts through content. In this approach, the components of language arts are integrated by focusing on themes or topics that provide the basis for all reading, writing, speaking, listening, and dramatic activities. Thus, in a theme of "Courage," students read material (articles, extracts, full-length books) about courage, they write about courage, speak about it (discussions, formal presentations), listen to others reading or talking about it, perform dramas on it. Skills are taught in the context of the various reading and writing activities. For example, learning the main idea is accomplished in part through the reading of a large number of books, extracts, and articles; in part through discussions and small group-directed reading activities focused on the meaning of specific works; and in part through writing about what has been read. Learning an editing skill such as quotation marks is accomplished primarily by having students engage in numerous composing activities, many of which will necessitate transcribing direct speech. Instruction in how to accomplish this is given at the point at which it is needed, and again during editing conferences if required. A theme-centered approach offers not only opportunities for integrating the various components of language arts (they are all drawn into the service of exploring the themes), but it also exposes students to a wide variety of written materials (fiction and nonfiction) without making it necessary to increase the time allocation to language arts. Finally, it addresses the "less is more" principle—students will be exploring topics in depth. If teachers are careful in their choice of basal reader series (i.e., if they choose ones that already organize their units around themes or topics), and have reduced the scope and sequence of skills to bare essentials, it should be possible to organize an integrated language arts curriculum within an existing basal language arts program rather than having to start from scratch with entirely teacher-made materials.

This approach does not by itself solve the problem of integrating language arts with content area instruction, but its use of content to connect the various components offers a significant clue to the solution. Instead of creating special themes or topics for use within language arts, suppose the content areas themselves were used as the basis for language arts activities? Thus, literature, history, geography, and science provide the topics about which students read and write. Another approach would be to use themes or topics that were not drawn from content areas, but examine them from literary, historical, geographical, or scientific perspectives. In either case, the barrier between language arts and content areas is broken down.

This raises an intriguing question: Is there a need for language arts as a separate subject area at all? Could language arts instruction be completely integrated within subject areas? This is a radical proposal, given that it is the subject areas themselves that have been almost eradicated from elementary school by an ever-spreading language arts curriculum. Yet if we take seriously the principle, suggested earlier, that reading and writing are language processes, not subject areas, then why not fully integrate them within the study of content? In such an approach, the language arts program is abolished as a separate entity, its time being reallocated to the subject areas. In these subject areas, students explore topics in science, in history, in geography, and in literature, spending extended periods of time gaining access to, enlarging, and communicating their knowledge through reading and writing. When students encounter difficulties in the process of reading or of writing, they receive assistance, including direct instruction in reading and writing strategies if they need it, but without a separate reading and/or writing program. I do not underestimate the difficulties in persuading elementary teachers and parents of elementary students of the practicality of this approach, but it does represent a logical application of the principle that reading and writing should be fully integrated with content.

While these proposals appear to favor an academic ideology (they stress content area learning as the major end of the elementary curriculum, including its language arts program), the principles that underlie it can be used to support other ideologies as well. Clearly it is the ends that are in dispute—academics favoring familiarity with classical literature and history, utilitarians favoring job-related literature and knowledge, romantics favoring personal literature and knowledge, and so on. Could an elementary curriculum be organized in such a way that students read and wrote for all of these ends? In other words, could these ends be balanced in such a way that some of the reading was academic, some utilitarian, some romantic, some cognitive-developmental, and some emancipatory? The complaint against a literacy skills ideology was that it represented none of the other ideologies' purposes for reading and writing: The present proposal ensures that there are genuine ends for language arts instruction, and that legitimately different ends are represented in the curriculum.

Balancing different ends might be accomplished in a variety of ways. Romantic goals could be stressed during the first two years of school, making the transition from home to school as natural as possible, and helping students to acquire reading and writing abilities within the context of highly meaningful and personal literature (for reading) and topics (for writing). As students become confident in their reading and writing abilities, and as they develop the capacity to "decenter," their curriculum might draw more from other ideologies (e.g., introduce students to a variety of genres of literature, including classical, contemporary, and didactic; balance different instructional approaches, such that, for example, students' own responses to literature are integrated with traditional "canonical" interpretations; encourage, perhaps challenge, students to raise their own consciousness with respect to stereotypes, to the representation of minorities, and to their own status as a reader and writer).

Another approach might be to forge a better balance between these ideologies right from the start, such that students are brought up within a framework that keeps the ideologies in tension with one another. For example, Gagnon (1988) has suggested that kindergartners should study "Reaching Out To Times Past" rather than "My Family"—a shift from what is called "the ever-expanding curriculum" to one in which the "ethical traditions of the major world civilizations" are studied. Why not study both of these, using the contrasts between the two to better understand both the present and the past? In studying literature, why should even the youngest students not be exposed to the best of classical and contemporary literature, and at the same time be encouraged also to read what they find enjoyable and rewarding?

PRACTICAL PROBLEMS IN REFORMING THE
ELEMENTARY LANGUAGE ARTS CURRICULUM

Choosing Between Competing Ideologies

There is no shortage of proposals for reforming elementary language arts programs. Indeed, all of the ideologies have associated with them either proposals or programs aimed at reforming traditional approaches.[4] The problem is this: How are teachers or schools to decide between these competing reform proposals? And once they have decided, how will they implement reforms? And once implemented, how will the reforms be maintained?

Choosing between competing ideologies is not an easy task, but it is also one that most teachers and schools do not consciously engage in; it is doubtful that many are even aware that what they have chosen as an approach to language arts is in fact a choice between competing ideologies. Indeed, my experience in elementary schools, both as a researcher and language arts consultant, leads me to believe that the majority of schools (even those that portray themselves as having a consistent and widely-shared set of beliefs for the teaching of language arts) have represented within them a variety of different philosophies. While one would expect teachers to have different philosophies from one another, it seems that teachers sometimes have competing philosophies within their language arts program: For example, a romantic (top-down) approach to writing, where children are ungrouped, free to choose their own writing topics, and work on editing skills solely in the context of their own compositions, contrasted to a literacy skills (bottom-up) approach to reading, where children are grouped according to reading level, read from a basal text, and work on skills in isolation. In some cases, this conflict can be explained in terms of a language arts program that is evolving from a literacy skills philosophy and has yet to change all the procedures; in most, my interpretation is that the two sets of practices (one for reading, one for writing) are simply two different approaches that a teacher has happened to choose for the teaching of reading and writing, and that the philosophical inconsistencies simply are not recognized.

In thinking about which ideology or ideologies should guide a language arts program, teachers should recognize that these ideologies represent legitimate ways of conceiving the ends and means of elementary education, even though proponents of particular ideologies routinely portray other approaches as illegitimate:

> Most theories associated with a subject like reading are simply prejudices; and like prejudices, these theories have a strong immunity to facts or the basic cannons (*sic*) of science . . . the quintessence of inadequate theories is one promulgated by Kenneth Goodman. . . . Goodman's theoretical contribution is the 'Whole Language' approach for teaching reading. The description of the theory is replete with romantic terms that apparently make teachers feel good all over. These nice words imply that anyone who fails to adopt whole language apparently doesn't care about children. . . . Where is the evidence that this approach works? There is none, despite the fact that the article quoted above [Altweger, Edelsky, and Flores (1987)] is followed by nearly a full page of references. (Engelmann, 1988)

> Let's not beat around the bush. Basal readers, workbooks, skills sequences, and practice materials that fragment the process are unacceptable to whole language teachers. Their presentation of language phenomena is unscientific, and they steal teachers' and learners' time away from productive reading and writing. Many whole language

teachers don't use basals at all, but build their programs around children's literature, often in thematic units. Some teachers salvage what
they can—whatever good children's literature there is in their
basals—to support the whole language program. But some programs—among them so-called mastery learning programs—are so
rigidly based on arbitrary skill drills and rigid pre-test, test, post-test
sequences that the program is at odds with whole language criteria.
Furthermore, rigid programs monopolize school time and turn
progress into progress-through-the-program, rather than progress in
real learning. Teachers are reduced to robots: technicians acting out
someone else's script. In fact, such tightly controlled programs are
often based on assumptions of teacher incompetence. Whole language
teachers have the right and obligation to reject them, on behalf of the
kids they teach and the professionalism they embody. (Goodman,
1986; p. 29)

From Engelmann's perspective, which rests heavily on assumptions
about direct instruction of reading skills, Goodman's approach is unsci-
entific because neither Goodman nor others supporting a "whole language" philosophy can produce the kinds of evidence that direct instruction supporters would accept as proof of its effectiveness. From
Goodman's perspective, direct instruction is inadequate not because of
poor results but rather because it takes a particularly narrow view of
what constitutes reading and writing. Clearly Goodman and Engelmann have quite different views on what constitutes literacy (i.e., what
are its components), how literacy is acquired, and how literacy should
be taught. Both are extremely persuasive advocates of their own particular approaches, and there are large numbers of teachers and schools
employing one or other of these approaches. Beneath the rhetoric on
both sides lie legitimate differences in the ends and means of elementary language arts instruction, and teachers need to take this into account as they examine their options for reform.

In elementary schools I have studied, I have seen two approaches to
choosing options, with several variations: One is adopting a single philosophy, the other multiple philosophies. The *single philosophy* approach
is typically driven by the philosophy of an external consultant, or a
member of the school's administration or teaching staff. In this approach, the school adopts (or adapts) a particular ideology, and sets
about implementing it. There may be variations in implementation—for
example, teachers may simply be required to adopt the new procedures,
or they may be encouraged to do so—but the goal is the same, namely
that the school will change its language arts instruction to conform to
the principles set out by the single philosophy. The program may be

presented as a set of specific practices (as in Distar), or as a set of guiding principles with examples of practice (as in Whole Language); it may require teachers to attend a series of highly structured workshops or set up study groups so that teachers can work out the teaching details for themselves. The advantage of a single philosophy approach is that it has been defined, and typically has been tried out elsewhere so that teachers can have some confidence in the approach's effectiveness, and learn how it should or can be done from those who have designed or used it. One of the problems with a single philosophy approach, however (especially where teacher "ownership" is an important principle of reform), is how teachers who have a different teaching philosophy are to be treated. Should they be required to bring their philosophy and practice into line with the program, or else leave? In most cases, teachers who do not adopt new procedures are simply left alone (they are often cut off from professional development opportunities other than those that support the new program); but leaving their programs intact seriously undermines the degree to which a school can claim it has reformed its curriculum. Single philosophy approaches also tend to cut themselves off from research and practice that do not support their own practices, creating instead their own literature, their own professional conferences, even their own publishing houses: While these maintain the integrity of the philosophy, they also stifle legitimate debate and polarize positions held by competing philosophies.

A *multiple philosophy* approach comes in at least two forms. The first is eclectic—this is an approach that recognizes the variety of philosophies and tries to represent each of them, either by deliberately sampling from a range of philosophies, or by giving individual teachers the freedom to choose their own teaching techniques. In one elementary school I studied, teachers are required to use a variety of teaching techniques drawn from quite different philosophies—the rationale being that by betting on all the horses, as it were, the school's language arts program is always a winner. By the same token, of course, it is always a loser. Techniques in vogue are simply added to an array of techniques that derive from all kinds of different assumptions about literacy and learning—and who will ever know which of these techniques were successful? In trying to represent the major instructional philosophies, it represents none of them adequately. If teachers are given complete freedom to choose their own teaching techniques, multiple philosophies will certainly be represented, but then the question arises: Will a laissez-faire language arts policy almost guarantee literacy experiences that are too haphazard and unpredictable for a school to want to be held accountable for? One rather conservative form of eclecticism is represented by the basal series; they are slow to incorporate new techniques, but they do try to represent the major competing philosophies. Eclectic approaches do avoid the potential narrowness of single philosophies, but they can create problems of narrowness and particularly shallowness by dipping into techniques. More importantly, they fail to synthesize competing philosophies.

A second form of a multiple philosophy approach is represented by an elementary school I have been working with that is trying to establish its own language arts philosophy by examining its practices and beliefs and synthesizing these with views of others in the professional literature. Rather than subscribe to a single philosophy (which would necessitate denying the beliefs of several members of the faculty who have quite divergent views on the teaching of reading and writing), the teachers have articulated what attributes they think an eighth grade reader and writer should have, and have sought out what seem to them, and to others in the field, the most appropriate pedagogical techniques. This approach might be thought of as eclectic, but it differs from the eclecticism described above in that it is an attempt to build a coherent set of practices, for kindergarten to eighth grade, such that some guarantees can be made about the literacy experiences of students who attend the school. It draws from both the direct instruction and whole language literatures, as well as others (e.g., literary criticism). The advantage of such an approach is that it not only respects the experience and knowledge of teachers, but also accommodates those with different philosophical views of language arts. The disadvantage lies primarily in the amount of time and effort that inevitably accompanies such a careful examination of the alternatives.

Obstacles To Be Overcome

Whether teachers adopt a single or multiple philosophy approach to reforming language arts, there are major obstacles in their path. One of the most difficult for reformers to accept is that most reforms ultimately fail:

> The major studies of curriculum reform have shown that where training, the introduction of materials, vertical political solidarity and staff and administrative commitment are brought together, there is considerable movement. Gradually, the school returns to the normative patterns which characterize most American schools and the innovations lose their steam. The problem is a worldwide one. (Hersh, et. al., 1981: quoted in Carnine, 1988)

Carnine (1988) has identified several methods that are used to cause innovations to fail: They can be discredited, delayed, distorted, or simply discontinued. Discrediting can be accomplished by "attributing (the innovation's) success to unique factors not found in other settings; objecting to the values represented by the innovation; questioning, criticizing, and ignoring any evaluation that judges the innovation to be effective; or even claiming that the innovative practice has already been incorporated into current practices" (p. 63). In a sense, discrediting is a natural defense mounted by teachers or administrators who feel that a hostile philosophy is being imposed on them. Carnine assumes they discredit even in the face of overwhelming evidence of an innovation's effectiveness, but they may also be discrediting on the basis of a genuine philosophical difference of opinion. Delaying an innovation is another technique, easily accomplished in large, bureaucratic school districts where implementing any curriculum reform takes a long time. In one school district I studied, teachers routinely ignored curriculum mandates they did not agree with, claiming that by the time anyone caught up with them, the district would have moved on to another mandate. Even in small schools, innovations can often easily be delayed by simply not engaging in them: After all, what are the penalties for not using particular techniques, and anyway, who will find out? Distorting an innovation comes about by making extensive modifications to it, such that it no longer even resembles the original design. Discontinuing an innovation is typically not difficult to do, especially given the high turnover of administrators and the lack of commitment to maintaining reforms in public education.

Carnine's analysis points to some reasons why innovations fail, especially when they are opposed. Innovations also do not work quite the way their designers had in mind for other reasons, too. First, teachers vary enormously in their willingness and ability to change, and in the changes they actually make. On a Friday, one teacher comes into contact with a philosophy that contradicts everything she has believed in and taught for fifteen years, and by Monday she is teaching from a new philosophical position. Another teacher, upon hearing that her school is adopting a new approach to language arts, and not wishing to be "left out," simply relabels her existing practices with the new terminology. Other teachers take five to ten years to effect a transition from one philosophy to another, because it takes that long to work through the implications of new ideas for teaching routines. Some teachers simply resist any change whatsoever. Long-term projects have made me aware of how unmindful consultants and curriculum developers are of how difficult it is for teachers to handle both the day-to-day teaching of reading and writing, and at the same time to reformulate their approach to language arts instruction. A full daily teaching schedule, school gover-

nance obligations, and family commitments understandably take prece-
dence over sustained professional reading. University consultants are
used to thinking about instructional philosophies and reflecting on practice, and they read deeply and widely—they also do not teach from
eight to three each day. Given what teachers are already committed to,
it should be no surprise that they sometimes need several years to accommodate new ways of thinking about reading and writing. Unfortunately, by the time they have done so, their school district may well
have moved on to another innovation.

Second, consultants routinely overestimate their impact on elementary language arts improvements, frequently equating their view of
what a program should be like with what the school accomplished
while they were a consultant to it. Schools are easily converted to a particular approach under the direct guidance of a persuasive consultant,
but the test is what is left of that approach three or four years after the
consultant has departed. I have been struck by the number of schools in
which hardly a trace of the influence of nationally-known consultants is
evident only after two years. Ironically, some of these projects ultimately fail because they were so successful: Teachers and administrators suddenly find that what they now know is either directly mar-
ketable (as independent consultants, or as more senior staff in other
districts), or could be if they pursued advanced degrees (as students in
the consultant's host university), leaving too few of the "reformed" staff
knowledgeable enough, nor perhaps powerful enough, to continue the
approach. If the reforms never really permeated the entire school, those
who either resisted the reforms or who preferred other approaches
could simply pick up where they left off.

Third, we need to clarify what is meant by the success of a language
arts reform. Traditionally, a program is declared successful if its students make better gains in reading or writing achievement tests than
control groups over a period of a year. It is not difficult to demonstrate
the superiority of an experimental group over a control group, especially if the pretest scores are low. Also, reading and writing achievement tests are very narrow in their definition of reading and writing.
But there are other considerations, too. The first is that success should
not be measured solely in terms of year-to-year gains, but rather in
terms of the cumulative effects of a particular approach. What is important is not whether a child has made such-and-such a gain in a given
year (especially if that was a year in which an innovative program was
introduced) but what effects a program has over the course of elementary school. This turns out to be very difficult to do, because a large
number of variables comes into play in determining the literacy out-

comes of elementary school. For one thing, there is no such thing as *an* elementary curriculum: The teaching and learning experiences over the course of a child's elementary school years are constantly in flux. Teachers are not constants—some are brand new, settling into routines; others are experienced but are trying out new techniques, some have settled into a rut. In any given year, a teacher might be having an off semester, as family, illness, or other professional commitments intrude. The child gets a succession of one year-long field trips with a teacher, and those experiences are carried forward into the next grade, influencing the next year's experiences. A child's literacy experiences are made up of a variety of encounters, both in and out of school. When we talk about the success of a particular approach to the teaching of reading and/or writing, we need to be able to describe what it was that students encountered, and what, cumulatively, was gained from those encounters. We are a long way from being able to state confidently that if a particular approach were used, be it direct instruction or whole language in its design, that particular outcomes could be guaranteed: We have little idea, given present evaluative techniques, about what kinds of literacy experiences elementary students have engaged in, kindergarten through eighth grade, let alone what the outcomes are. It may be wise to argue for particular approaches to literacy instruction on philosophical grounds, rather than on the basis of measured success, at least until measurement of literary experiences becomes a great deal more sophisticated than it is at present.

Clearly there are major obstacles to reform, and they seem to work equally effectively against innovations from all ideological perspectives. Given the educational establishment's lack of patience with long-term projects, and with complex solutions to complex problems, these obstacles are likely to remain as serious challenges to those who would reform elementary language arts programs.

CONCLUSION

In this essay, I have tried to make a constructive response to the current rash of critiques of the elementary literacy curriculum. Rather than defend existing practices, I have used the opportunity to reflect on the implications of the critiques for reconceptualizing language arts instruction. It is clear from the discussion on educational ideologies that there are quite different—yet legitimate—notions of what counts as reading and writing, and what are the proper ends of elementary schooling. I have suggested some ways in which teachers and schools might address themselves to the concerns raised by different ideologies' notions about literacy and literacy instruction: I conclude that elementary schools cannot properly meet these concerns without a major restructuring of their elementary language arts curriculum.

It is clear that maintaining a largely separate language arts program in elementary school (separate in two senses—separate components within language arts, and a language arts program separate from content areas such as social studies and science) is no longer the only viable option for elementary schools. If we are to restore content to the elementary curriculum—and I think we should—then we either will have to lengthen the school day,[5] or will have to find ways to make the various components of language arts fit together better, and make language arts fit better with content areas. I have proposed several ways to pursue the latter course, including establishing a better balance within traditional components of language arts, and between language arts and content areas; a theme-centered approach in which content drives all language arts instruction and experiences; and an approach in which language arts is dropped entirely as a separate entity and is fully incorporated within content areas. While I do not underestimate the challenges—the half-life of educational innovations is extremely short—I am quite optimistic that if different views on literacy can be synthesized rather than polarized, genuine progress can be made. At the very least, we need to continue to explore our options for reforming elementary language arts, even if the changes we make do not turn out to be as permanent as we hoped.

This is not an apology for an eclectic approach to elementary language arts, rather a plea for greater awareness of the legitimacy of different conceptions of what it means to be literate, and of different pedagogies to achieve literacy. Our own approaches to language arts can only be strengthened by a clearer understanding of why others take a different path.

The University at Albany

10

Reconstructing the Classroom: Literacy and the Problem of Choice

LIL BRANNON

In response to a college placement essay topic, "Smoking should be banned in public places. Argue for or against," Danny writes in the fifty minutes allotted to him:

> Fifth National Bank, Adams and Alexrio's are public places that entertain in the most elegant and fashionable style. The sofisicated atmosphere pronounce for enduce an unwimeing sprit of the soul, searching, in the mis of poetic ventilation, smoking should not be banned in public places.

Danny, in effect, is writing for his life, a life at this moment he can only imagine.[1] He must construct needs of readers he has never, and probably will never meet, in order to gain access to a conversation he can only barely conceive. The imaginative will that gives Danny the courage to try to enter the college world is tempered, even constrained, by his lack of control over the conventions of language and processes of composing that most entering college freshmen take for granted. Danny's text is, after all, insufficient for that world. He could produce less than fifty words in the time given him to write. The second sentence is virtually incomprehensible. His text lacks clear indications of sentence boundaries, of spelling conventions, and of organizational control. Danny needs help if he is going to "make it" in the world of the academy: help in finding themes and in constructing and elaborating arguments, help in controlling the language practices that now place him on the far boundaries of academic life. The question, then, becomes not "what needs to be done?" but "where to begin?"

In most academic programs designed to help students like Danny, the first priority of instruction is to socialize him into the language practices of the educated class by attacking the most obvious of barriers, the stigmatizing paucity of conventional language use. A teacher working with Danny, then, would begin with sentence structure, the location of

165

nouns and verbs, and in placing ideas in a logical, grammatical order. The teacher's aim would be to bring Danny's English "up to par," to make Danny's acts of language more in line with those expected of college students. It's difficult to complain about that. After all, for Danny to engage fully in education as we now have it, he must become socialized into those practices. The problem is more in how this socialization should happen and whether the emphasis on grammatical skill is the best route. Yet the question of "how" is often not posed because of the "commonsensical" conception of literacy that dominates American education. Functional literacy—the ability to write a simple sentence, fill out a job application, write a business letter—has conceptual power because surely, people reason, anyone should be able to do such simple tasks. Teaching grammar looks like a logical starting point and has been so much a part of the American educational scene that it appears almost rooted in the world. And this "self-evident" quality of the functionalist argument makes its limitations very difficult to reveal,[2] closing off other potentially generative conceptions of literacy that might offer students like Danny more advantage.

Berger and Luckman (1967) call this "self-evident knowledge" our "knowledge of everyday life"—the unselfconscious knowledge that we live by, the knowledge that guides the "self-evident" routines of life in the school or community—what appears to be commonsensical—what everybody already knows. Knowledge of everyday life consists of the experiences that parents accept as part of being parents or teachers accept as part of what it means to be a teacher. It is knowledge accepted without critique.

Berger and Luckman contrast "knowledge of everyday life" with "theoretical knowledge"—our discursive, self-conscious knowledge that is subject to examination and change, knowledge represented in books or academic conversations or in professional journals. Theoretical knowledge is more easily malleable because we see it as knowledge created by ourselves. Knowledge of everyday life, however, is much more difficult to change precisely because we forget that it is human. When we live by this certain knowledge—when we take it for granted—it takes the shape of "how things are in the world." When teachers accept as "fact" that students must be tested, for example, they have made testing a permanent feature of the life world of the school. While they may complain that such testing adds to competition in the classroom, that it can give a distorted view of some students, that tests fail to measure accurately this or that skill, they will not raise the question, "Why test at all?" precisely because it appears necessary to "measure" in some way just what students have learned; so necessary, in fact, that abolishing testing appears impossible. Educators might change their theories of testing, always seeking more humane or more accurate modes, yet the fact of testing remains, impervious to question or critique.

The obvious advantage of our knowledge of everyday life is that we don't have to puzzle over every single choice that we make throughout our day. Such questioning would, of course, render us incapable of action. The disadvantage, however, is that we forget that we are making choices and, therefore, lose our flexibility to change when there may be good reason to do so. Our concepts become ossified; we can imagine no alternatives. Reflecting on action—theorizing—scrutinizing the commonsense knowledge of our daily routines in light of theoretical alternatives recreates the possibility of choice and therefore the possibility of change. Perceiving alternatives, however, is very difficult not only because of the force of traditional values but also because the language we use to share our understanding of the world itself forces us to think of what we do in particular ways. When we talk of "correcting" or "marking" or "grading" student writing, for instance, we have closed off the possibility that we might read it as an interested adult and respond to it as a interested reader and not as an authority or a judge.

Perceiving alternatives, then, is impeded by the language we use to construct our "normal" understandings of what it means to be literate. According to Jerome Bruner (1986), we grow accustomed to "the way things are" in schools because we have named those events in particular ways. Our language shapes those events and over time continues to shape them, making those events seem ordinary, making daily habits seem inevitable and not a human construction. I was reminded of Bruner's caution when I was working with a small group of elementary teachers who were attempting to change the ways they were teaching writing. The teachers had learned a new approach to writing instruction, one that challenged functional literacy practices, through a series of in-service workshops conducted by well respected leaders in composition, and the teachers felt comfortable with and excited about the strategies they learned for implementing their new writing program. The teachers wanted to use whatever method might be helpful to assist the development of children and so began to use the ideas from the workshops, allowing me to observe them as they did so. What I noticed was that they continued to teach writing virtually in the same ways they had traditionally taught (in other words, functional practices were enforced). The new strategies were simply superimposed onto the normal routines of the classroom. More problematic for me, though, was that those traditional methods were used more energetically and argued for more forcefully with students in the lower ability groups. The teachers were impeded from implementing new theories in their regular or gifted and talented classrooms by the ways they constructed their commonsense knowledge of schooling, and they failed altogether to see the connection between the theory and the remedial classroom, because the language "problems" that students exhibited seemed too pressing to permit any other kind of instruction.

Although the teachers were troubled by the fact that remedial students always remained in remediation, that all their work never assisted students into the "mainstream," they rationalized their actions by continuing to react to students' "grammatical mistakes," not questioning the fact that most of the remedial students were minorities and/or the poor. In many cases, the teachers failed to acknowledge that the students were even using the English language at all, in effect denying students the language they brought to the school. By saying that the students had "no language," the teachers could begin at square one—with nouns and verbs and adjectives, each taught "properly." Their testing system showed that students were "progressing" toward "standard" English, but never fast enough to catch up with the students who came to the classroom already speaking in language patterns characteristic of the middle class, language patterns that catagorized a child as more intelligent and better educated, not in need of remediation, not in need of finding a language. While remedial students were spending time on grammar drills, the other students were reading books and going on field trips. While remedial students were copying words from the board and filling in dittoed exercises, other students were composing stories and discussing their scientific experiments.

The powerful force of functional literacy constructed the ways teachers talked about the students and their needs, which in turn shaped what they noticed happening to those students during the school day. The insistence on "proper" language first distorted the potential for any other kind of instruction: imaginative exploration, for example. Perhaps this illustration from one of my visits to a fourth grade remedial classroom will show how difficult it is to argue for, even for teachers to see the necessity for, choosing different avenues for the teaching of reading and writing. In this class session, the aim of the lesson was to have students write an imaginative story approximately a paragraph in length that followed a logical sequence of events. The story was to be written as part of a schoolwide writing contest that occurred every six weeks during the academic year. Every student in the school had to submit an essay that was scored holistically using the statewide writing assessment scoring guide. The teachers got practice in using the scoring guide, and the principal insured that every student wrote at least one essay every marking period. The teachers, however, found the contest to be an imposition that interrupted their normal classroom activities, and that finally had very little instructional value for the children. On this day, the students were to write an imaginative story, and the children were to use the following sentence as the story starter: "I opened the door and I saw . . ." The teacher began the class by writing the story starter on the board and explaining to the students that they were going to write a story for the Writers' Gallery contest. In order to help the children decide what to say in their stories, the teacher decided to have a few children get up from their desks, open the classroom door, and say what they saw. She thought this talk would be a heuristic for the children—a stimulus to their imaginations—that would spur other children to make their own imaginative leaps. The first child got up and walked toward the door while the teacher read: "I opened the door and I saw . . .". The child opened the door and said, "I see the lockers; I see the hallway." The teacher told the child that his response was not what she had in mind. While the child walked back to his seat disappointed that he had not understood the teacher, the teacher walked over to me and whispered, "Now what would you do? These children simply lack imagination."

Because the child had failed to move beyond the literal reporting of what he saw, the teacher's belief that the child could not imagine was reinforced. In fact, the story-starter itself implied that the teachers or at least the contest officials believed the children needed some external nudge to get the imagination started. From my vantage point, however, the child's response did not seem at all out of place. Almost every day those children are in the classroom, the use of language is restricted to copying, memorizing, and reciting. They are penalized if they do not follow explicit instructions. The classroom, in other words, is grounded in the here and now. On this particular day when the children attempted to engage in the everyday routines of schooling they were penalized because their understanding of school reality did not extend to the particular practices their teacher had in mind, practices that in fact depended on their perceiving the inappropriateness of their customary ways of responding to school demands. They had available to them, in the teacher's commands to perform in certain ways, an understanding of acceptable behavior; but because the practice intended by the teacher's new commands was inaccessible to them, their response was customary, which then confirmed the teacher's beliefs that they were "unimaginative" and fit only for the rote learning that formed so large a part of their school experience. The teacher's "common knowledge" that students in low-ability classes need certain kinds of instruction and cannot respond to other kinds was confirmed.

I do not wish to indict teachers. Giving children opportunity to en-gage their imaginations is much more difficult than merely mustering the desire to do so. Teachers are, in fact, struggling to educate their students into the values and educational customs of their communities, and functionalism supports many existing social values, specifically those associated with the hierarchical and meritocratic structure of the American workplace. What can be more logical, given the constraints of American economic life, than grouping students by practical "skill levels" that follow similar groupings beyond school? In literacy programs focused on the "least able" (who also tend to be at the bottom of the so-cioeconomic "ladder"), students are perceived to be "slow" and "unimaginative" and, therefore, instruction remains concrete and en-tirely referential, regulatory and unimaginative. The teacher tells the students what they are to know. The students' only obligation is to take that knowledge down and be able to retrieve it on call. The children are rewarded daily for paying attention, following directions, being neat and polite, and copying and recording literally what they see and hear. These routines of daily classroom life are preoccupied with the literal re-call of information that fosters subordination to authority and discipline, the very values necessary to maintain a "good" working-class life. Meanwhile, students outside of the "lower groups" (i.e. those who tend to come from more privileged positions in the socioeconomic hierarchy) have greater opportunity to read and write, to engage in classroom dis-cussion of their ideas, to develop exploratory and imaginative uses of language. Their curriculum honors the myth of functionalism—hence the basal readers and competency exams. But it does not restrict them in the same ways, recognizing that they are being prepared for managerial positions, which require not docility and a limited capacity to work from other people's directions, but some flexibility of mind, a knack for problem solving, and a capacity for administrative self-direction.

A measure of the truth of this interrelationship between functional-ist curricula and the world of work is the fact that there is remarkably little student movement from level to level within the curricular divi-sions of school life. While functional programs, featuring sequential pro-gressions of skill, create the illusion of progress by documenting how a child is mastering each distinctive competence, in fact it allows few chil-dren ever to escape the programs to which they are assigned. The slow learner in grade school enters the remedial program of high school and the basic-skill program of the junior college, effectively maintaining the power structures now in place. While such superficial "progress" from grade to grade, school to school, fails to move most people beyond the literal-mindedness that remediation is designed to encourage, it does prepare them for a life of obedience, of following orders, of repetitious work. Meanwhile, the overwhelming majority of gifted and talented students in high school, who come primarily from upper-middle- and upper-class families, go on to the top colleges and universities, and finally take their place in mid- and top management positions.

In short, functional literacy does not produce a nation of critically alert readers and writers because it is not intended to do so. The outcome of functional priorities is that students who enter school already practicing the uses of language sanctioned by schools move ahead, while those who happen to use less prestigious dialects of English or come from homes where the activities of reading and writing are not particularly valued are channeled into remedial or vocational programs. This sorting system is then rationalized by the testing industry, which appeals to American confidence in objectivity and technical know-how in order to "explain" why some students do very well while others seem not to prosper no matter how many "second chances" they receive, no matter how many times they make one more try at mastering "the basics." In this fashion, schools maintain the status quo, albeit at cost of leaving unfulfilled their extravagant promises of offering opportunity for all students to reach their intellectual potential.

Because of the self-interested complexity of our educational system, its "commonsensical" dependency on functionalism, and the elaborate testing mechanisms in place to insure that functional priorities are enforced, students who depend on schooling to acquire the abilities to read and write are carefully prohibited from the independence of mind that alternative forms of literacy might encourage. That's what is wrong with, or at least limiting about, functionalism. Students' inability to perform well on functional tasks appears rooted in their own ignorance, not in a conceptual system which not only stifles their capacities as readers and writers but also fails to demonstrate to them the power that such practices might have in their lives. Limiting literacy to "grammatical competence" and designing a sequential curriculum based on the mastery of skills, while it appears streamlined, efficient, and accountable, does not offer students insight into how writers and readers actually use those abilities when composing, nor does it give them the motive to want to learn to read and write—which stems, in large part, from a critical understanding of the potentially transforming power that literacy can have. For students whose home environments have already encouraged reading and writing abilities, functional curricular rituals are harmful enough, creating exasperation and boredom. But they become a serious problem, indeed, for students who are dependent on schooling to provide their context for literacy, particularly when the curriculum seldom asks them to participate in literate activities. For them, skills become an illusory means to an end—and for too many of them, these skills become barriers rather than access to literacy.

The conceptual innovations in literacy instruction over the last two decades that have begun to define alternative educational goals and methods are based on a competing definition of what constitutes language learning. "Critical literacy" offers a challenge to the traditional functional view of reading and writing by conceiving of literacy as a transforming process, a political act of naming the world for oneself, an ability to think critically by using reading and writing as a means of intervening in one's own social surroundings. Reading and writing, then, are not simply the mastery of skills, but entail the quality of human consciousness as well. Reading and writing are symbolic acts, not merely the processes of decoding and encoding, but the ability to comprehend and create texts that manifest new ways of being and perceiving the world.[3] Yet for critical literacy to have much impact on the ways students are taught to read and write will mean a fundamental reconceptualizing not only of the everyday world of the classroom but of the social role that schools have typically played. The most important change is in conceiving of "knowledge" as an activity, not a condition or state. If one believes that the act of "knowing" is the engagement of the individual mind in the making of connections among the materials of her experience, the classroom must be a place for dialogue and the pursuit of individual needs and concerns. Teaching, then, can no longer be a one-way transmitting of ideas, but must become a conversation, an interaction among peers and teacher, an exploration, a process of learning. Literacy defined in these terms, where "dialogue" becomes the dominant metaphor for teaching, would have to be the concern of all faculty members rather than the domain of the remedial teacher, for the act of composing is part of the activity of coming to know a subject.

If one believes that writing and reading are not prior to the understanding of content but integrally connected with it, the difficulty of teaching within a functionalist conception becomes apparent. When composing means the constructing and organizing of ideas in order for writers to express something that matters to them to someone who matters to them, teachers would need opportunity and time to read and respond to student work and to write to and interact with their students. (Within a functionalist perspective, English teachers can work with 150 students a day, simply because they are expected only to lecture and correct.) When literacy becomes the ability to create and understand symbolic meanings constructed as verbal texts, critical literacy is the ability to construct the world through written language and the ability to reconstruct the world through reflection and critique. Critical literacy moves beyond narrowly prescribed incremental instruction by over-looking ethnic and class dialect differences and by offering students the power to "speak," requiring only that they engage in the active constru-ing and constructing of their world. Such acts of composition also re-quire individuals to reflect on the statements they make, to be account-able for the material of their experiences, to see that they structure and are structured by their encounters with language. Critical literacy opens up to all children the imaginative, the creative, and the critical; it offers them the possibility of engaging with ideas and people whom they can only encounter through the medium of text. In this perspective, they are no longer restricted to the here and now, the immediate idea, but are re-quired to explore, to expand, to push beyond the ordinary, to critique the complexity of their experiences. Literate individuals in this perspec-tive do not simply encode and decode, but come to know that texts are situated historically, and therefore can be interpreted and reinterpreted, examined and challenged. In this model of literacy, texts and the con-struction of texts become powerful means of knowing and changing the world.

Danny, the student whose text began this essay, was lucky enough to have a teacher devoted to critical literacy.[4] Her response to Danny's exam was to have a conference with him where she invited him to talk about his text. She asked him what he intended to say. Below is a por-tion of a transcript where Danny talks with his teacher about the prob-lematic second sentence:

> Teacher: Dan, would you tell me about your first sentence. How does it relate to the exam question?
>
> Danny: They are all public places. They allow smoking. They allow drinking. There is enough space for one to enjoy.
>
> Teacher: OK. Well, I became confused in the second sentence. I'm just not sure what you mean by "pronounce to induce."
>
> Danny: It's like when you go somewhere, you know, and you get in there and you just be sitting there and then somebody'll start play-ing the music and you start feeling tipsy, you know . . . You start get-ting grooving . . . it pulls you into it, you know, the music, you know, the people, you see the people, so it's comin' all at you, you know, and so den you accept it and den you just absorb yourself into it and den you just relax . . . here I am.
>
> Teacher: So is that what you mean by "an unwinding spirit"?
>
> Danny: Yeah, I mean you move in. You're around socializing. If you found somebody to dance with, you go dancing, you know, if

you're talking, you're alive, you, you're spirited and you be sexy.

Teacher: So tell me about "searching."

Danny: That's like you (pause) that's like when you first walk in a place and you can feel the music and you can hear it at the same time but it don't do anything to you. You just sit there, you know. Then from all of a sudden, I guess from watching girls come by, from watching how they move and all that, you know, you start to wondering, you know, then you want to move and say I want to dance with her and you start to pick out your certain people.

Teacher: OK. I think I'm catching on now. "In the mis of poetic ventilation"?

Danny: Candlelights, you know, candlelights. Some clubs when you walk in they have candlelights burning on the table or when you get to the table a waitress will come along, and she'll light a little candlelight, you know, and you'll be sitting across from whoever you're sitting across with, the light glowing up on their face and that seems to have some type of stimulation.

Teacher: "Ventilation?"

Danny: 'Cause the air's so pleasant, soothing, it's so . . . so . . . it's responding between two people, like a (like a) not verbally understood but a mentally understood that (um) I want to socialize with ya, I want to be with ya, to understand, to appreciate, yeah, all this air between us, baby, just you and me.

Teacher: So your argument is?

Danny: I think a smoker needs to come in and say, you know, I need a break to (uh, to uh, to uh) get my composure back. Uh, you may dance four or five times and you just want to kick back and light up (makes a puffing sound). Oh I'm having a good time, so, you know, that's why smoking is there.

By allowing Danny to express his intentions through conversation, the teacher could better understand Danny's essay and thereby assist him as a writer. Her first priority for Danny was fluency. She wanted Danny to use his gift of description and his imaginative energy to construct what he wished to express. Danny's teacher asked that he "free" write, without worrying about spelling or sentence structure or paragraph form. He already possessed a powerful language, an eye for detail, a sense of humor. She wanted him to work from those strengths as he moved from fluency to clarity of expression. Correction would come much later, when Danny had confidence enough to explore and confront the institutional barriers to dialects other than those used by the white middle class. Danny's teacher believed that the motive to say something within the conventions of academic discourse would come only after the students believed they had something to say.

Another teacher working in a prekindergarten program enabled her students to write, even before they knew how to spell or read.[5] She engaged her students from the start with stories that she read to them and stories that the children presented to the class. The children wrote daily and "read" their work to her and to their peers. Pieces from one of her student's portfolios are located in figures 10.1 to 10.5. Figure 10.1 shows the teacher that Jessica has been read to, in fact knows that writing fills up a page moving from the left to the right. Later that month (figure 10.2) Jessica writes, "I love Casey," her new best friend. By October Jessica has written her first extended piece and is able to read it to the teacher, who writes underneath Jessica's handwriting the words she intends to express. As the year progresses, because of the literacy environment prepared by the teacher and her attitude toward critical literacy, Jessica is able to compose more fluently and, incidently, more correctly as she goes. Jessica's emergent literacy is a powerful confirmation of a critical literacy perspective. Jessica is able to write, to express herself, to construct her understandings of the world, without penalty and in conversation with her teacher. Such an enabling environment gave Jessica opportunity and motive to feel a part of the world of words and ideas.

No matter the successes of their students, teachers who advocate critical literacy meet a predictably intense resistance. Yet through the

FIGURE 10.1

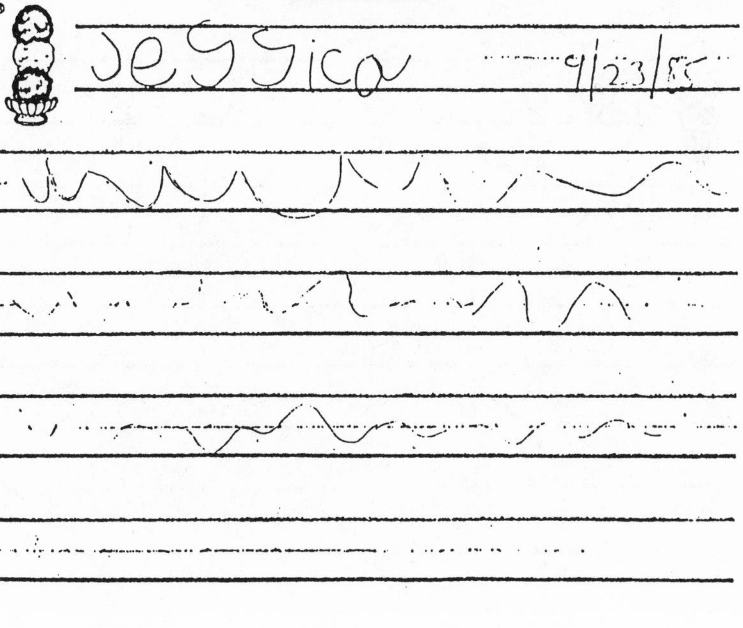

FIGURE 10.2

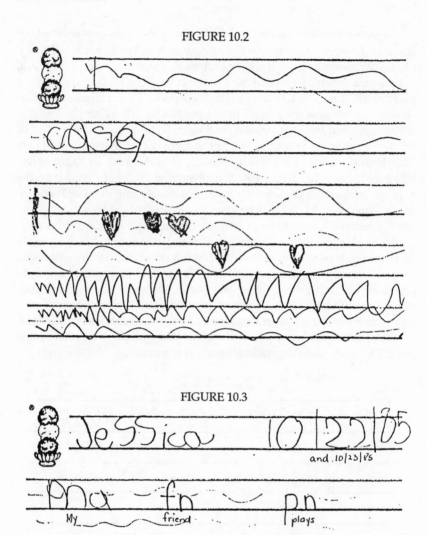

FIGURE 10.3

FIGURE 10.4

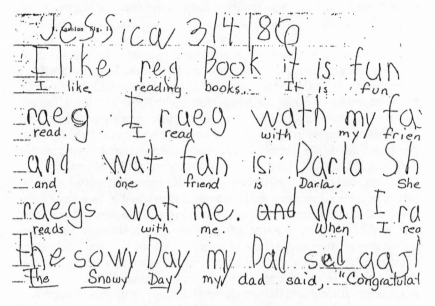

Jessica 3/4/86

I like reg Book it is fun
I   like   reading books.   It   is   fun

raeg. I raeg wath my fa
read.   I   read   with   my   frien

and wat fan is: Darla Sh
and   one   friend   is   Darla.   She

raegs wat me. and wan I ra
reads   with   me.   When   I   rea

the sowy Day my Dad sed gaɹ
The   Snowy Day,   my   dad   said,   "Congratulat

FIGURE 10.5

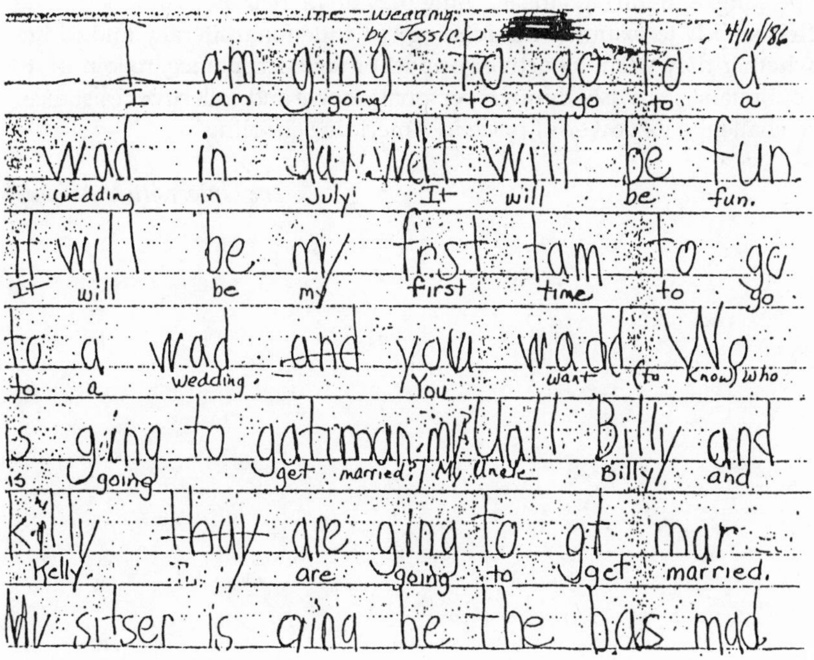

the wedding
by Jessica   4/11/86

I am ging to go to a
I   am   going   to   go   to   a

wad in Jul.welt will be fun.
wedding   in   July   It   will   be   fun.

It will be my frst tam to go
It   will   be   my   first   time   to   go

to a wad and you wad Wo
to   a   wedding   You   want (to know) who

is ging to gatiman:myUall Billy and
is   going   get married? My Uncle   Billy   and

Killy thay are ging to ot mar
Kelly.   are   going to get married.

My sitser is ging be the bas mad

work of these and other teachers, educational priorities are being redirected, and the institutional realities that support functional literacy are being deliberately critiqued. Change is slow and the arrangements of curricula still need to be rearticulated; the uses of resources still need to be reassessed; such "basic" yet persistently insoluble problems as class size, teacher workload, classroom materials, and teachers' authority in their classrooms and their schools need to be addressed. In other words, the supplanting of functionalist priorities with those of critical literacy requires systemic change, an imaginative restructuring of the current practices of schools in the context of a reexamination of the realities of American life. Little wonder if teachers should sigh and regard such a daunting list of challenges as an improbably quixotic undertaking.

Dedicated teachers have begun to claim more authority for themselves in their classrooms and schools, and gradually they have been gaining that authority. Writers like Paulo Freire, Ann Berthoff, Ira Shor, and Dixie Goswami, to name a few, have spoken strongly and effectively about alternative possibilities for school literacy programs. Change is not only possible, it is inevitable, because social realities always change. Teachers who believe that a functionalist definition of literacy is insufficient and dehumanizing have opportunities to intervene in the process of change—through political action, through writing and speaking, and through the teaching they do in their own classroom. The first step is to examine the ideology of functional literacy and judge whether they wish, by active support or tacit acceptance, to join in its continuance, or wish, through personal resolve and collective resistance, to challenge its powerful place in American schooling.

The University at Albany

11

Skills That Aren't Basic in a
New Conception of Literacy

CATHERINE E. SNOW
AND
DAVID K. DICKINSON*

Discussions of literacy, its nature, its determinants, and its consequences can typically be categorized as falling within one of two traditions, which have unfortunately had rather little contact with or influence upon one another. There is a tradition of talking and thinking about literacy that emerges from the discipline of reading education and emphasizes the psycholinguistic processes involved in literate behavior and the cognitive accomplishments that literacy represents. In this view, literacy is essentially private, internal, psychological. This view maps roughly onto the etic approach as Wagner (this volume) describes it: Performance criteria are established that can be applied across settings and will qualify one as being more or less literate.

A second view of literacy that emerges from a more ethnographic, anthropological, and sociological research perspective emphasizes the ways in which literate practices are embedded in cultural norms and values, and stresses the need for descriptive studies of group process rather than psychometric studies of individual processes in order to understand literacy. In this perspective literacy is classed as a social, cultural phenomenon and what counts as being literate may vary by setting. Such ethnographic accounts correspond to the type of work that Wagner describes as being consistent with the emic approach to the study of literacy.

In our view, both these perspectives have offered considerable insight into the nature, determinants, and consequences of literacy. The social/cultural view has enabled us to recognize the importance of such phenomena as continuities between oral and literate behaviors and to identify the cultural sources of organization in narratives, arguments, explanations, and other rhetorical forms. The social/cultural view of literacy has reminded us of the need to recognize extreme diversity in the forms literacy takes, the uses to which it is put, and the values it ex-

179

presses. While the cultural view of literacy sidesteps issues of assessment and facilitation that are crucial to educators, it nonetheless provides welcome insights about the nature of the phenomenon being assessed, and about the complexity of its relationships to other factors in its cultural context.

The psycholinguistic/cognitive orientation toward literacy has equally informed and enlightened its practitioners. Research emerging from this tradition has made abundantly clear the degree of individual effort involved in achieving literacy skills, some of the sources of individual variation in that achievement, and the contributions of specific instructional practices to their accomplishment. The psycholinguistic/cognitive view of literacy has provided a basis for analyzing the skills involved in "being literate," for seeing how they are interrelated, and for recognizing the role of both instruction and practice in their acquisition. Whereas one can justifiably fault the rather uninsightful procedures for assessing literacy skills that have sometimes been employed by practitioners of the psycholinguistic tradition, nonetheless one cannot deny that they have shaped our understanding of the complexity of literacy in a way that concentrating on group-level literacy alone would not have done.

We believe that both views of literacy are correct and generative, and that greater gains in understanding literacy would be possible if the gulf between the practitioners of these two views were narrowed. In the research program we are engaged in, we have made an effort to incorporate insights from both these research traditions, in the hopes that the results will be of interest to both groups of researchers. In this essay, we will outline the conception of literacy that underlies this research program, and discuss ways in which psychological and anthropological research paradigms can be joined to study the nature and determinants of literacy development.

A NOTE ON TERMINOLOGY

The term *literacy* has achieved such popularity that it has come to be used in ways that ignore tradition and etymology, and that threaten to undermine communication. In locutions like "cultural literacy" and "computer literacy," *literacy* means nothing more than skill, competence, or knowledge. On the other hand, expressions like "literate conversation" and "literate stories" reflect metaphorical use of the term, stretching *literacy* to encompass a wide variety of behaviors (certain ways of talking, thinking, and dealing with the world) that are typical of literate people. The implication is that these behaviors are directly related to the literate status of their originators. There are lively on-going discussions about exactly what behaviors and modes of thought can be related to the introduction of literacy into a culture (e.g., development of a metalinguistic vocabulary, emergence of a tradition of discourse about the meaning of texts, separation of the intentions of speakers from the meanings literally conveyed by their words). But the causal links between print and these modes of thought and discourse are not firmly established. And even if such links were clear, they typically do not relate to changes brought about as a result of a particular individual's experiences with print; rather they refer to changes that affect entire speech communities. For those of us who are interested in talking about the emerging abilities of individuals (who happen to operate in environments replete with print and with experts in literacy), it is important that we be able to use the term *literacy* to refer to those behaviors that require direct engagement with print. Accordingly, in this essay we will use a traditional, limited, etymologically pure meaning for *literacy*—the reading and writing of graphic representations of language. While this definition is toward the "etic" end of the etic/emic continuum (e.g., Wagner's Oum Fatima would not be classified as being "literate"), it does allow for accommodation to cultural variation, if one accepts culturally and socially specific definitions for the individual level of attainment and the individual uses of print that merit the attribution "literate."

In addition to the metaphorical uses of the term *literacy* mentioned above—those which do not necessarily entail any reference to print or print-related competencies—there are uses such as "functional literacy" and "emergent literacy" that refer to certain levels of attainment of print-related competencies. Finally, there are uses of the term such as "Koranic literacy," which refer to the culture-specific patterning of uses for literacy. Such uses of *literacy* have utility as a means of referring to clusters of print-related competencies. However, we believe they have utility only as long as they are used within the theoretical contexts that support their usage, and that using such terms without care in juxtaposition to other uses can be misleading. For example, a graduate of a Koranic school in Morocco who is properly referred to as literate may have no more decoding ability than someone referred to in the United States as a functional illiterate. Similarly, the term "emergent literacy" properly stresses the continuity between prereading and reading abilities, but at the cost that it may blur the centrality of specific print-related competencies to the achievement of conventional literacy. In the discussion that follows of the emergence of literacy in young children, we will describe particular competencies that develop during the period before conventional literacy and that clearly show continuity to conventional literacy, but we will try to identify specific competencies such as phonemic awareness, print recognition skills, and decontextualized language abilities rather than referring to such emergent abilities as a global achievement with relevance to literacy.

A COMPONENTIAL VIEW OF LITERACY

Although the mere existence of the term *literacy* implies that it is a single thing, there is considerable evidence to suggest that what one acquires in the process of becoming literate in fact includes a number of skills that may be relatively independent of one another. The claim for independence is a difficult one to make precisely because it is theoretical and not statistical independence we are arguing for. Under normal circumstances, one's abilities at the various components of literacy are likely to be correlated, since they are acquired in the same contexts, and since use of one component may offer opportunities for practice of another. Nonetheless, it is possible to imagine and to find circumstances under which the components are not so closely related.

What components are we discussing here? Many decompositions are possible, and it is not our purpose to promote one as superior to the rest, in part because the specific breakdown is probably partly a function of developmental level (and no doubt also of the orthographic system being learned). It seems quite clear that at all developmental levels one must consider reading skills as separate from writing skills (Stotsky, 1984); one recent study, for example, found that reading comprehension correlated only .26 with writing for first graders (Juel, Griffith, and Gough, 1986). Many discussions of reading ability reflect the notion that word recognition and comprehension skills must be viewed as separable; this view has even been called the "simple view" (Gough and Tunmer, 1986; Juel, Griffith, and Gough, 1986). Of course, each of the subskills is then also susceptible to its own analysis; for example, evidence has been presented that word recognition depends on both phonemic analysis and orthographic exposure (Stanovich, Cunningham, and Feeman, 1984; West and Stanovich, 1979), and many would argue that oral exposure to nonregular lexical items is also crucial (Curtis, 1980). Writing skill can similarly be decomposed into more mechanical skills associated with spelling and punctuation and the ideational, creative skills associated with production of connected text. In the cases of reading and writing both, the print-specific skills reflect acquisition of knowledge of print-sound relationships while comprehension and writing production skills are more closely related to language abilities. Whatever the specific set of components identified, the basic point is widely accepted that literacy can be analyzed into some list of subskills, each of which might well have its own developmental course and its own set of facilitating circumstances.

DIFFERENT DEVELOPMENTAL PATHWAYS,
DIFFERENT SOCIAL FACILITATORS

Although reading comprehension is not possible without some level of skill in word recognition, and recognition of unknown words is in the course of normal reading greatly facilitated by higher levels of comprehension, nonetheless, reading comprehension and word recognition can develop at quite different rates. Under pathological conditions, it is even possible for word recognition to be highly developed in readers who have no comprehension skills at all (so-called word-callers). Alternatively, intelligent and sophisticated second language readers can often perform quite well in comprehending texts containing words most of which the reader would fail to read correctly on a word recognition task. Thus, under certain conditions it is possible for word recognition and comprehension to show extremely different levels of achievement within the same individual.

Similarly, word recognition and reading comprehension may have different precursor accomplishments, and may be promoted by rather different instructional and social conditions. For low-income children in elementary school classrooms, Snow, Barnes, Chandler, Goodman, and Hemphill (1991) found that highly structured teaching techniques, use of workbooks, use of basal readers, and time devoted to reading instruction predicted gains in word recognition, whereas use of trade books and other varied literacy materials, time devoted to silent reading, and use of class time for discussion, library visits, and field trips predicted growth in reading comprehension. Thus word recognition was promoted by structure, whereas reading comprehension was promoted by challenge, two very different approaches to reading instruction (see also Chandler and Hemphill, 1983).

In the same study, Snow and her colleagues found different social factors in the home related to children's abilities in word recognition and in reading comprehension. Home factors that related to high levels of word recognition skill were the same as those that related to vocabulary: time spent with adults, provision of literacy materials to the child, maternal education, and maternal literacy. Reading comprehension, on the other hand, was not strongly related to any single factor; it was, instead, influenced by a wide variety of home factors: time with adults, an absence of stress in the home environment, maternal education, frequent use of literacy by others in the home, the presence of rules for television use, parental interest and participation in the child's school, and help with homework, among other variables. The wide pattern of influence on comprehension contrasts with the rather specific set of home factors that related to word recognition skills.

Of course, it is not theoretically necessary that either homes or classrooms foster development of one set of skills at the expense of the other. Unfortunately this too often happens in typical classrooms. Additionally, it should be noted that various instructional and social conditions might have differential effects at different ages. For school-aged children who already understand the functions of literacy and the social value of literacy skills, the type of structured practices observed by Snow and her colleagues probably results in acquisition of developmentally appropriate knowledge. However, imposition of such practices on preschool-aged children, or on children from backgrounds which have not displayed the value and uses of literacy, may have quite different effects, given the more limited metalinguistic knowledge of these children and their relative unfamiliarity with the entire enterprise of reading. For example, in a recent study of the uses of language and literacy in Head Start classrooms, Dickinson (1989) observed 'Big Books' (books with enlarged pictures and text) being read aloud with the children as the teacher pointed to the text. In these classrooms, one of which was rich with challenge, children became interested in the activity of reading, seemed to acquire greater language competence, and began to acquire rudimentary understandings about the correspondence between print and speech. While similar amounts of time could have been spent on structured print-specific activities, it is highly unlikely that the benefits would have been as great as those provided by exposure to structured print-oriented activities in the elementary grades.

In order to determine the effects of instructional experiences on literacy development, we need to take into consideration the age of the child and patterns of previous exposure to an assortment of experiences. The experiences of importance span home and school environments and include diverse print-related activities, activities that facilitate language growth, as well as activities that support general knowledge acquisition.

PATTERNS OF RELATIONSHIP OF COGNITIVE AND LINGUISTIC ABILITIES

If the various components of literacy are truly separate from one another, it makes sense to expect that they will relate in identifiably separate ways to oral language abilities. In fact, some aspects of literacy skill may not be particularly dependent on oral language abilities at all, whereas others may be highly associated with achievements in the realm of oral language. For example, individual differences in the sorts of skills one associates with literacy for the first grader—reading and writing fairly simple words and short texts—are probably mediated more by differences in print knowledge than by differences in oral language skills, whereas individual differences in achieving age-appropriate levels of reading and writing for sixth graders may well be much more closely tied to achievements in oral language use.

Some evidence for these claims derives from the widely varied set of relationships that has been found between preschool accomplishments and reading achievement. The status of "precursor to true reading" has been claimed for print skills (knowing the alphabet, recognizing familiar words and logos, writing one's own name), for phoneme segmentation skills (rhyming, pronouncing words without the first or last letter), for pretend reading and writing, for dictating stories and oral storytelling, and for creative spelling/writing. (For reviews see Dickinson, 1987; Mason and Allen, 1987; Teale and Sulzby, 1986). While considerable evidence confirms that abilities in all of these areas are greater for children who are likely to become good readers, the question remains how any of these divergent prereading abilities directly facilitates or leads to the acquisition of true reading. We believe the conclusion is inevitable that they do so through different pathways. Print skills and phoneme segmentation facilitate the acquisition of word recognition ability, whereas pretend reading and writing and oral storytelling skills facilitate comprehension abilities.

Of particular interest as a precursor to high-level literacy skills including reading comprehension is skill in "decontextualized" oral language. We use the term "decontextualized" here with considerable sensitivity to the complaints of those who say that all language must be understood in some context or other, and thus that "decontextualized language" is an oxymoron. We do not deny the ultimately social nature of language use, but nonetheless find it useful to distinguish between language that is communicatively effective only in the context in which it is uttered, and language that is effective across a wider variety of contexts. We use "decontextualized" to refer, in a shorthand sort of way, to language of this second sort, in which the message is sufficiently complete, referents are sufficiently explicit and nonindexical, and the perspective of an absent audience sufficiently taken into account, that the language would "work" in a variety of contexts and for a variety of listeners.

There is evidence that skill at the decontextualized uses of language predict literacy and school achievement better than skill at other challenging language tasks that are not specifically decontextualized. Decontextualized tasks can be distinguished from contextualized language tasks in terms of three dimensions: absence of an interactive, conversational partner; absence of the presumption of shared knowledge with the audience; and complexity of the message (Snow, 1987). Children who perform well on one decontextualized oral language task also perform well on other ones, indicating that it does make sense to abstract the dimensions of similarity across such tasks (Davidson, Kline, and Snow, 1986). Furthermore, children who perform well on such tasks show higher standardized achievement scores, particularly in areas related to reading (Snow, Cancino, Gonzalez, and Shriberg, 1989; Velasco, 1987).

It is of particular importance to note that task difficulty is not the dimension that enables decontextualized oral language tasks to distinguish between better and poorer school learners. A very challenging conversational task, for example, shows up large individual differences among children, but those differences do not relate to literacy skills (Snow and Dolbear, 1988). Thus, we would argue that language proficiency has to be seen as a composite of a variety of theoretically and empirically distinguishable skills, just as we have been arguing literacy must be viewed (see also Torrance and Olson, 1985). Furthermore, we would contend that some of the separable language skills are relatively irrelevant in explaining individual differences in literacy accomplishment, whereas others are crucial precursors to aspects of literacy achievement.

The connection between skills at producing and understanding oral decontextualized language on the one hand and skill at reading comprehension on the other seems to us to be quite obvious. "Comprehension" in reading means being able to build a new knowledge structure based on text. The texts presented for comprehension are, typically, decontextualized—which means they make use of certain linguistic structures that are unnecessary and thus rare in face-to-face conversation. Understanding these structures, and developing fluency in using and recognizing them, is easier if children have encountered them in oral language—where the additional burden of print processing is not present. We predict, then, that children who have heard more decontextualized talk, and on whom demands have been made to produce such talk, will fare better in comprehending what they read than other children whose word recognition skills are equivalent but whose oral decontextualized language skills are inferior.

ENVIRONMENTAL SUPPORTS FOR
DECONTEXTUALIZED ORAL LANGUAGE

While considerable research attention has already been given to the social-interactive facilitators of syntactic and lexical development in young children, we know almost nothing about the types of social interactions that help children develop skills with decontextualized language— telling stories, giving descriptions, and giving explanations about complex matters to unfamiliar interlocutors (Snow, 1983, 1989). Such skills are, however, important components of normal language development starting around age four, and they are, furthermore, strongly related to literacy and school achievement in older children.

If we are to understand how such emerging linguistic competencies are related to experiences in the home and school, we need to know more about children's experiences than can be captured by the type of global descriptions of home and school experiences discussed earlier. We also need to know the frequency and types of encounters that occur between adults and children which are theoretically supportive of decontextualized language abilities. Most importantly, we need to know the effects of these encounters on subsequent competencies with oral and written language.

We know from work done by Tizard and Hughes (1984) that, in British nursery schools, extended interactions between children and their preschool teachers are rather rare. For children from working-class backgrounds such encounters are especially infrequent in nursery school. Limitation in the number of opportunities for children to practice decontextualized language skills also may be the rule in preschools in the United States. Dickinson (in press [a]) has recently analyzed conversations in a high-quality preschool and found relatively few occasions when children engaged in talk that required decontextualized strategies such as recounting personal narratives, planning future events, or explaining ideas.

It may be the case that the typical organization of teacher-child relationships in preschool provides children with limited opportunities to develop the language abilities that support literacy, except for times spent reading and discussing books (Cochran-Smith, 1984; Dickinson and Keebler, 1989). The supposition that preschools may not be well adapted to support decontextualized language abilities is bolstered by the finding that working-class children attending high-quality, academically oriented day care centers still score well below middle-class children on decontextualized oral language abilities (Dickinson and Snow, 1987).

It is essential that we know what conversational opportunities children have at home that might support the skills needed to understand and produce decontextualized talk. Tizard and Hughes (1984) found that homes provided a richer context for children to engage in extended conversations, the type of interactions more likely to support decontextualized skills. Also, in a study of nonschool factors associated with reading development, researchers recently stumbled across the finding that time spent at the dinner table was significantly associated with reading (Anderson, Wilson, and Fielding, 1988). Anderson and others interpreted this finding as reflective of general family stability. On the other hand, dinner table conversations can be rich with opportunities to develop and extend a line of thought (Ochs, Smith, and Taylor, 1988; Perlmann, 1983). It could be the case that participation in dinner table conversations is related to facilitation of later reading development because it supports acquisition of decontextualized language abilities.

A very similar argument could, of course, be made for the effect of book-reading on children's development. Parental reading of books to and with preschool-aged children has been widely reported to relate to the children's later literacy skills and school achievement (reviewed by Goldfield and Snow, 1984). While this effect has typically been interpreted as one mediated by the positive direct effects of book-reading on children's literacy skills, it could also be argued that book-reading episodes have their most potent effect on children's language skills (Snow, 1983). Traditional measures of sentence-level linguistic competence (e.g., syntactic measures) will not capture the oral language competencies developed in such encounters. We know this because, in his longitudinal study of language development, Wells (1985) found significant links between book-reading and school success, but few links between his sentence-level measures of language and school success. Instead of supporting acquisition of sentence-level syntax, the important characteristic of periods of book-reading may be that they provide opportunities to engage in extended discourse on a single or related series of topics, and exposure to areas of world knowledge and to vocabulary not frequently encountered in other types of interaction.

A componential view to literacy will enable us to take a more fine-grained, analytic approach to examining the factors that support its development. Such an approach to literacy will allow us to understand better exactly what literacy is—the skills, orientations, and knowledge it draws upon and leads to—and to begin to understand with some precision the linkages between environmental factors and psycholinguistic and cognitive processes.

RELEVANT RESEARCH

A proper test of the claim concerning the componential nature of literacy and its resultantly complex relationships to precursor achievements, to social/instructional facilitators, and to decontextualized oral language skills requires a longitudinal study in which evidence about all these domains is tapped. Since the components of literacy skills do not emerge as fully differentiated until the middle school years, a relatively long-term longitudinal study is necessary to reveal relationships between aspects of interaction during the preschool period to literacy development and to school achievement. We currently are engaged in such a study of the social prerequisites to the language and literacy skills of low SES children.

In this study, we are following working-class children from the preschool through the early school years, assessing their literacy and decontextualized oral language skills in kindergarten and regularly during the elementary school years. In addition, the children are being observed in interaction with their caregivers and in group care settings in order to assess aspects of the interaction that contribute to the children's conversational and decontextualized oral language skills.

Home data. When the children were three and four we made two home visits during which we observed each child interacting with a caregiver during toy-play and book-reading sessions. We also asked the caregiver to elicit a personal report from the child, in order to assess adult strategies for helping the child construct a coherent narrative. Parents also taped a family mealtime, transcripts of which are being analyzed for the occurrence of narratives and of talk about world knowledge versus concrete, context-tied topics. Finally, at each home observation session, we administered extensive interviews to the child's primary caregiver dealing with demographic variables, information about child-care arrangement and daily routines, and information about parental goals and aspirations for their children.

School data. We also gathered data in children's preschool classrooms. In order to obtain information about the language environment of preschools, spontaneous measures of child performance, conversations of each target child and of the lead teacher were recorded throughout the morning using tape recorders carried in backpacks. These tapes enable us to determine the amount and nature of the talk occurring in different contexts (e.g., narratives, explanations, controlling behavior of others). Additionally, group meeting times and any group book-reading time were videotaped and these tapes are being analyzed to determine teacher book-reading style and target child involvement and responsivity. Also, as in the home, teachers are asked to encourage each child to tell about some experience the child has had at home. Additional information about the target child is gained by asking teachers to assess a variety of the target child's language abilities.

In addition to the interactional data being collected, we learn as much as possible about classroom routines by recording the location, variety, and uses of print in the room and noting general aspects of the curriculum that can be inferred from materials and areas that are visible. Also, at half-hour intervals observers note what activities children are engaged in and whether they are alone or in a small group. Finally, teachers have been interviewed to determine the general nature of their program and their attitudes related to supporting development of language and literacy.

Data analyses. The basic logic of our data analysis distinguishes three types of data: data about the child's linguistic and literate environments at home and in group care settings; data about the child's oral language skills; and data about the child's literacy skills and school achievement. We expect there will be relationships among all of these, but we expect especially strong links from certain aspects of home and preschool environments (e.g., opportunities for extended talk about sequences of past or future events) to oral decontextualized language skills, and in turn from oral decontextualized language skills to reading comprehension. We expect other strong links between print-specific experiences (e.g., daily recitation of the alphabet) and early decoding. The strength of these varied relationships will be compared to alternative explanatory pathways, for example, the pathway that links literacy exposure at home and in preschool to print skills at entry to first grade, and in turn to reading comprehension at grade four.[1]

CONCLUSION

The enterprise we are engaged in here will contribute, we hope, to adjustments in both the social/cultural and the psycholinguistic/cognitive perspectives on literacy. We see literacy, first of all, as a set of cognitive accomplishments, each with its own precursors and consequences for cognitive functioning. At the same time, we see literacy skills as the product of a set of social and cultural forces that translate themselves into specific interactive environments for children. What children can learn about print in those environments depends to a large extent on the access they have been given to information about the nature and value of literacy in the society as a whole.

The widespread tendency to associate literacy with, and ultimately define it in terms of, a wide variety of phenomena with which it happens to co-occur does not, in our view, contribute to our understanding of literacy. There are, of course, many characteristics more likely to be true of literate than of nonliterate individuals, including ownership of books, experience in schools, and specific decisions about oral language use, but the co-occurrence of these with the ability to read and write may not illuminate the nature of literacy any more than does its co-occurrence with ownership of Saabs, experience in airports, or particular sartorial decisions.

Many questions arise regarding the nature of literacy and about its course of development that cognitive/psychological approaches can address. For example, observational and experimental work can continue to help identify crucial, central, defining capacities (e.g., metalinguistic competences, language, memory, problem-solving strategies, analytic strategies) that individuals who can read and write display, which nonliterate individuals either do not display or display in different patterns. Longitudinal observational work, such as ours, can help establish causal relations among such cognitive capacities by determining temporal relationships among them and, in so doing, help us better understand how literacy develops.

In addition to deepening our understanding of the intrapsychic processes associated with reading and writing we need to understand better how the social world supports the emergence of the literacy-related skills which the cognitive/psychological work is helping to identify. Careful observational work in settings where literacy is transmitted is needed to augment our understanding of the factors that promote the development of these capacities. It is especially important that such work be done in settings where, based on demographic data, we can assume the participants may not achieve high literacy levels. Furthermore, work is needed that follows the same at-risk individuals across settings so that we can learn both how children display literacy-related abilities in varied contexts and what opportunities children have to acquire prerequisite skills.

Finally, carefully monitored intervention studies in schools, communities, and homes can augment knowledge gained from experimental and observational research. Such work can shed light on questions about the interrelationships among cognitive skills and it also can help us better understand the role and nature of social networks in facilitating—or, as Wagner notes in this volume, impeding—literacy development.

In conclusion, we hope that the research program on which we have embarked will help us to address both questions related to the emergence of cognitive abilities and questions about the nature of social supports for literacy development. In particular, we hope to provide information about the degree to which literacy must be conceived of as componential, and to explore the complex sets of relationships among social precursors and specific literacy skills, as well as among achieved literacy skills and their cognitive consequences.

Harvard University and Clark University

DOCUMENTATION

CHAPTER 1:
INTRODUCTION

References

Faure, E., et al. (1972). *Learning to Be: The World of Education Today and Tomorrow.* Paris: UNESCO.

Goody, J. (1986). *The Logic of Writing and the Organization of Society.* Cambridge: Cambridge University Press.

Lazarus, Mel. (1970). "Miss Peach" syndicated cartoon strip, April 6.

Mayor, Federico. (1988). "The World Decade for Cultural Development." *The Courier* (November): 5-6.

von Bertalannfy, Ludwig. (1966). "The Tree of Knowledge." In G. Kepes, ed., *Sign, Image, Symbol.* New York: Braziller.

CHAPTER 2:
LITERACY AS CULTURE: EMIC AND ETIC PERSPECTIVES

References

Bennett, J. A. H., and Berry, J. W. (1987). "The Future of Cree Syllabic Literacy in Northern Canada." In D. A. Wagner, ed., *The Future of Literacy in a Changing World.* New York: Pergamon Press.

Berry, J. W., and Dasen, P. (1974). Introduction. In J. W. Berry and P. Dasen, eds., *Culture and Cognition: Readings in Cross-cultural Psychology.* London; Methuen.

Chall, J. (1987). "Developing Literacy . . . in Children and Adults." In D. A. Wagner, ed., *The Future of Literacy in a Changing World.* New York: Pergamon Press.

Clanchy, M. T. (1979). *From Memory to Written Record.* Cambridge, MA: Harvard University Press.

Eickelman, D. F. (1978). "The Art of Memory: Islamic Education and Its Social

Reproduction." *Comparative Studies in Society and History*, 20: 485-516.

Eisenstein, E. L. (1979). *The Printing Press as an Agent of Change*. Cambridge: Cambridge University Press.

Fagerlind, I., and Saha, L. J. (1983). *Education and National Development: A Comparative Perspective*. New York: Pergamon Press.

Gilmore, P. (1986). "Sub-rosa Literacy: Peers, Play and Ownership in Literacy Acquisition." In B. B. Schieffelin and P. Gilmore, eds., *The Acquisition of Literacy: Ethnographic Perspectives*. Norwood, NJ: Ablex.

Giroux, H. A. (1983). *Theory and Resistance in Education*. South Hadley, MA: Bergin and Garvey.

Goody, J., and Watt, I. (1968). "The Consequences of Literacy." In J. Goody, ed., *Literacy in Traditional Societies*. Cambridge: Cambridge University Press.

Graff, H. J. (1981). *Literacy and Social Development in the West: A Reader*. Cambridge: Cambridge University Press.

Heath, S. B. (1983). *Ways with Words*. New York: Cambridge University Press.

Mickulecky, L. (1986). "The Status of Literacy in our Society." Paper presented at the National Reading Conference, Austin, TX.

Miller, G. (1988). "The Challenge of Universal Literacy." *Science*, 241: 1293-1299.

Pike, K. L. (1966). *Language in Relation to a Unified Theory of the Structure of Human Behavior*. The Hague: Mouton.

Scribner, S., and Cole, M. (1981). *The Psychology of Literacy*. Cambridge, MA: Harvard University Press.

Snow, C. E., Barnes, W. S., Chandler, J., Goodman, I. F., and Hemphill, L. (1991). *Unfulfilled Expectations: Home and School Influences on Literacy*. Cambridge, MA: Harvard University Press.

Street, B. V. (1987). "Literacy and Social Change: The Significance of Social Context in the Development of Literacy Programmes." In D. A. Wagner, ed., *The Future of Literacy in a Changing World*. New York: Pergamon Press.

Tambiah, S. (1968). "Literacy in a Buddhist Village in North-East Thailand." In J. Goody, ed., *Literacy in Traditional Societies*. Cambridge: Cambridge University Press.

Teale, W. H., and Sulzby, E. (1987). "Literacy Acquisition in Early Childhood: The Roles of Access and Mediation in Storybook Reading." In D. A. Wagner, ed., *The Future of Literacy in a Changing World*. New York: Pergamon Press.

Wagner, D. A. (1986). "When Literacy Isn't Reading (and Vice-versa)." In M. E. Wrolstad and D. F. Fisher, eds., *Towards a New Understanding of Literacy.* New York: Praeger.

―――. (1988). "Appropriate Education and Literacy in the Third World." In P. Dasen, J. W. Berry, and N. Sartorious, eds., *Psychology, Health and Culture.* Beverly Hills: Sage.

―――. ed. (1987). *The Future of Literacy in a Changing World.* New York: Pergamon Press.

―――. (1990). "Literacy Assessment in the Third World: An Overview and Proposed Schema for Survey Use." *Comparative Education Review,* 33:112-138.

Wagner, D. A., and Lotfi, A. (1980). "Traditional Islamic Education in Morocco: Socio-historical and Psychological Perspectives." *Comparative Education Review,* 24: 238-251.

―――. (1983). "Learning to Read by 'Rote'." *International Journal of the Sociology of Language,* 42: 111-121.

Wagner, D. A., Messick, B. M., and Spratt, J. E. (1986). "Studying Literacy in Morocco." In B. B. Schieffelin and P. Gilmore, eds., *The Acquisition of Literacy: Ethnographic Perspectives.* Norwood, NJ: Ablex.

Wagner, D. A., and Spratt, J. E. (1988). "Intergenerational Literacy: Effects of Parental Literacy and Attitudes on Children's Reading Achievement in Morocco." *Human Development,* 31: 359-369.

CHAPTER 3:
LITERACY, ECONOMIC STRUCTURES, AND INDIVIDUAL AND
PUBLIC POLICY INCENTIVES

References

Bequele, A., and Boyden, J. (1988). "Child Labour: Problems, Policies, and Programmes." In A. Bequele and J. Boyden, eds., *Combatting Child Labor.* Geneva: International Labour Office, pp. 1-27.

Blaug, M. (1966). "Literacy and Economic Development." *School Review,* 74: 393-418.

Carr-Hill, R. A. (1988). *The Information Base for the Planning of the Diversified Educational Field.* Paris: International Institute of Education (Research Report #68).

Carron, G., and Bordia, A. (1985). *Issues in Planning and Implementing Literacy Programmes.* Paris: International Institute for Educational Planning.

Colclough, C. (1983). "The Impact of Primary Schooling on Economic Development: A Review of the Evidence." *World Development*, 10: 167-185).

Cotlear, D. (1986). *Farmer Education and Farm Efficiency in Peru: The Role of Schooling*. Washington, D.C.: World Bank Discussion Paper, Education and Training Series.

Datta, L. E. (1982). "Employment Related Basic Skills." In H. F. Silberman, ed., *Education and Work*. Chicago: University of Chicago Press for the National Society for the Study of Education.

Duke, C., ed. (1985). *Combatting Poverty Through Adult Education: National Development Strategies*. London: Croom Helm for the International Council on Adult Education.

Foster, P. (1987). "The Contribution of Education to Development." In G. Psacharopoulos, ed., *The Economics of Education: Research and Studies*. New York: Pergamon Press, pp. 93-100.

Foster, P., and Purves, A. (1988). "Literacy and Society with Particular Reference to the Non-Western World." (Draft).

Freire, P. (1985). *The Politics of Education*. Boston: Bergin and Garvin Publishers, Inc.

Fuller, B., Edwards, J. H. Y., and Gorman, K. (1987). "Does Rising Literacy Spark Economic Growth? Commercial Expansion in Mexico." In D. Wagner, ed., *The Future of Literacy in a Changing World*. New York: Pergamon Press, pp. 319-340.

Grosse, R. N., and Auffrey, C. (1989). "Literacy and Health Status in Developing Countries." *Annual Review of Public Health*, 10: 281-297.

Hunter, C. (1989). "Literacy in Local Communities: The Influence of Economic and Social Factors." Paper prepared for Workshop on Literacy, World Conference on Education For All Secretariat, New York, NY.

Hyde, K. A. L. (1989). "Improving Women's Education in Sub-Saharan Africa: A Review of the Literature." Report prepared for the Education and Employment Division, The World Bank, Washington, D.C.

Jamison, D., and Lau, L. J. (1982). *Farmer Education and Farm Efficiency*. Baltimore: Johns Hopkins University Press for the World Bank.

Jamison, D., and Moock, P. (1984). "Farmer Education and Farm Efficiency in Nepal: The Role of Schooling, Extension Services, and Cognitive Skills." *World Development* , 12: 67-86.

Levin, H. M., and Rumberger, R. W. (1986). *Educational Requirements for New Technologies: Visions, Possibilities, and Current Realities*. Stanford, CA: Institute for Research in Educational Finance and Governance.

Limage, L. J. (1986). "Adult Literacy Policy and Provision in an Age of Auster-ity." *International Review of Education*, 32: 399-412.

Lind, A., and Johnston, A. (1986). *Adult Literacy in the Third World: A Review of Objectives and Strategies*. Stockholm: Swedish International Development Authority.

Lockheed, M. E., Jamison, D., and Lau, L. J. (1980). "Farmer Education and Farm Efficiency: A Survey." *Economic Development and Cultural Change*, 29: 37-76.

Lourie, S., and Reiff, H. (1988). "Towards an International Strategy of Basic Ed-ucation for All." (Draft).

Lowe, J. (1982). *The Education of Adults: A World Perspective*. Paris: UNESCO (sec-ond edition).

Morsy, Z., ed. (1987). *Illiteracy in Industrialized Countries: Situation and Action*. Special issue of *Prospects: Quarterly Review of Education*, Vol. 17.

Myers, W. (1988). "Alternative Services for Street Children: The Brazilian Ap-proach." In A. Bequele and J. Boyden, eds., *Combatting Child Labour*. Geneva: International Labour Office, pp. 125-143.

Schultz, T. P. (1989). "Returns to Women's Education." Report prepared for the Education and Employment Division, The World Bank, Washington, D.C.

Stewart, F. (1985). *Basic Needs in Developing Countries*. Baltimore: Johns Hopkins University Press.

Sticht, T. G. (1989). "The Intergenerational Transfer of Literacy and Workplace Literacy: Linking the Literacy Development of Children and Adults." Paper prepared for Workshop on Literacy, World Conference on Education for All Secretariat, New York, NY.

UNICEF (1988). "Moving Towards Basic Education for All." Report prepared for meeting of the International Working Group on Education, Paris, France, November 23-25.

Windham, D. M. (1988). "Effectiveness Indicators in the Economic Analysis of Educational Activities." *International Journal of Educational Research*, 12: 575-665.

World Bank (1980). *Education Sector Policy Paper*. Washington, D.C.: World Bank.

Zelizer, V. A. (1985). *Pricing the Priceless Child: The Changing Social Value of Chil-dren*. New York: Basic Books.

CHAPTER 4:
LITERACY AND THE POLITICS OF LANGUAGE

Notes

1. Laitin, David. (1989). "A Political Scientist Looks at the Role of Language in National Conflicts." *University of Chicago Reports of the Division of Social Sciences* No. 9 Spring, pp. 9-12. Game theory first emerged as a branch of mathematics concerned with the optimal behavior of participants in games of strategy. It is concerned with resultant equilibria where every participant strives for maximum advantage. In these circumstances final outcomes depend not only on an individual's actions but on the environmental framework and the actions of other players whose interests may be similar or opposed. Thus the theory encompasses notions of conflict of interest as well as possible cooperation.

Such an approach can be applied to relationships between groups as well as individuals, and game theory has made significant contributions to economic theory. However, it is clear that such an orientation has major implications for the study of political behavior in "pluralist" societies.

CHAPTER 5:
THE TEXTUAL CONTRACT: LITERACY AS COMMON KNOWLEDGE AND CONVENTIONAL WISDOM

Notes

1. The same may also be applied to formal oral discourse and probably to informal discourse as well (Akinnaso, 1985). The special property of literate activity is that it involves physical and visible language.

References

Akinnaso, F. N. (1985). "On the Similarities between Spoken and Written Language." *Language and Speech*, 28: 323-359.

Anderson, R. C., Spiro, R. J., and Montague, W. E. (1977). *Schooling and the Acquisition of Knowledge*. Hillsdale, NJ: Erlbaum.

Applebee, A. M. (1978). *The Child's Concept of Story: Ages Two to Seventeen*. Chicago: University of Chicago Press.

Bateson, G. (1972). *Steps to an Ecology of Mind*. New York: Ballentine.

Bereiter, C., and Scardamalia, M. (1981). "Information Processing Demands of Text Production." Paper presented at the Deutsches Institut fur Fernstudien an der Universitat Tubingen.

Bloom, H. (1973). *Anxiety of Influence: A Theory of Poetry*. New York: Oxford University Press.

Carroll, J. (1960). "Vectors of Prose Style." In T. A. Sebeok, ed., *Style in Language.* Cambridge, MA, and New York: Technology Press and Wiley.

Chomsky, N. M. (1968). *Language and Mind.* New York: Harcourt, Brace and World, Inc.

Cole, M. (1985). "Education and the Third World: A Critical Discussion and Some Experimental Data." In E. Bok, J. P. P. Haanen, and M. A. Walters, eds., *Education for Cognitive Development.* The Hague: SVO/SCO.

Cole, M., Gay, J., Glick, J. A., and Sharp, D. W. (1971). *The Cultural Context of Learning and THinking.* London: Methuen and Co. Ltd.

Cole, M., and Scribner, S. (1974). *Culture and Thought.* New York: John Wiley and Sons Inc.

deSaussure, F. (1916). *Cours de linguistique général.* Lausanne: Payot.

Engeström, Y. (1987). *Learning by Expanding: An Activity-Theoretical Approach to Developmental Research.* Helsinki: Orienta-Konsultit.

Fish, S. (1980). *Is There a Text in This Class? The Authority of Interpretive Communities.* Cambridge, MA: Harvard University Press.

Galperin, P. J. (1979). *Johdatus Psykologiaan.* Helsinki: Kansankulttuuri. (Russian original "Introduction to Psychology" published in 1976.)

Gaur, A. (1985). *A History of Writing.* New York: Scribner's.

Gelb, I. J. (1952). *A Study of Writing.* Chicago: University of Chicago Press.

Glenn, E. S. with Glenn, C. G. (1981). *Man and Mankind: Conflict and Communication Between Cultures.* Norwood, NJ: Ablex.

Goody, J. (1977). *The Domestication of the Savage Mind.* Cambridge: Cambridge University Press.

———. (1986). *The Logic of Writing and the Organization of Society.* Cambridge: Cambridge University Press.

Gumperz, J. J., and Hymes, D. (1974). *Directions in Sociolinguistics: The Ethnography of Communication.* New York: Holt Rinehart and Winston.

Guthrie, J. T. and Kirsch, I. S. (1984). "The Emergent Perspective on Literacy." *Phi Delta Kappan,* 351-355.

Halliday, M. A. K., and Hasan, R. (1976). *Cohesion in English.* London: Longman.

Heath, S. B. (1983). *Ways with Words.* New York: Cambridge University Press.

Hirsch, E. D. (1987). *Cultural Literacy: What Every American Needs to Know.* Boston, MA: Houghton Mifflin.

Hofstede, G. (1980). *Culture's Consequences.* Berkeley, CA: Sage.

Hymes, D. (1974). "Sociolinguistics and the Ethnography of Speaking." In B. Blount, ed., *Language, Culture, and Society.* Cambridge, MA: Winthrop Publishers.

Kachru, B. (1982). *The Other Tongue: English across Cultures.* Urbana, IL: Illinois University Press.

Kádár-Fülop, J. (1988). "Culture and Education in Written Composition." In A. C. Purves, ed., *Contrastive Rhetoric.* Written Communication Annual, Beverley Hills, CA: Sage.

Kaplan, R. B. (1966). "Cultural Thought Patterns in Intercultural Education." *Language Learning,* 16: 1-20.

Kintsch, W., and van Dijk, T. A., EDS. (1983). *Strategies in Discourse Comprehension.* New York: Academic Press.

Leontev, A. A. (1973). "Some Problems in Learning Russian as a Foreign Language." *Soviet Psychology,* 111-117.

Lord, A. B. (1964). *The Singer of Tales.* Cambridge, MA: Harvard University Press.

Lowes, J. L. (1930). *Convention and Revolt in Poetry.* Boston: Houghton Mifflin.

Markova, A. K. (1979). *The Teaching and Mastery of Language.* London: Croom Helm.

Miller, G. A. (1956). "The Magical Number Seven, Plus or Minus Two: Some Limits on our Capacity for Processing Information." *Psychological Review,* 63: 81-97.

Olson, D. R. (1977). "From Utterance to Text: The Bias of Language in Speech and Writing." *Harvard Educational Review,* 47: 257-281.

Ong, W. J. (1982). *Orality and Literacy: The Technologizing of the Word.* New York and London: Methuen Co. Ltd.

Polanyi, M. (1958). *Personal Knowledge.* London: Routledge and Kegan Paul.

Purves, A. C. (1971). "Evaluation of Learning in Literature." In B. S. Bloom, J. T. Hastings, and G. Madaus, eds., *Handbook of Formative and Summative Evaluation of Student Learning.* New York: McGraw-Hill.

———. (1973). *Literature Education in Ten Countries: An Empirical Study. International Studies in Evaluation.* Stockholm: Almqvist and Wiksell.

———. (1984a). "The Teacher as Reader: An Anatomy." *College English,* 46: 259-265.

——— . (1984b). "In Search of an Internationally-valid Scheme for Scoring Compositions." *College Composition and Communication*, 35: 426-438.

——— . (1984c) "The Potential and Real Achievement of U.S. Students in School Reading." *American Journal of Education*, 93: 82-106.

——— . (1986). "On the Nature and Formation of Interpretive and Rhetorical Communities." In T. N. Postlethwaite, ed., *International Educational Research: Papers in Honor of Torsten Husén*. Oxford: Pergamon Press.

Purves, A. C., and Purves, W. (1986). "Culture, Text Models and the Activity of Writing." *Research in the Teaching of English*. 20: 174-197.

Purves, A., and Rippere, V. (1968). *The Elements of Writing About a Literary Work: Research Monograph No. 10*. Champaign, IL: National Council of Teachers of English.

Purves, A., and Takala, S., eds. (1982). *An International Perspective on the Evaluation of Written Composition: Evaluation in Education: An International Review Series*, Vol. 5, No. 3. Oxford: Pergamon Press.

Reder, S. (1987). "Comparative Aspects of Functional Literacy Development: Three Ethnic American Communities." D. A. Wagner, ed., *The Future of Literacy in a Changing World*. Oxford, Pergamon Press.

Richards, I. A. (1929). *Practical Criticism*. New York: Harcourt Brace.

Rosenblatt, L. M. (1978). *The Reader, the Text, the Poem: The Transactional Theory of the Literary Work*. Carbondale, IL: Southern Illinois University Press.

Said, E. (1983). *The World, the Text and the Critic*. Cambridge, MA: Harvard University Press.

Scardamalia, M., and Paris, P. (1984). "The Function of Explicit Discourse Knowledge in the Development of Text Representation and Composing Strategies." Occasional Paper No. 5. Centre for Applied Cognitive Science. Toronto: Ontario Institute for Studies in Education.

Scribner, S., and Cole, M. (1981). *The Psychology of Literacy*. Cambridge, MA: Harvard University Press.

Shaughnessy, M. P. (1977). *Errors and Expectations*. New York: Oxford University Press.

Stenhouse, L. (1967). *Culture and Education*. New York: Weybright and Talley.

Takala, S. (1983). "Achievement in Written Composition." Unpublished manuscript. Urbana, IL: IEA Study of Written Composition.

——— . (1984). "On Word, Meaning and Vocabulary in the Context of General Soviet Theory of Psycholinguistics." Jyvaskyla, Finland: Institute For Educational Research Bulletin 244.

—— . (1987). "Student Views on Writing in Eight Countries." In R. E. Dagenhart, ed., *Assessment of Student Writing in an International Context*. Jyvaskyla, Finland: Institute for Educational Research.

Takala, S., Purves, A. C., and Buckmaster, A. (1982). "On the Interrelationships Between Language, Perception, Thought and Culture, and Their Relevance to the Assessment of Written Composition." *Evaluation in Education: An International Review Series*, 5: 317-342.

Törnebohm, H. (1973). "Perspectives on Inquiring Systems." Department of Theory of Science, University of Gothenburg, Report No. 53.

Vygotsky, L. S. (1956). *Izbrannye Psikhologicheskie Isseldovaniia*. Moscow: RSFR Academy of Pedagogical Sciences.

Weinreich, U. (1963). *Languages in Contact: Findings and Problems*. The Hague: Mouton.

CHAPTER 6:
LITERACY AND INDIVIDUAL CONSCIOUSNESS

References

Akinnaso, F. N. (1981). "The Consequences of Literacy in Pragmatic and Theoretical Perspectives." *Anthropology and Education Quarterly*, 12: 163-200.

—— . (1982a). "On the Differences Between Spoken and Written Language." *Language and Speech*, 25: 97-125.

—— . (1982b) "The Literate Writes and the Nonliterate Chants: Written Language and Ritual Communication in Sociolinguistic Perspective." In William Frawley, ed., *Linguistics and Literacy*. New York: Plenum Press.

—— . (1985). "On the Similarities Between Spoken and Written Language." *Language and Speech*, 28: 323-359.

—— . (1988). "The Sociolinguistics of Communication in Speech and Writing." In Wendy Leeds-Hurwitz, ed., *Communication and the Evolution of Civilization*. Needham Heights, MA: Ginn Press.

Cole, M., and Scribner, S. (1974). *Culture and Thought*. New York: Wiley.

Cook-Gumperz, J., ed. (1986). *The Social Construction of Literacy*. Cambridge: Cambridge University Press.

Foster, P. J. (1971). "Problems of Literacy in Sub-Saharan Africa." In T. A. Sebeok, ed., *Linguistics in Sub-Saharan Africa (Current Trends in Linguistics, 7)*. The Hague: Mouton.

Goody, J. (1977). *The Domestication of the Savage Mind*. Cambridge: Cambridge University Press.

————. (1986). *The Logic of Writing and the Organization of Society*. Cambridge: Cambridge University Press.

————. (1987). *The Interface Between the Written and the Oral*. Cambridge: Cambridge University Press.

Goody, J., and Watt, I. (1963). "The Consequences of Literacy." *Comparative Studies in Society and History*, 5: 304-345.

Langer, J. A. (1986). "A Sociocognitive Perspective on Literacy." In J. A. Langer, ed., *Language, Literacy, and Culture: Issues of Society and Schooling*. Norwood, NJ: Ablex.

Meggit, M. (1968). "Uses of Literacy in New Guinea and Melanesia." In J. Goody, ed., *Literacy in Traditional Societies*. Cambridge: Cambridge University Press.

Scribner, S., and Cole, M. (1973). "Cognitive Consequences of Formal and Informal Education." *Science*, 182: 553-559.

————. (1981). *The Psychology of Literacy*. Cambridge, MA: Harvard University Press.

Sherzer, J. (1983). *Kuna Ways of Speaking*. Austin: University of Texas Press.

Street, B. V. (1984). *Literacy in Theory and Practice*. Cambridge: Cambridge University Press.

Vygotsky, L. S. (1962). *Thought and Language*. Cambridge, MA: MIT Press.

————. (1978). *Mind in Society: The Development of Higher Psychological Processes*. Cambridge, MA: Harvard University Press.

Wertsch, J. V., ed. (1985a). *Culture, Communication, and Cognition: Vygotskian Perspectives*. New York: Cambridge University Press.

————. (1985b). *Vygotsky and the Social Formation of Mind*. Cambridge, MA: Harvard University Press.

CHAPTER 7:
BECOMING LITERATE IN A MULTI-ETHNIC SOCIETY

Acknowledgements

I am grateful to the editors and to the participants at the First Gutenberg Conference for their many helpful suggestions regarding this essay. I would also like to thank Nyi Akinnaso, Ana Mari Cauce, Débora Ferdman, and Janet Powell for carefully reading and thoughtfully commenting on earlier versions of the essay. An earlier version appeared in *Harvard Educational Review*, 60: 181-204.

Notes

1. This debate itself forms part of the interethnic relations in the society. The lines dividing various points of view often follow ethnic boundaries. Moreover, the approach that is adopted has implications not just for pedagogy, but also for ethnic stratification.

2. Note, for example, the spread of a "mainstreaming" policy for special populations that were previously segregated within the educational system.

3. It must be noted that Roth's use of the term "culture" is somewhat imprecise and is more general than my usage of the term in this essay. She seems to use "culture" as a synonym for "dominant group" or "mainstream society." In either case, her use of the first person ("our" culture) is appropriate only for those groups adequately represented by the school. For those whose culture is different from that (or those) of the school, read "their" in place of "our."

4. As Kochman (1987) puts it, "[o]utgroup members are too far removed from the context in which such distinctive ingroup cultural patterns are displayed. Ingroup members, on the other hand, are often too close to their own culture to be able to see it" (p. 224).

5. So, for example, while for some groups, maintenance of the native language may function as a core value, for others the centrality of the family, or religious life, may play this role (Smolicz, 1981).

6. Social identity may refer to any type of social group (see Tajfel, 1981; Ferdman, 1987). Thus, the concept is too broad if we are interested in focusing specifically on the individual's relationship with ethnic groups. The notion of ethnic identity, as it is defined here, is intended to serve this purpose.

References

Akinnaso, F. N. (1982). "On the Differences Between Spoken and Written Language." *Language and Speech*, 25: 97-125.

――――. (1985). "On the Similarities Between Spoken and Written Language." *Language and Speech*, 28: 324-359.

Babad, E. Y., Birnbaum, M., and Benne, K. D. (1983). *The Social Self: Group Influences on Personal Identity*. Beverly Hills, CA: Sage.

Ball, P., Giles, H., and Hewstone, M. (1984). "Second Language Acquisition: The Intergroup Theory with Catastrophic Dimensions." In H. Tajfel, C. Fraser, and J. Jaspars, eds., *The Social Dimension: European Developments in Social Psychology*, vol. 2.Cambridge: Cambridge University Press.

Banks, J. A. (1977). *Multiethnic Education: Practices and Promises*. Bloomington, IN: Phi Delta Kappa Educational Foundation.

———. (1981). *Multiethnic Education: Theory and Practice*. Boston: Allyn and Bacon.

———. (1987). *Teaching Strategies for Ethnic Studies*, 4th ed. Boston: Allyn and Bacon.

Berry, J. W. (1983). "Acculturation: A Comparative Analysis of Alternative Forms." In R. Samuda and S. Woods, eds., *Perspectives in Immigrant and Minority Education*. New York: University Press of America.

———. (1986). "Multiculturalism and Psychology in Plural Societies." In L. H. Ekstrand, ed., *Ethnic Minorities and Immigrants in a Cross-cultural Perspective*. Berwyn: Swets North America.

Boekestijn, C. (1988). "Intercultural Migration and the Development of Personal Identity: The Dilemma Between Identity Maintenance and Cultural Adaptation." *International Journal of Intercultural Relations*, 12: 83-105.

Cook-Gumperz, J., ed. (1986). *The Social Construction of Literacy*. Cambridge: Cambridge University Press.

Cummins, J. (1986). "Empowering Minority Students: A Framework for Intervention." *Harvard Educational Review*, 56: 18-36.

de Castell, S., and Luke, A. (1983). "Defining 'Literacy' in North American Schools: Social and Historical Conditions and Consequences." *Journal of Curriculum Studies*, 15: 373-389.

———. (1987). "Literacy Instruction: Technology and Technique." *American Journal of Education*, 95: 413-440.

Deschamps, J. (1982). "Social Identity and Relations of Power Between Groups." In H. Tajfel, ed., *Social Identity and Intergroup Relations*. Cambridge: Cambridge University Press.

Erickson, F. (1984). "School Literacy, Reasoning, and Civility: An Anthropologist's Perspective." *Review of Educational Research*, 54: 525-546.

Ferdman, B. M., and Hakuta, K. (1985). "Group and Individual Bilingualism in an Ethnic Minority." Paper presented to the American Psychological Association, Los Angeles.

Flores, J. (1985). "'Que assimilated, brother, yo soy asimilao': The Structuring of Puerto Rican Identity in the U.S." *Journal of Ethnic Studies*, 13: 1-16.

Ginorio, A. B. (1987). "Puerto Rican Ethnicity and Conflict." In J. Boucher, D. Landis, and K. A. Clark, eds., *Ethnic Conflict: International Perspectives*. Newbury Park, CA: Sage.

Giroux, H. A. (1987). "Critical Literacy and Student Experience: Donald Graves'

Approach to Literacy." *Language Arts*, 64: 175-181.

Goody, J. (1977). *The Domestication of the Savage Mind*. Cambridge: Cambridge University Press.

————. (1982). "Alternative Paths to Knowledge in Oral and Literate Cultures." In D. Tannen, ed., *Spoken and Written Language: Exploring Orality and Literacy*. Norwood, NJ: Ablex.

Goody, J., and Watt, I. (1963). "The Consequences of Literacy." *Comparative Studies in Society and History*, 5: 304-345.

Graves, T. D. (1967). "Psychological Acculturation in a Tri-ethnic Community." *Southwestern Journal of Anthropology*, 23: 337-350.

Guillaumin, C. (1972). *L'idéologie Raciste: Genèse et Langage Actuel*. Paris: Mouton.

Guiora, A. Z. (1985). "The Psychodynamic Aspects of Bilingualism." Paper presented to the American Psychological Association, Los Angeles.

Hakuta, K., Ferdman, B. M., and Diaz, R. M. (1987). "Bilingualism and Cognitive Development: Three Perspectives." In S. Rosenberg, ed., *Advances in Applied Psycholinguistics. Volume 2: Reading, Writing and Language Learning*. New York: Cambridge University Press.

Heath, S. B. (1986). "The Functions and Uses of Literacy." In S. de Castell, A. Luke, and K. Egan, eds., *Literacy, Society, and Schooling: A Reader*. Cambridge: Cambridge University Press.

Heller, M. (1987). "The Role of Language in the Formation of Ethnic Identity." In J. S. Phinney and M. J. Rotheram, eds., *Children's Ethnic Socialization: Pluralism and Development*. Newbury Park, CA: Sage.

Herman, S. N. (1977). *Jewish Identity: A Social Psychological Perspective*. Beverly Hills, CA: Sage.

Hirsch, E. D. (1987). *Cultural Literacy: What Every American Needs to Know*. Boston: Houghton Mifflin.

Jones, J. M. (1988). "Racism in Black and White: A Bicultural Model of Reaction and Evolution." In P. A. Katz and D. A. Taylor, eds., *Eliminating Racism: Profiles in Controversy*. New York: Plenum.

Kádár-Fülop, J. (1988). "Culture and education in written composition." In A. C. Purves, ed., *Contrastive Rhetoric*. Written Communication Annual, Beverly Hills, CA: Sage.

Keefe, S. E., and Padilla, A. M. (1987). *Chicano Ethnicity*. Albuquerque: University of New Mexico Press.

Kochman, T. (1987). "The Ethnic Component in Black Language and Culture."

In J. S. Phinney and M. J. Rotheram, eds., *Children's Ethnic Socialization: Pluralism and Development*. Newbury Park, CA: Sage.

Matute-Bianchi, M. E. (1986). "Ethnic Identities and Patterns of School Success and Failure Among Mexican-descent and Japanese-American Students in a California High School: An Ethnographic Analysis." *American Journal of Education*, 95: 233-255.

McEvedy, M. R. (1986). "Some Social, Cultural and Linguistic Issues in Teaching Reading to Children Who Speak English as a Second Language." *Australian Journal of Reading*, 9: 139-152.

Montero, M. (1987). "A Través del Espejo: Una Aproximacion Teórica al Estudio de la Conciencia Social en América Latina." In M. Montero, ed., *Psicología Política Latinoamericana*. Caracas: Editorial Panapo.

Ong, W. (1982). *Orality and Literacy: The Technologizing of the Word*. London, New York: Methuen.

Roth, R. (1984). "Schooling, Literacy Acquisition and Cultural Transmission." *Journal of Education*, 166: 291-308.

Said, E. W. (1983). *The World, the Text, and the Critic*. Cambridge, MA: Harvard University Press.

Scollon, R., and Scollon, S. (1981). *Narrative, Literacy and Face in Interethnic Communication*. Norwood, NJ: Ablex.

Scribner, S. (1986). "Literacy in Three Metaphors." In N. L. Stein, ed., *Literacy in American Schools: Learning to Read and Write*. Chicago: University of Chicago Press.

Scribner, S., and Cole, M. (1981). *The Psychology of Literacy*. Cambridge, MA: Harvard University Press.

Smolicz, J. (1981). "Core Values and Cultural Identity." *Ethnic and Racial Studies*, 4: 74-90.

Tajfel, H. (1978). *The Social Psychology of Minorities*. London: Minority Rights Group.

———. (1981). *Human Groups and Social Categories*. Cambridge: Cambridge University Press.

Tajfel, H., and Turner, J. C. (1986). "The Social Identity Theory of Intergroup Relations." In S. Worchel and W. Austin, eds., *Psychology of Intergroup Relations*. Chicago: Nelson-Hall.

Taylor, D. M., and MicKirnan, D. J. (1984). "A Five-stage Model of Intergroup Relations." *British Journal of Social Psychology*, 23: 291-300.

Triandis, H. C. (1972). *The Analysis of Subjective Culture.* New York: Wiley.

Trueba, H. T. (1984). "The Forms, Functions, and Values of Literacy: Reading for Survival in a Barrio as a Student." *NABE Journal,* 9: 21-38.

Wallace, C. (1986). *Learning to Read in a Multicultural Society: The Social Context of Second Language Literacy.* Oxford: Pergamon Press.

CHAPTER 8:
LITERACY AND THE BETTERMENT OF INDIVIDUAL LIFE

References

Adler, M. J. (1978). *Aristotle for Everybody: Difficult Thought Made Easy.* New York: Macmillan.

———. (1985). *Ten Philosophical Mistakes.* New York: Macmillan.

Appignanesi, L., and Maitland, S. (1989). *The Rushdi File: Fourth Estate Limited.* London: Classic House.

Baltes, P. B. (1987) "Theoretical Propositions of Life Span Developmental Psychology." *Developmental Psychology,* 23: 611-626.

Bandura, A., and Walters, R. H. (1963). *Social Learning and Personality Development.* New York: Holt.

Bhola, H. S. (1979). *Evaluating Functional Literacy.* Tehran: Hulton Educational Publications in Cooperation with the International Institute for Adult Literacy Methods.

Bok, S. (1978). *Lying: Moral Choice in Public and Private Life.* New York: Random House.

Burroughs, J. (1902). *Literary Values and Other Papers.* Boston: Houghton Mifflin.

Chandler, M. (1987). "The Othello Effect: Essay on the Emergence and Eclipse of Skeptical Doubt." *Human Development,* 30: 137-159.

Dann, H. O. (1986). *"Reconstruction and Validation of Teachers' Interaction-Relevant Subjective Theories."* Paper presented at the Third European Conference on Personality, Gdansk, Poland.

Davidson, J., and Koppenhauer, D. (1988). *Adolescent Literacy: What Works and Why.* New York: Garland.

Eco, U. (1988). "The Future of Literacy." *Brown Alumni Monthly,* 89(1): 220-226.

Erikson, E. H. (1968). *Identity: Youth and Crisis.* New York: W. W. Norton.

———. (1974). *Dimensions of a New Identity.* New York: W. W. Norton.

Freire, P. (1970). *Pedagogy of the Oppressed*. New York: Seabury Press.

———— . (1987). *Education for Critical Consciousness*. New York: The Continuum Publishing Company.

Furnham, A. F. (1988). *Lay Theories: Everyday Understanding of Problems in the Social Sciences*. Elmsford, NY: Pergamon Press.

Furnham, A., and Lewis, A. (1986). *The Economic Mind*. Brighton, Sussex: Wheatsheaf.

Hamilton, E. (1942). *The Greek Way to Western Civilization*. New York: W. W. Norton.

Hare-Mustin, R. T., and Maracek, J. (1988). "The Meaning of Difference: Gender Theory, Postmodernism, and Psychology." *American Psychologist*, 43: 455-464.

Hirsch, E. B., Jr. (1987). *Cultural Literacy: What Every American Needs to Know*. Boston: Houghton Mifflin.

Kekes, J. (1986). "Moral Intuition." In *Re reading* (pp. 25-40). Albany, NY: Center for the Arts and Humanities, SUNY/Albany.

Kelly, G. A. (1963). *A Theory of Personality: The Psychology of Personal Constructs*. New York: W. W. Norton.

Kohlberg, L. (1969). "State and Sequence: The Cognitive-Developmental Approach to Socialization." In D. Goslin, ed., *Handbook of Socialization Theory and Research*. Chicago: Rand McNally.

Kohlberg, L., Boyd, D., and Levine, C. (1985). *The Return of Stage 6: Its Principle and its Moral Point of View* (mimeo). Cambridge: Harvard University.

Kohlberg, L., and Mayer, R. (1972). "Development as the Aim of Education." *Harvard Educational Review*, 43: 245-257.

McGuffey, W. (1907). *McGuffey's Third Eclectic Reader* (revised edition). New York: American Book Co.

McVey, R. (1986). "The Wayang Controversy in Indonesian Communism." In M. Hobart and R. Taylor, eds., *Context, Meaning and Power in South East Asia*. Ithaca, NY: Cornell University, South East Asia Program.

Mulyono, I. S. (1981). *Human Character in the Wayang*. Singapore: Gunung Agung.

Perry, W. G., Jr. (1970). *Forms of Intellectual and Ethical Development in the College Years: A Scheme*. New York: Holt, Rinehart and Winston.

Richmond, E. B. (1986). *A Comparative Survey of Seven Adult Functional Literacy*

Programs in Sub-Saharan Africa. Lanham, MD: University Press of America.

Rosch, E. (1973). "On the Internal Structure of Perceptual and Semantic Categories." In T. E. Moore, ed., *Cognitive Development and the Acquisition of Language.* New York: Academic Press.

Rosch, E., and Mervis, C. B. (1975). "Family Resemblances: Studies in the Internal Structure of Categories." *Cognitive Psychology,* 7: 573-605.

Shils, E. A. (1981). *Tradition.* Chicago: University of Chicago Press.

The Shoemaker's Present: or How a Boy Became Obedient (author unknown), p. 12-13. London: Blackel and Son Limited.

Streufert, S., and Streufert, S. (1978). *Behavior in the Complex Environment.* Washington: V. H. Winston.

Van Ness, E. C., and Prawirohardjo. (1985). *Javanese Wayang Kulit.* Oxford: Oxford University Press.

Watzlawick, P., ed. (1984). *The Invented Reality: Contributions to Constructivism.* New York: W. W. Norton.

Woolfolk, R. L., and Richardson, F. E. (1984). "Behavior Therapy and the Ideology of Modernity." *The American Psychologist,* 39(7): 777-786.

CHAPTER 9:
LITERACY IN THE ELEMENTARY CLASSROOM

Notes

1. Writing, literature, and content areas are not the only subjects that elementary teachers have to contend with. Increasingly, elementary schools have become agents of public health agencies and have to spend considerable amounts of time engaged in teaching such topics as drugs, AIDS, bus and fire safety, care of animals, and so on. In an era when so many parents work, teachers also find themselves having to make up for gaps in children's literacy experiences at home.

2. The focus of most of these programs appears to be on giving bright students additional time and attention to pursue projects they are interested in, rather than offering an academic curriculum in Western literature and history. One program, *Junior Great Books,* which is sometimes used in gifted and talented programs and with top reading groups, does represent the academic philosophy, but its use in elementary schools is not widespread, even with these two groups of students.

3. One reason is that in general elementary classroom teachers are much better trained to teach reading than they are history, geography, or science. Another is that until quite recently, elementary students were expected to be pro-

ficient in reading (and tested to ensure their proficiency) but no similar expectations were made for their historical, geographic, or scientific knowledge. A frequent complaint of elementary teachers is that they simply do not have time left over from reading instruction to give full attention to these content areas.

4. Even the Literacy Skills ideology is not immune from proposals for its reform. For some educators, the basal reader approach is not sufficiently skills-oriented, and should be replaced or supplemented with much stricter approaches (e.g., Carnine and Silbert, 1979).

5. What I fear most about lengthening the school day (or the school year) is that given more time, teachers will simply do more of the same (e.g., they will spend forty minutes a day with the same spelling series they used to spend twenty minutes a day with). If the elementary curriculum were reformed along the lines I have proposed in this chapter, additional time would most likely not be needed.

References

Altweger, B., Edelsky, C., and Flores, B. M. (1987). "Whole Language: What's New?" _The Reading Teacher_, 41(2): 144-154.

Applebee, A. N. (1989). _A Study of Book-length Works Taught in High School English Courses_. Albany, NY: Center for the Learning and Teaching of Literature, State University of New York at Albany.

Anyon, J. (1979). "Ideology and United States History Textbooks." _Harvard Educational Review_, 49(3): 361-386.

Ashton-Warner, S. (1963). _Teacher_. New York: Bantam Books.

Atwell, N. (1987). _In the Middle: Writing, Reading and Learning with Adolescents_. Portsmouth, NH: Heinemann.

Beach, J. D. (1988). "Writing Tasks and the Integration of Reading and Writing in American Basal Reader Series: A Descriptive and Analytical Study." Unpublished doctoral dissertation. Albany, NY: State University of New York at Albany.

Bennett, W. J. (1988). _James Madison Elementary School: A Curriculum for American Students_. Washington, DC: United States Department of Education.

Bereiter, C. (1972). "Development in Writing." In L. W. Gregg and E. R. Steinberg, eds., _Cognitive Processes in Writing_. Hillsdale, NJ: Erlbaum.

Cambourne, B. (1988). _The Whole Story: Natural Learning and the Acquisition of Literacy in the Classroom_. New York: Ashton-Scholastic.

Carnine, D. (1988). "How to Overcome Barriers to Student Achievement." In S. J. Samuels and P. D. Pearson, eds., _Changing School Reading Programs:_

Principles and Case Studies. Newark, DE: International Reading Association.

Carnine, D., and Silbert, J. (1979). *Direct Instruction Reading.* Columbus, OH: Merrill.

Chall, J. S. (1983). *Stages of Reading Development.* New York: McGraw-Hill.

Clarke, M. A. (1987). "Don't Blame the System: Constraints on 'Whole Language' Reform." *Language Arts,* 64(4): 384-396.

Engelmann, S. (1988). "Theories, Theories, Theories: A Critique of Logic of Whole Language Arguments." *Association for Direct Instruction News,* 7(3): 5-6.

Freire, P. (1970). *Pedagogy of the Oppressed.* New York: Seabury Press.

Freire, P., and Macedo, D. (1987). *Literacy: Reading the Word and the World.* South Hadley, MA: Bergin and Garvey.

Gagnon, P. (1988). "The California Framework: Turning Point for Social Studies Reform?" *American Educator,* 12(3): 36-40, 48.

Goodman, K. S. (1986). *What's Whole in Whole Language?* Portsmouth, NH: Heinemann.

Graves, D. H. (1978). *Balance the Basics: Let Them Write.* New York: Ford Foundation.

———. (1983). *Writing: Teachers and Children at Work.* Portsmouth, NH: Heinemann.

Grosvenor, M. (1985). "Geographic Ignorance: Time for a Turnaround." *National Geographic Magazine,* 167(6): iv.

Hersh, R. H., et. al. (1981). "The Education Professions and the Enhancement of Classroom Productivity." Eugene, OR: University of Oregon, CEPM Education Professions Committee.

Hirsch, E. D., Jr. (1987). *Cultural Literary: What Every American Needs to Know.* Boston: Houghton Mifflin.

Holdaway, D. (1979). *The Foundations of Literacy.* Portsmouth, NH: Heinemann.

Huck, C. S. (1977). "Literature as the Content of Reading." *Theory Into Practice,* 16(4): 363-371.

Kohlberg, L., and Mayer, R. (1972). "Development as the Aim of Education." *Harvard Educational Review,* 48(3): 449-496.

Moffett, J. (1967). *Teaching the Universe of Discourse.* Boston: Houghton Mifflin.

Mullis, I. V. S., and Jenkins, L. B. (1988). *The Science Report Card: Elements of Risk and Recovery. Trends and Achievement Based on the 1986 National Assessment.*

Princeton, NJ: Educational Testing Service.

Northcutt, N. (1975). *Adult Functional Competence: A Summary*. Austin, TX: University of Texas at Austin.

Perry, W. G., Jr. (1970). *Forms of Intellectual and Ethical Development in the College Years: A Scheme*. New York: Holt, Rinehart and Winston.

Petty, W. T., and Finn, P. J. (1981). "Classroom Teachers' Reports on Teaching Written Composition." In S. Haley-James, ed., *Perspectives on Writing in Grades 1-8*. Newark, DE: International Reading Association.

Piaget, J. (1969). "The Intellectual Development of the Adolescent." In G. Caplan and S. Lebovici, eds., *Adolescence: Psychological Perspectives*. New York: Basic Books.

Ravitch, D. (1985). *The Schools We Deserve: Reflections on the Educational Crises of Our Time*. New York: Basic Books.

Ravitch, D., and Finn, C. (1987). *What Do Our 17-year-olds Know? A Report on the First National Assessment of History and Literature*. New York: Harper and Row.

Rich, S. J. (1985). "Restoring power to teachers: the impact of 'Whole Language'." *Language Arts*, 62(7): 717-724.

Rosenblatt, L. M. (1949). "The Enriching Values of Reading." In W. S. Gray, ed., *Reading in an age of mass communication*. New York: Appleton-Century Crofts.

———. (1978). *The Reader, the Text, the Poem: The Transactional Theory of the Literary Work*. Carbondale, IL: Southern Illinois University Press.

Shannon, P. (1983). "The Use of Commercial Reading Materials in American Elementary Schools." *Reading Research Quarterly*, 19: 68-85.

Sizer, T. R. (1985). *Horace's Compromise: The Dilemma of the American High School*. Boston: Houghton Mifflin.

Spring, J. H. (1975). *A Primer of Libertarian Education*. New York: Free Life Editions.

Tyson-Bernstein, H. (1988). *The Textbook Fiasco: A Conspiracy of Good Intentions*. Washington, DC: Council for Basic Education.

Veatch, J. (1986). "Individualized Reading: A Personal Memoir." *Language Arts*, 63(6): 586-593.

Venezky, R., et al. (1987). *The Subtle Danger: Reflections on the Literacy Abilities of America's Young Adults*. Princeton, NJ: Educational Testing Service.

Walmsley, S. A. (1981). "On the Purpose and Content of Secondary Reading Programs: An Educational Ideological Perspective." *Curriculum Inquiry*, 11(1): 73-93.

Walmsley, S. A., and Walp, T. P. (1989). *Teaching Literature in Elementary School.* Report 1.3. Albany, NY: Center for the Learning and Teaching of Literature, State University of New York at Albany.

———. (1990). "Integrating Literature and Composing into the Language Arts Curriculum: Philosophy and Practice." *Elementary School Journal*, 90(3): 251-274.

CHAPTER 10:
RECONSTRUCTING THE CLASSROOM:
LITERACY AND THE PROBLEM OF CHOICE

Notes

1. David Bartholomae's essay "Inventing the University" in *When a Writer Can't Write* edited by Mike Rose (New York: Guilford, 1985), pages 134-165, provides a very important discussion of the complexity of students' imaginative powers in attempting to construct for themselves the needs of academic readers.

2. For a complete discussion and critique of the functionalist conception of literacy, see Myron Tuman, *A Preface to Literacy: An Inquiry into Pedagogy, Practice, and Progress*, Tuscaloosa: University of Alabama Press, 1987.

3. For a full discussion of critical literacy, see Paulo Freire's *Pedagogy of the Oppressed*, New York: Seabury, 1975; Henry A. Giroux's *Theory and Resistance in Education: A Pedagogy for the Opposition*, South Hadley, MA: Bergin and Garvey, 1983, particularly pages 226-231; and Myron C. Tuman's *A Preface to Literacy: An Inquiry into Pedagogy, Practice, and Progress*, Tuscaloosa: University of Alabama Press, 1987.

4. I am indebted here to the work of Pamela Gay, assistant professor at SUNY-Binghamton, and the important work she has done over the years to improve the quality of life of developing writers.

5. I am indebted to the work of Nancy Cashion, a teacher in East Windsor, New Jersey, for her important work with prekindergarten children, and for the copies of Jessica's writing.

References

Bartholomae, D. (1985). "Inventing the University." In M. Rose, ed., *When a Writer Can't Write*. New York: Guilford.

Berger, P., and Luckman, T. (1967). *The Social Construction of Reality*. Garden City, NY: Doubleday.

Berthoff, A. (1981). *The Making of Meaning.* Portsmouth, NH: Boynton/Cook.

Bruner, J. (1986). *Actual Minds, Possible Worlds.* Cambridge, MA: Harvard University Press.

Freire, P. (1975). *Pedagogy of the Oppressed.* New York: Seabury Press.

Giroux, H. (1983). *Theory and Resistance in Education: A Pedagogy for the Opposition.* South Hadley, MA: Bergin and Garvey.

Goswami, D., and Stillman, P., eds. (1986). *Reclaiming the Classroom.* Portsmouth, NH: Boynton/Cook.

Shor, I. (1980). *Critical Teaching and Everyday Life.* Chicago: University of Chicago Press.

Tuman, M. (1987). *A Preface to Literacy.* Tuscaloosa: University of Alabama Press.

CHAPTER 11:
SKILLS THAT AREN'T BASIC IN A NEW CONCEPTION OF LITERACY

Acknowledgements

*We would like to express our appreciation to the Ford Foundation, which is funding our work on the social prerequisites to decontextualized oral language skills and literacy. We would also like to thank the many child-care centers, Head Start programs, parents, and children who have agreed to participate in the study, and Patton Tabors for her helpful comments on an earlier version of the essay.

Notes

1. For early reports of data from this study see Dickinson (in press a; in press b) and Snow and Dickinson (1990).

References

Anderson, R. C., Wilson, P. T., and Fielding, L. G. (1988). "Growth in Reading and How Children Spend Their Time Outside of School." *Reading Research Quarterly,* 23: 285-303.

Chandler, J., and Hemphill, L. (1983). "Models of Classrooms as Effective Literacy Environments for Low-income Children." Manuscript, Harvard Graduate School of Education.

Cochran-Smith, M. (1984). *The Making of a Reader.* Norwood, NJ: Ablex.

Curtis, M. E. (1980). "Development of Components of Reading Skill." *Journal of Educational Psychology,* 72: 656-669.

Davidson, R., Kline, S., and Snow, C. E. (1986). "Definitions and Definite Noun

Phrases: Indicators of Children's Decontextualized Language Skills." *Journal of Research in Childhood Education*, 1: 37-48.

Dickinson, D. K. (in press b). "An Environmental Approach to Informal Evaluation in Preschools." *Linguistics in Education*.

――――. (in press a). "Teacher Stance and Setting: Constraints on Conversation in Preschools." In A. McCabe and C. Peterson, eds., *Developing Narrative Structure*. Hillsdale, NJ: Erlbaum.

――――. (1987). "Oral Language, Literacy Skills, and Response to Literature." In J. Squire, ed., *The Dynamics of Language Learning*. Urbana, IL: The Educational Resources Information Center.

――――. (1989). "Effects of a Shared Reading Program on a Head Start Language and Literacy Environment." In J. Allen and J. Mason, eds., *Risk Makers, Risk Takers, Risk Breakers*. Portsmouth, NH: Heineman.

Dickinson, D. K., and Keebler, R. (1989). "Variation in Preschool Teachers' Styles of Reading Books." *Discourse Processes*, 12: 353-375.

Dickinson, D. K., and Snow, C. E. (1987). "Interrelationships Among Prereading and Oral Language Skills in Kindergartners from Two Social Classes." *Early Childhood Research Quarterly*, 1: 1-25.

Goldfield, B. A., and Snow, C. E. (1984). "Reading Books with Children: The Mechanics of Parental Influence on Children's Reading Achievement." In J. Flood, ed., *Understanding Reading Comprehension*. Newark, DE: International Reading Association.

Gough, P. B., and Tunmer, W. E. (1986). "Decoding, Reading, and Reading Disability." *Remedial and Special Education*, 7: 6-10.

Juel, C., Griffith, P. L., and Gough, P. B. (1986). "Acquisition of Literacy: A Longitudinal Study of Children in First and Second Grade." *Journal of Educational Psychology*, 78: 243-255.

Mason, J. M., and Allen, J. (1986). "A Review of Emergent Literacy with Implications for Research and Practice in Reading." In C. Z. Rothkopf, ed., *Review of Research in Education*, vol. 13. Washington, D.C.: American Educational Research Association.

Ochs, E., Smith, R., and Taylor, C. (1988). "Putting Problems on the Table: Dinner and Literacy." Paper presented at Boston University Conference on Language Development.

Perlmann, R. (1983). "Variations in Socialization Styles: Family Talk at the Dinner Table." Doctoral dissertation, Boston University.

Snow, C. E. (1983). "Literacy and Language: Relationships During the Preschool

Years." *Harvard Educational Review*, 53: 165-189.

————. (1987). "Beyond Conversation: Second Language Learners' Acquisition of Description and Explanation." In J. Lantolf and A. Labarca, eds., *Research in Second Language Learning: Focus on the Classroom*. Norwood, NJ: Ablex.

————. (1989). "Understanding Social Interaction and Language Development: Sentences Are Not Enough." In M. Bornstein and J. Bruner, eds., *Interaction in Human Development*. Hillsdale, NJ: Erlbaum.

Snow, C. E., Barnes, W. S., Chandler, J., Goodman, I. F., and Hemphill, L. (1991). *Unfulfilled Expectations: Home and School Influences on Literacy*. Cambridge, MA: Harvard University Press.

Snow, C. E., Cancino, H., Gonzalez, P., and Shriberg, E. (1989). "Giving Formal Definitions: An Oral Language Correlate of Literacy." In D. Bloome, ed., *Classrooms and Literacy*. Norwood, NJ: Ablex.

Snow, C. E., and Dickinson, D. K. (1990). "Social Sources of Narrative Skills at Home and at School." *First Language*, 10: 87-103.

Snow, C. E., and Dolbear, M. (1988). "The Relation of Conversational Skill to Language Proficiency in Second Language Learners." Manuscript, Harvard Graduate School of Education.

Stanovich, K. E., Cunningham, A. E., and Feeman, D. J. (1984). "Intelligence, Cognitive Skills, and Early Reading Progress." *Reading Research Quarterly*, 29: 278-303.

Stotsky, S. (1984). "Research on Reading/Writing Relationships: Synthesis and Suggested Directions." In J. M. Jensen, ed., *Composing and Comprehending*. Urbana, IL: National Council of Teachers of English.

Teale, W., and Sulzby, E. (1986). "Introduction: Emergent Literacy as a Perspective for Examining How Young Children Become Writers and Readers. In W. Teale and E. Sulzby, eds., *Emergent Literacy: Writing and Reading*. Norwood, NJ: Ablex.

Tizard, B., and Hughes, M. (1984). *Young Children Learning*. Cambridge, MA: Harvard University Press.

Torrance, N., and Olson, D. R. (1985). "Oral and Literate Competencies in the Early School Years." In D. R. Olson, N. Torrance, and A. Hildyard, eds., *Literacy, Language, and Learning*. New York: Cambridge University Press.

Velasco, P. (1987). "Oral Decontextualized Language Skills and Reading Comprehension in Bilingual Children." Paper presented to Boston University Child Language Conference.

Wells, G. (1985). "Preschool Literacy-Related Activities and Success in School." In

D. R. Olson, N. Torrance, and A. Hildyard, eds., *Literacy, Language, and Learning*. New York: Cambridge University Press.

West, R. F., and Stanovich, K. E. (1979). "The Development of Automatic Word Recognition Skills." *Journal of Reading Behavior*, 11: 211-219.

INDEX

Compiled by James Bradley